Shakespeare on the Noongar Stage

Clint Bracknell

Clint Bracknell is a Noongar song-maker and Professor of Music at the University of Western Australia investigating connections between song, language, landscapes, and improving Indigenous community access to cultural heritage collections. Cosmos Magazine named him one of 50+ Indigenous People Changing the World. Clint releases music under the name Maatakitj.

Kylie Bracknell

Kylie Bracknell is an actor, director, and writer responsible for ground-breaking productions including Hecate, which *The Australian* lauded in its 'Best of 2020' year-in-review, and the Noongar dub of Bruce Lee's film *Fist of Fury* retitled *Fist of Fury Noongar Daa*. Kylie has over two decades experience working in Australia's creative industries and is a 2020 recipient of Australia's prestigious Sydney Myer Performing Arts Award.

Clint Bracknell & Kylie Bracknell

Shakespeare on the Noongar Stage

Language Revival and Hecate

UPSWELL

First published in Australia in 2024
by Upswell Publishing
Perth, Western Australia
upswellpublishing.com

Upswell operates in the city of Perth, on ancient country of the Whadjuk people of the Noongar nation who remain the spiritual and cultural custodians of this beautiful land. We acknowledge their continuing connection to country and express gratitude to elders past and present for their strength and creativity...Always was, always will be, Aboriginal land.

ISBN: 978-0-645-24808-1

NATIONAL LIBRARY OF AUSTRALIA
A catalogue record for this book is available from the National Library of Australia

Cover design by Chil3, Fremantle
Typeset in Foundry Origin by Lasertype
Printed by McPherson's Printing Group

Upswell Publishing is assisted by the State of Western Australia through its funding program for arts and culture.

GOVERNMENT OF WESTERN AUSTRALIA
Department of
Local Government, Sport and Cultural Industries

Contents

Everyone knew the name Shakespeare, but he was from another century, another world. Then he came into our world long after he was gone and helped promote our language.

Going back in time to when you're running around as a kid with people frightened to talk language aloud in public, I would never have imagined for this to be able to come about at all.

Those that didn't understand the language before had an awakening within themselves, you know. It was a beautiful experience to be part of.

Just watching everybody, the expressions on their faces. There were tears too, flooding inside the room.

Roma Yibiyung Winmar

Foreword

Kate Mulvany

Kaya.

You are about to witness history.

Within these pages are words and ideas and songlines that are some of the oldest in the known universe.

Think about that for a moment...

If language is a galaxy, then these words are the first scattering of glimmering stars, and the English language hasn't even started to form. These two languages are separated by thousands of years. One is a mere embryo to the other. And yet, shamefully, the younger language is revered worldwide, and the older language was almost lost entirely...

Almost.

Because despite the horrors of colonisation that saw so many First Nations people and languages and cultures separated and decimated, a knowledge was passed on. Ancestors spoke to Elders who shared with their children and grandchildren and great-grandchildren...And a galaxy of words began to shine again.

Kylie and Clint Bracknell were taught the importance of these words, these worlds. They and their team of Aboriginal storytellers took the ancient Noongar language and breathed new life into it through the most unlikely of allies: Shakespeare. In 2020, partnered by the Perth Festival, Yirra Yaakin Theatre Company and Bell Shakespeare, they brought these words and worlds to audiences who sat captivated – many of whom were hearing words they had been taught by their Elders, but told by strangers not to say.

Not to think. Not to feel. To forget.

The words and ideas and songlines on these pages were brought to a stage on Noongar *boodjar*. They were spoken. Sung. Wailed. Laughed. Whispered. Honoured. And shared.

Imagine if we could tell Shakespeare that his Macbeth would be translated into an ancient language and communicated with audiences from all walks of life. I wonder what he would say. I wonder if he would believe.

I reckon he'd be awestruck.

I was honoured to be asked to dramaturg this work, but truly I sat as an observer and a listener as it formed in front of me. I was a *nyidiyang* witness to something astoundingly ancient and yet resoundingly immediate. I was invited into a world I knew shamefully little about, and I left with a small sparkle of knowledge from an ancient galaxy of Dreaming.

The result of Kylie Bracknell and Clint Bracknell and their storytelling team is *Hecate*. The story of Macbeth, told through the Noongar experience. Told from the heart of Aunty Hecate. And through the eyes of history.

In your hands, you hold a powerful knowledge and an ancient culture. A shining sky of *djindang*!

Respect it. Honour it. Enjoy it. Learn from its wisdom. And let us never let it be forgotten again.

1
Introduction

Clint Bracknell

Performed entirely in the endangered Noongar language from the southwest of Western Australia (also spelled Nyungar and Nyoongar), including the capital city of Perth, *Hecate* is an audacious reinterpretation of William Shakespeare's *Macbeth* through a Noongar lens. It foregrounds Hecate, queen of the witches, as an embodiment of Country surviving the consequences of Macbeth's descent into moral corruption. 'Country' is capitalised in Aboriginal contexts to indicate 'nourishing terrain' – living, multidimensional, and intertwined with culture.[1] The Noongar term for Country, *boodjar* – and the related term *boodjari* (pregnant) – evokes the concept of 'mother earth'. Hecate is the first character to appear in our production. She sings 'boodjar baal waaliny' (Country she crying), echoing issues of ecological crisis and settler-colonisation. Emerging after almost a decade in development with Yirra Yaakin Theatre Company and Bell Shakespeare to premiere at Perth Festival 2020, *Hecate* is a landmark production as the first complete adaptation of a Shakespearean work in one Aboriginal language of the place now known as Australia.[2] It asserts Noongar power over a canonical English text and builds upon decades of Noongar cultural resilience, perseverance, and language revitalisation. As a testament to both the power of the piece itself and the story of language survival it embodies, every performance of *Hecate* has elicited a standing ovation.[3]

As part of his initial agenda as artistic director at Yirra Yaakin Theatre Company, Kyle J. Morrison devised the original idea to present a

Shakespearean work in the Noongar language in 2009. Kylie Bracknell and I co-translated *Hecate* with editorial guidance from Roma Yibiyung Winmar, a senior Noongar language teacher with over three decades of experience revitalising the language. Kylie adapted and directed, while I served as musical director, composer, and sound designer. The original cast included actors Della Rae Morrison, Maitland Schnaars, Bobbi Henry, Trevor Ryan, Kyle J. Morrison, Ian Wilkes, Rubeun Yorkshire, Mark Nannup, and Cezera Critti-Schnaars. Mark Howett was the lighting designer and cultural consultants included Judy Bone, Jill Dewar, and Mitchella Waljin Hutchins. The decade of development towards *Hecate* provided a unique opportunity for a troupe of Noongar creatives to be immersed in our endangered Aboriginal language.

Australia is home to enormous linguistic diversity, with more than 200 distinct Indigenous languages spread across the continent, each of which is associated with a unique local region and people.[4] Around 700,000 Aboriginal and Torres Strait Islander people in Australia account for approximately 3 per cent of the nation's total population.[5] Australia's continuing legacy of settler-colonialism and successive cultural assimilation policies have combined to position most of these languages in various states of endangerment and silence.[6] Linguist Arthur Capell explained in 1964, 'government policy looks forward to the loss of Aboriginal languages so that the Aborigines may be assimilated'.[7] Half a century later, the 2014 National Indigenous Languages Survey indicated that only 'around 120' Indigenous languages are still spoken and that 'about 13 can be considered strong', spoken across all generations.[8] Many Aboriginal and Torres Strait Islander communities are engaged in processes to revitalise and sustain their languages as they simultaneously respond to ongoing social, cultural, and economic marginalisation. These languages are not just important to Aboriginal and Torres Strait Islander peoples, but also vital to maintaining intimate relationships with the unique and diverse landscapes they emanate from.

The Noongar language has been dramatically impacted by colonisation since the early 1800s and was actively suppressed until the 1970s. Over 30,000 Aboriginal people in the predominantly urban/rural southwest corner of Western Australia identify as Noongar, adapted from a word meaning 'person', 'man', 'ally' or even 'mankind/humanity' in the local Aboriginal language and used today to refer to the Aboriginal people, country, language, and culture of the region.[9] The need for 'Noongar' to serve as a catch-all term arose with colonisation. Describing people's lives before British invasion, the late Noongar statesman Ken Colbung explains:

> They existed when there was no necessity for any name. They were the good, the enlightened people. They were the people who know about the laws of nature and the laws of the spirit. They built a great civilisation, a great culture, and a unique social order.[10]

Noongar constitutes one of the largest Aboriginal cultural blocs in Australia in terms of geography and population. However, in the last Australian census less than 5 per cent of Noongar people reported that they use Noongar language at home.[11] Nevertheless, Noongar vocabulary has been widely co-opted into Australian English vernacular courtesy of official placenames such as Joondalup, Coolbellup, and Quairading, along with colloquial terms to describe local fauna and flora, including quokka (*Setonix brachyurus*), tammar (*Notamacropus eugenii*), and jarrah (*Eucalyptus marginata*, plus implements like a gidgee (fishing spear). As a result, many people regularly employ a smattering of Noongar in everyday speech. Despite the ubiquity of Noongar terms in everyday speech, the language is rarely heard strung together in full sentences and conversations. Annual global language reference publication *Ethnologue* lists the Noongar language and its regional variants as dormant or extinct,[12] which makes *Hecate* even more remarkable.

Building on centuries of Noongar performance traditions and more recent performance history,[13] *Hecate* is the first full work of Western-style theatre presented entirely in the Noongar language, and one of very few theatrical adaptations presented entirely in an Aboriginal language of Australia, the first being *Ngundalehla Godotgai*, a 1997 version of Samuel Beckett's *Waiting for Godot* performed in the Bundjalung language of northern New South Wales. Presented with English surtitles by the Bangarra National Indigenous Dance Troupe at 1997 Festival of the Dreaming in Sydney, *Ngundalehla Godotgai* was directed by non-Indigenous Irish theatre specialist Clara Mason. Presented completely in Noongar language without surtitles and led by a Noongar director and creative team, *Hecate* is more than a significant creative achievement; it is an embodiment of Noongar self-determination. The challenge of performing Shakespeare in Noongar has provided a range of very rare opportunities for Noongar and the broader public to actively engage with the Noongar language.

Language and Country

The south of Western Australia has always been home to Noongar people who carry living oral histories stretching back beyond the last ice age and an expressive culture that was once routinely musical and intrinsically linked to local landscapes.[14] Western Australia was claimed by the British in 1829 and became part of the nation state of Australia in 1901. Over the past two centuries, most Noongar families have been marked by experiences of sanctioned and arbitrary settler-colonial violence and rigorous government policies of segregation and cultural assimilation.[15] In Western Australia today, arts organisations increasingly promote agendas that are avowedly pro-Indigenous, pro-environmental, and pro-sustainability, but they are also increasingly reliant on funding from environmentally destructive industries. The increased public acknowledgement of 'Noongar culture' in recent decades masks the fact that we Noongar are among the poorest and most incarcerated people in our own homelands, now one of the wealthiest places on earth.

As a Noongar and Yamatji man with a lifelong love of theatre, Kyle J. Morrison was one of the youngest artistic directors ever appointed to lead a major Australian theatre company when he took charge of

Yirra Yaakin in 2009. As Morrison explains, *Hecate* brings together two things he intensely values – Shakespeare and Noongar language – and makes both more accessible and relevant for Noongar people and broader audiences.

> This whole idea of elitism in art and culture does not exist in Noongar culture. The Western world's ideas of taking art and culture away from everybody is annoying. I hate it, because when you have your culture belittled, separated, and disenfranchised from you, you have a weaker sense of your own self in a lot of ways. I would love to see the people that are pushing the prams and trolleys through the shopping centre in Gosnells [a suburb on the southeast outskirts of Perth] on a Thursday afternoon, I want them at my audience for opera, I want them to hear Shakespeare, I think Shakespeare should be available for all human beings. I think Shakespeare has a wealth of knowledge to teach humanity, and I think Noongar language has a wealth of knowledge to teach Western Australians, and so if every single West Australian could access the knowledge of Noongar language, we could all grow together, and if Noongars could access the beauty, the strength of opera, the ballet, the orchestra, and Shakespeare then they're all growing in a way, they're being stronger Noongars for it.

Morrison's unique vision for a *Macbeth* in the Noongar language inspired more than a novel translation of Shakespeare's play about power, greed, and violence in eleventh-century Scotland. *Hecate* is driven by the idea that by working together and engaging with our language on our Country, we can become strong enough to stand alongside anyone – even the coloniser's purportedly greatest writer – and tell a story bigger than *Macbeth*: a story about the power of language and culture to connect us to each other and connect us to Country.

Languages can represent 'the distillation of the thoughts and communication of a people over their entire history'.[16] For Aboriginal peoples, that history stretches back more than fifty thousand years.[17] As distinguished senior Akarre woman Margaret Kemarre Turner OAM explains:

> Not only you speak that language, but generation upon generation upon generation of your families have also spoken it. And so language is really, really important. Your own language. And that language really recognises you, gives you identity, and who you are and what is you and how you're connected to that Land, and how you hold the Land.[18]

The relationship between landscapes and language is reciprocal. Aboriginal people will often describe Country as being happy when it hears the local Aboriginal language. Yorta Yorta and Dja Dja Wurrung singer and scholar Lou Bennett, who was in *Hecate*'s first audience, considers language as something that belongs *to* Country.[19]

Although the English language certainly does not belong to Australia, it dominates social, cultural, and civic life here. Any language can be used to speak about all manner of topics in all kinds of ways, but settler-colonists have imposed words like 'Australia', 'Aboriginal', and 'nomadic' to codify Country and its peoples within a narrow and limiting worldview. 'Aboriginal' denies cultural and linguistic diversity. 'Nomadic' undermines regionally specific Indigenous systems of land management and ownership. 'Australia' accomplishes both. As Tuck and Yang explain,

> To codify is to manage, to arrange in an order that is meaningful to the coder. Coding is something we do to objects. Codes stand in for objectified living things. Codes become objects themselves, to be treated objectively, in the way that the living things would not allow.[20]

In this way, the English language has been used as a tool to deny the sovereignty and cultural diversity of Aboriginal peoples. It has also been used to perpetuate a deficit vision of Country.

Lexicographer Jay Arthur explains that because the English language is imbued with ideals and expectations associated with English landscapes, settler-colonists have 'created this new country haunted by the image of the Default country, which was narrow, green hilly and wet – which meant that Australia was understood as vast, brown, flat and dry'.[21] Arthur finds the English language 'constantly disappointed' in its descriptions of Australian landscapes, where drought is normal and waterways are periodically bare.[22] Rather than use terminology predisposed to frame Australia in terms of deficiency, she asks if it would be better to have 'another language in which more truly to imagine Australia'.[23] Of course, we already have many languages fit for this purpose. Unburdened by historical echoes of the English countryside, Aboriginal languages can ably describe their local landscapes, often in deep and profound ways. For example, *bily* in Noongar describes both a waterway and the navel. Rather than creating expectations of England's brimming lakes and flowing rivers, this polysemy poetically conveys the normal infrequency of local water regimes. It also intimately links landscapes to the body, dissolving anthropocentric/ecocentric boundaries between people and the rest of existence.[24]

Noongar language links us to landscapes. *Kaat* is head and hill, *bookal* is lower back and knoll, *koongat* is shoulder and the side of a hill, *bonitj* is island and knee, *maarr* is wind and *maar* is hand, *ngaangk* is sun and mother. Humanities researchers have long suggested that environmental crisis may not just be the result of flawed science and economics, but also a disconnection between culture and nature.[25] Ideally, a local language can underpin nuanced ecological understandings and encourage environmental stewardship, or 'caring for Country'. A resurgence in the use of Indigenous languages like Noongar will not necessarily halt environmental degradation. However, this kind of restorative cultural change could certainly increase the diversity of perspectives on how to appreciate and interact with local landscapes.

Shakespeare waangkiny

The English language is by no means incapable of expressing pro-environmental and anti-colonial ideologies. Shakespeare's work is certainly interwoven with ecological concerns, such as deforestation and climate change, which were topical in early seventeenth-century England.[26] Indigenous peoples frequently use settler-colonial languages to articulate their own distinctive worldviews.[27] In recent decades, theatre makers have even attempted to recuperate and reframe plays about racial vilification like *Othello* and *The Merchant of Venice* as 'woke' critiques of racism.[28] For most Noongar people, however, Shakespeare looms not as an environmentalist or humanist, but as the colonial power's most lauded writer.

Noongar understandings of Shakespeare are often associated with experiences of compulsory English-language schooling as part of the Australian Commonwealth Office of Education's 'planned, vigorous and maintained drive for English'.[29] Speaking about Australian government attitudes to Indigenous languages, Roma Yibiyung Winmar explains:

> Our languages aren't valued. They never have been...Kids going into missions and having to learn English because their own mother tongue wasn't acceptable.

For many Noongar, Shakespeare is symbolic of imposed settler-colonial ideas about high culture and, indirectly, the suppression of Noongar culture. Like ballet, opera, and Western art music, Australian institutions have supported and promoted Shakespeare on a scale incommensurate with the paltry support recently extended to Indigenous languages – languages that past governments invested in wiping out.

Hecate subverts and capitalises on Australia's deference to British and European high culture. Ironically, engaging with something as canonically English as Shakespeare was crucial to *Hecate*'s success as an act of language revitalisation. As professor of theatre studies Ric Knowles observes:

> That the show relied upon audiences' familiarity with the Shakespeare 'original' for their full understanding spoke to the cultural authority of the classic text; that it asserted the equal cultural authority, expressiveness, and value of Nyungar spoke to Indigenous resurgence in Western Australia.[30]

Prior experience of Shakespeare's *Macbeth* in schooling, theatre, films, and popular culture would have already primed most Noongar and non-Noongar audiences to understand *Hecate*'s narrative arc, even without comprehending the Noongar language. Shakespeare's cultural cache also attracted the government and philanthropic support, media attention, and audience interest to support the long development period required for the cast to reclaim and learn to perform in their Noongar language.

Shakespeare's work is so enshrined in global popular culture that *Macbeth* has been adapted and presented in various non-European cultural and linguistic contexts, particularly in Akira Kurosawa's samurai film *Throne of Blood* (1957), Vishal Bhardwaj's Bollywood film *Maqbool* (2003), Abhaya Simha's Tulu language film *Paddayi* (2018), non-Indigenous director Anita Maynard-Losh's stage version of *Macbeth* partially presented in the Tlingit language (2007), and Inuvialuit, Cree and Dene writer Reneltta Arluk's reimagined *Pawâkan Macbeth* staged partially in Cree.[31] *Hecate* is not alone in its mobilisation of Shakespeare to address local concerns, particularly in contexts of language endangerment.[32] Based on a 1945 te reo Māori translation of *The Merchant of Venice*, the feature film *Te Tangata Whai Rawa o Weniti* (2002) was produced to bolster Māori language revitalisation.

As an anomaly in Australian theatre history, 1999 saw Indigenous actors constitute at least half of the cast in three separate Australian Shakespearean productions: *As You Like It* (Company B), *Romeo and Juliet in Black and White* (Bell Shakespeare) and *Romeo and Juliet* (La Boite and Kooemba Jdarra). However, all actors performed in English. Before *Hecate*, Australia's only other mainstage Shakespearean work with an all-Indigenous cast – Malthouse Theatre's 2013 adaptation of *King Lear* titled *The Shadow King* – featured a linguistic mélange of English, Yumpla Tok (Torres Strait Creole), Kala Lagow Ya (Torres Strait Creole), Gupapuynga (Yolngu), Baard, and Katherine Kriol, and was guided by a non-Indigenous director.

In contrast to all prior productions of Shakespearean work involving Indigenous peoples or languages in Australia, *Hecate* was unequivocally Noongar-led, with a Noongar director, composer, lighting designer, and cast of nine actors. Maitland Schnaars played the role of Macbeth in *Hecate* and began his tenure as the new artistic director of Yirra Yaakin Theatre Company in 2023. In the context of Australia's arts sector, he considers *Hecate*'s creative team unique and unparalleled:

> It's so significant. I mean for the Noongar people. I've worked a bit on the east coast too, and they look down on us Noongars, they think we're a bit crazy...And I get [frustrated] when I see NITV (National Indigenous Television), 'cause to me NITV is not NITV. It's east coast TV. Also, when you go to even the state gallery here [in Perth], you see these Aboriginal art exhibitions and they're all from Pilbara, Kimberley way. So even on Noongar Country you see jack shit that's Noongar. So *Hecate* for me is like saying, 'we're as good as everyone else, we can create stuff which other mob can't'. 'Cause on the east coast there's no way can they pull nine actors, a director, sound, lighting, that's twelve key creatives from the one language group. They can pull twelve blackfellas, but not from the one language group. Only us here in Noongar Country can do that.

Using this Noongar-centric approach, Kylie Bracknell and Kyle J. Morrison formed the creative team around the most skilled practitioners in Western Australia, ensuring gender equilibrium and honouring longstanding relationships with Noongar people and Country. Yamatji movement director Janine Oxenham and stage manager Susan Fenty Studham were key collaborators, enriching *Hecate* with their specialist skills.

In addition, Yirra Yaakin Theatre Company's Kyle J. Morrison invited Bell Shakespeare, Australia's national theatre company specialising in the works of William Shakespeare, to collaborate as a partner in 2017. Via dramaturg Kate Mulvany and associate directors James Evans and Peter Evans, Bell Shakespeare effectively supported the Noongar creative team in realising a collective Noongar vision for *Macbeth*, rather than asserting control. Bell's artistic director Peter Evans saw *Hecate* as vital to the company's remit, to present Shakespeare in ways it had never been done before, preventing it from being 'stuck in the past' and reorienting it as a 'lens through which we can explore and question the present and imagine our future'.[33] Uncompromisingly immersing its audience, performers, and creative team in Noongar language for eighty minutes each night, *Hecate* certainly aimed to provoke questions and dream up new paths ahead.

Reverence – for Shakespeare in the arts community and Noongar language in the Noongar community – raised the stakes for *Hecate*. Kyle J. Morrison describes how the cast and creative team approached the dual challenge of being creative in the context of language endangerment and the theatre establishment:

> We really needed to learn the difference between respect and reverence, that was the biggest lesson that we learnt from working with Bell Shakespeare...Peter Evans started talking about the difference between respect and reverence. You can respect anything right up until you are full of its respect and still change it and edit it and augment it, but if you revere something, you're not going to change it. The level of reverence for Shakespeare in this country is stupid, but with the right respect, you can invest in it. It's the exact same idea with Noongar language, you know, there's this reverence around Noongar language and this fear that you can't get it wrong. Do you know how many times I've got Noongar language wrong? I've been in front of hundreds of people and got Noongar language wrong but I'm not going to stop, you've got to fall over and get back up, you've got to stumble. So, there was this idea that you can't make a mistake in Shakespeare, and you can't make a mistake in Noongar language because of reverence, but as soon as we get rid of reverence of anything, then with all respect you can create everything anew.

Despite overwhelming challenges to its continued vitality, most Noongar people value their language highly as a marker of identity and a connection to their ancestors.[34]

In various contexts of language endangerment, the deep respect people have for their Indigenous language can even deter them from speaking for fear of making mistakes.[35] Trauma connected to the suppression or absence of language can also inhibit language revitalisation and make communities wary of sharing their languages.[36] Even so, there is a long and established practice of Aboriginal languages being shared and spoken far and wide. As in the past, most speakers of Aboriginal languages today are highly multilingual, with individuals often able to speak many languages from surrounding areas.[37] While some Aboriginal stories and song repertoire are necessarily restricted to special people, places, and purposes, other kinds of stories and songs, including Aboriginal travelling corroboree songs, were once Australia's popular and widespread music.[38] Throughout the twentieth century, European and North American modes of cultural expression became increasingly ubiquitous in the south of Western Australia, subsuming the travelling corroborees which were once the staple of people's lives.

It was Morrison's formative experiences of Shakespeare refracted through popular culture that underpinned his impetus to present *Macbeth* in Noongar. He describes how:

> Shakespeare was always a high, elite thing, but I didn't see it as elite as a kid. I saw it as esoteric, hidden. You'd see Looney Tunes make references to Shakespeare, you had Bugs Bunny doing the 'to be or not to be' with Daffy's skull in his hands. Even though it was satirical, there was always this deep respect. Even Bugs Bunny had a deep respect for *Romeo and Juliet* and *Othello* and *Hamlet* and things like that. When I was fourteen and realised that *The Lion King* was actually *Hamlet*. I kind of went 'How was that story told?', and I just realised that Shakespeare's stories have been retold and redone. And as a sixteen-year-old I remember I had this dream of having this dark *Macbeth*, the three witches and how that works in a blackfella context. I didn't know why back then, but I do know now, because I suppose I could see the themes underlying *Macbeth*, the themes of femininity and Country and the land, and how nature is affected and infected by our decisions.

Obliterating notions of high culture and centralising Noongar language on Noongar Country, Kylie Bracknell's adaptation and co-translation juxtaposes Shakespearean and Noongar ideas about femininity and Country. Shakespeare's *Macbeth* demonstrates the potential for power to corrupt as the titular character commits increasingly violent acts to gain power over others. *Hecate* explores the broader ecological impact of that corruption. It frames Macbeth as acting against the laws of nature and mother earth herself, embodied by Hecate, a role often omitted from productions of *Macbeth* but brought forward here as the titular character.[39] Morrison explains that although the play is performed entirely in Noongar:

> it was Kylie's idea to keep the Scottish names, just to be able to tell that story with all that clarity and all that strength in Noongar language meant that our community was safer, that our community could go in there and it wasn't *about* them, it was *for* them. Do you know how much theatre that involves Indigenous people is actually for us? Not very much, 'cause everybody wants to tell stories about us.

Hecate is Shakespeare's *Macbeth* refracted through a radical Noongar lens. The promotional tagline at *Hecate*'s premiere read, 'In a world where the Noongar language is spoken by all, a yarn about a Scottish king is retold'. It was purposefully a well-known story from the European canon presented in Noongar language with a distinctly Noongar sensibility. Morrison points out:

> I could foresee the difficulties and problems if we told any Western Australian or Noongar stories in Noongar language, there would have been a lot more pushback. If we would have told a Dreaming story or if we would have told a contemporary story, if we would have connected to Noongar Country, too much reverence and ownership would have stopped us from being creatively explorative. I always understood that we could not tell our stories here in Noongar language yet, not the first time, so with the safety of telling a story that's so far removed from us physically, but so much closer to us philosophically, people accepted it a lot better, Noongar accepted a telling. But I don't think they really got it until they were in the audience, because they thought they were going to see Shakespeare and they weren't, they were going to see a Noongar story. It wasn't until they really

got in there that they forgot all about Shakespeare. One of the Elders goes, 'I forgot what I was watching until somebody said "Macbeth *yoowarl koorliny*" – 'oh that's right, we're watching *Macbeth*'!

Hecate broke down the barriers of silence and shame associated with Indigenous language loss and revitalisation, providing an unprecedented immersive audience experience. It also received critical acclaim.

Hecate's first season closed on 16 February 2020, exactly one month before a state of emergency was declared in Western Australia due to the pandemic caused by COVID-19. Although the Helpmann Awards, Australia's major performing arts awards, were cancelled, *Hecate* headlined *The Australian*'s review of best stage shows of 2020 and was awarded eight Performing Arts WA Awards, including Best Mainstage Production and Best New Work. Kylie Bracknell also received the prestigious Sidney Myer Performing Arts Award for her work on *Hecate*. These achievements paled in comparison with the language revitalisation gains over the decade-long timeframe necessary to adapt and translate the work, engage with senior Noongar speakers, and develop a Noongar acting ensemble. In the long lead-up to *Hecate*, many Noongar people including performers Irma Woods, Gina Williams, Dennis Simmons and Ebony McGuire participated in language gatherings to help nourish a community of speakers. While some of these gatherings were directly connected to developing and casting the production, others were far less formal, held outside or in donated venues and involved Noongar from all walks of life, often with their children in tow. Throughout the whole process, *Hecate* paid homage to the senior Noongar speakers who retained the language through the harshest years of injustice and assimilation.

2
Waabarangkar! A Noongar Ensemble

Clint Bracknell

Along with deeply considered work on the language, script, and story, making *Hecate* crucially involved the formation of a Noongar ensemble who could perform in their endangered language. This process really began in 2011 with an email that Kyle J. Morrison, then artistic director of Yirra Yaakin Theatre Company, received from Shakespeare's Globe Theatre in London. They were preparing to hold an international festival of Shakespeare's plays including 37 works presented in 37 different languages as part of the cultural festival called the Cultural Olympiad. As Malthouse Theatre's *The Shadow King* was not going to be ready in time for inclusion, the Globe suddenly had an empty slot in the program for an adaptation of *King Lear* from Australia. Given his interest in presenting Shakespeare in Noongar, Kyle explored the opportunity, recalling that:

> After a week of no sleep and numerous project plans, phone calls and meetings with artists, it became obvious that a project of this scale and significance would require a lot more time than the ten months we had for this project. I also could not work out why as a Noongar man I would want to tell the story of King Lear, it seemed like it was a story that white people could tell about 'Aboriginal' people but as a Noongar man, I could not see why I would want to tell it, why my community would need this story, or how I would even begin telling it.[1]

He responded to the Globe Theatre, explained the difficulty that the short timeframe posed, and questioned why, if they wanted to include Indigenous languages of Australia, they had not approached an Indigenous theatre company with the opportunity in the first place. The Globe responded with an invitation to instead present several of Shakespeare's sonnets translated into Noongar language as part of 'Sonnet Sunday' to open the festival.

Morrison thought that working with sonnets would be a good way to build towards eventually presenting a fully translated Noongar work. However, not everyone shared his enthusiasm:

> Unfortunately, none of the people I approached at that time could see the value of translating Shakespeare into Noongar language. I was disheartened by this setback and was talking through my disappointment with Kylie Bracknell, Kylie Farmer at the time. Kylie then very clearly reminded me that I was searching in the wrong places. Kylie then looked me in the eye and said, 'Bro, I can do this'. That moment of clarity still inspires me to this day. Not only is Kylie Bracknell an experienced Noongar language speaker, but she is also a brilliant Shakespearean actor.

Kylie would go on to boldly create interpretive translations of sonnets 18, 44, 45, 46, 127, and 134, with editorial guidance from Roma Yibiyung Winmar. Those interpretive translations are included in this book, along with Sonnet 71 which was translated in 2020. Receiving the first Noongar sonnet was profoundly moving for Morrison:

> To this day I can recall all the emotions I felt the first moment I held that page. The paper was still warm in my hand and the words leapt directly off the page straight to my soul: 'Birok kidala, ngany kaaditj nyoona' (Shall I compare thee to a summer's day). This was the first line I read of a Noongar adaption of Shakespeare's work and from that very second, I knew that Noongar language was alive. I silently cried while standing next to the office printer with the page still warm in my hands and the ambition of performing Noongar

> Shakespeare transitioning from a boyhood dream to material reality in my own hands.[2]

With Kylie able to translate and perform the sonnets alongside Kyle, he approached a third performer to join them. Noongar and Yamatji man Trevor Ryan had studied at the National Institute of Dramatic Art in Sydney, but was living back in Perth and dancing with Wadumbah dance group when Kyle noticed his 'commitment, passion and outright skill' and invited him to join the project as a performer. As Trevor explains:

> Kylie Bracknell and Aunty Roma Winmar taught me the Noongar language before I went to the Globe Theatre in London. It was quite difficult at first to learn, which is quite strange even saying that because it is my mother tongue. To come to the realisation of struggling to even speak your own native tongue was quite frustrating. You start to question yourself, the history of our country, and what has happened to our people all throughout Australia. But with the previous experience I had from the Globe I felt more confidence in going into the *Hecate* rehearsals with the other cast members.[3]

Before leaving for London, Kyle, Kylie, and Trevor performed the Noongar sonnets for a small Noongar community audience at the Yirra Yaakin Theatre Company's office in East Perth. The emotional audience included Kyle's grandmother, one of the most senior Noongar women still alive today. Many of the eventual *Hecate* creative team were there too.

After the 'Sonnet Sunday' performance in London, Ian Wilkes and Irma Woods joined the troupe to perform the sonnets again for the opening event of Perth Festival 2013. Della Rae Morrison, who would play Hecate herself, and I were there as backing singers for headlining act Archie Roach. In 2016 Kylie read her interpretation of sonnet 127 in Noongar for a national television audience on the Australian Broadcasting Corporation's *Q&A* program, with *Hecate*'s eventual dramaturg, acclaimed actor and writer Kate Mulvany, reading the original English version. In the ensuing discussion *Q&A* host Tony

Jones announced the impending Noongar adaptation of *Macbeth*, but there was still much work to be done. At that point, Kylie did not have a contract to adapt the work, let alone direct it.

Throughout the early sonnet project and up to the premiere of *Hecate*, Kylie led biannual, week-long workshops involving up to fifteen Noongar performers. As none were fluent Noongar language speakers, these workshops provided a rare space for Noongar artists, as well as invited senior language speakers, to collectively address intergenerational trauma associated with language loss and reclaim the language together as an ensemble. Maitland Schnaars describes his experiences coming into the workshops which would lead to *Hecate*:

> I had no [Noongar language] experience at all. There's always [Noongar] words which everyone knows, stuff like that. The biggest thing I had to confront when I started learning it, I knew I'd have issues with regards to the white institutions and anger against them for taking away my language, but what surprised me that I didn't expect was anger towards my family. I was hit with this anger like 'Why did Kylie's family keep language and mine didn't?' I had to realise that it was a different time back then, and they did what they thought was best for the family. It wasn't them, they shouldn't have been put in that position in the first place where they had to give up language. But yeah, it was a challenge 'cause when you're younger, it's easier to learn language. It's hard and more a challenge when you're older.

Bobbi Henry, who played opposite Schnaars as Lady Macbeth, also had to work through emotions associated with not having prior opportunities to learn Noongar language.

> Learning the language for me was both challenging and rewarding. I had some knowledge of Noongar language but not enough to have a fluent conversation. I found myself angry early in the process about not being taught my language earlier, angry with the people who took the language and sometimes people who did not teach me but taught others. After conversations with other Elders, they simply told me you weren't ready, but now you are.

The significance of the actors becoming able to speak and comprehend Noongar for themselves cannot be overstated. For *Hecate* to work pragmatically as both a theatre production and an overt act of language revitalisation, the ensemble needed to do more than memorise and repeat Noongar dialogue. Actors had to be aware of their cue lines and be able to react and improvise during any point of the performance to unintended deviations from the script.

To increase the ensemble's Noongar comprehension and communicative skills, Kylie embedded a 'Noongar-only' hour, in which participants could only interact using the Noongar language, into each workshop and rehearsal day. This approach functioned as a scaled-down version of successful language immersion methods used in revitalisation programs across New Zealand and Hawaii.[4] In the beginning, Noongar-only hour could bring silence to the room. This challenging activity often triggered discomfort and, on more than one occasion, participants were so overwhelmed during the hour that they left the space altogether. Even so, they always returned. The workshops and rehearsals provided a challenging environment, while also functioning as a sanctuary. They allowed flexible space and time for contemplation and group discussion, enabling the development of not just skills in Noongar language, but courage to continue to engage and keep growing in the language.

Although Kylie invited many senior Noongar language speakers to visit the ensemble during the Noongar-only hours, few took up the challenge. The senior people who did take up the invitation to spend time with the actors mostly offered phrases and words before the commencement of the hour for the actors to practise. Most stayed after the Noongar-only hour concluded, joining the group in discussing the difficulty of avoiding English after having it mandated in our lives for so long. The performers and creative team had to depend on each other during the Noongar-only hour to communicate. This interdependence strengthened bonds among the ensemble and between the actors and the senior language speakers, helping to solidify a stronger Noongar language-speaking community. As one of the younger cast members, Mark Nannup, remembers,

> In the beginning it was very scary, I was thinking, 'What the hell did I get myself into?' but I had the drive and determination to make it work. I loved the old people being in the room and helping us with language.

With the right support in place, the ensemble embraced the challenge of Noongar-only hour so much that by 2016, Kylie observed that it was 'hard to get sixty seconds of quiet time amongst them'.[5]

Brave spaces

After years of community and performer workshops, *Hecate*'s formal production process consisted of three major phases: six weeks of studio rehearsals, two weeks of technical rehearsals leading to three previews, and the subsequent performance season. Daily rehearsals consistently involved a core group including director Kylie Bracknell, nine Noongar cast members including Kyle J Morrison, Yamatji movement director Janine Oxenham, and stage manager Susan Fenty Studham. Although not Indigenous, Susan has a long history of cross-cultural collaboration and had previously worked with Morrison, other cast members, and myself on a range of Noongar-led theatre projects. We shared a pre-established relationship and trust that she would support us in her role as stage manager, maintaining the structure of rehearsals, planning for technical rehearsals, communicating with all departments through daily schedules and reports, and working to ensure the rehearsal space was safe for performing artists and theatre makers.

Although that last element of a stage manager's job description could be described as creating a 'safe space', there are many ways to interpret 'safety'. In the case of Noongar actors learning to perform in their endangered mother tongue, physical, emotional, and cultural safety are incredibly important. However, the term 'safe space' is ill-fitting for this context as it does not allow for any kind of discomfort.[6] Working towards staging *Hecate* was far from 'safe'; it challenged the whole team to bravely respond to the long-term suppression of Noongar language and culture. The actor who played Hecate herself, Della Rae Morrison, describes *Hecate* as the 'biggest highlight of my career', but also 'terrifying'. Reflecting on *Hecate*'s development, she states 'I loved every step, every moment, every challenge of every day'. The youngest member of the ensemble, Cezera Critti-Schnaars, reflects on the impact of hearing sustained Noongar dialogue:

> The day where they had the first reading of the first draft of the first scene, I got to hear that. I didn't understand the impact of it at the time, but I just remember all the men went really quiet, and all the women started crying, because for everyone there, for most of us there, it was the first time we'd heard our language spoken like that.

The *Hecate* company frequently participated in challenging dialogue, took risks to enable more authentic conversations, and, when necessary, sat with discomfort. These kinds of practices required a 'brave space'.[7] A simple definition of a brave space is 'a space where we can sit with discomfort but can also look after each other's well-being'.[8] While the intent is still always that participants remain physically and emotionally unharmed, 'brave spaces' allow for growth and development in ways that 'safe spaces' may inhibit. Learning one's endangered language is an act of bravery, especially in the context of performing arts.

Each stage of *Hecate*'s production could trigger trauma associated with colonisation and language loss, and this risk was compounded by pressure on the cast to seamlessly deliver dialogue in a recently learned endangered language. In every *Hecate* development workshop, grief over language loss would cause a performance block for at least one actor. Fostering a brave space meant ensuring flexibility to respond to daily triggers experienced by the ensemble over the entire production process, which crucially involved holding space and listening. As director, Kylie would initiate a dordong waangk (circle talk) at various stages of the rehearsal process. Held inside rehearsal rooms or outside on Country as required, the circle was a trusted space for the team to air and address discomfort. Dordong waangk became so integral to the production process that it would be formally included in daily rehearsal and technical rehearsal schedules as pressure on the ensemble increased ahead of the premiere season.

As the development and rehearsal of *Hecate* progressed, Kylie would increasingly direct in Noongar and the ensemble followed suit, the company becoming more confident incorporating more Noongar vocabulary daily to the point at which Noongar became the dominant language of the rehearsal room. Cezera Critti-Schnaars remembers how rehearsing lines with her father, Maitland Schnaars, after coming home from rehearsals helped expand her language repertoire:

> I got to learn more than I guess I had to, in the sense that Dad had a bajillion lines and I had twenty-five. So through him I actually learnt more Noongar by practising with him. And then it was really exciting being surrounded by it and slowly kind of picking up on it, like I still can't really respond properly, but I remember we started doing notes in Noongar and there was one time when I understood all of the notes that I got.

It was not just the cast who dramatically increased their Noongar language competence. Non-Indigenous stage manager Susan Fenty Studham had to develop her understanding of the language to keep track of the development of the show, off-book comments, intention, blocking, and technical cues. In addition, as stage manager, Fenty Studham had to call out any forgotten lines to prompt the actors to continue. Like the actors, Susan was working between two languages. The challenging and culturally nuanced nature of producing a Noongar language adaptation of *Macbeth* increased the importance of establishing and maintaining a brave space and developing a range of tailored strategies to support the ensemble's language reclamation journey.

Voice work

Most of the actors had formally trained at institutions including the Western Australian Academy of Performing Arts, the Victorian College of the Arts, and the National Institute of Dramatic Art, and performed in English-language acting for many years so were skilful in creating the forward-projected sounds expected in that arena.[9] In addition to the way that Australian policies of assimilation violently supressed the sounds of Indigenous languages, traditional approaches to actor voice training 'favour the white middle-class somatic norm and dominant listening ear within the performing arts'.[10] As a result, at the time rehearsals for *Hecate* commenced, the Noongar language ability among the ensemble of nine Noongar actors varied from knowledge of a few key words to some functional language skills, mostly acquired through prior involvement in performances of sonnets in Noongar. The whole cast shared English as their first language and had to learn to perform in Noongar as a second or third language. Mark Nannup explains his lack of prior opportunities for Noongar language immersion and how much he values learning to perform in his language:

> I had grown up in the desert and only came down to Perth for holidays to see family, but not many people were speaking the language when we came down. I knew very little Noongar growing up, but now as an adult I can't get enough of it. It makes you feel connected to place and how nature, people, and animals are all connected through language. By speaking language on stage it allows you to be free in who you are and showcase the complexities and beauty of language.

As some actors had grown up hearing family members speaking Noongar words and phrases, if not full conversation, they were familiar with some of the language's characteristic sounds and articulation. Imagining most Noongar sounds as emerging from the back of the mouth, as opposed to the way English articulation is projected forwards, was useful for the ensemble.

Although literacy is fundamental to most Indigenous language revitalisation movements, Noongar included, written Noongar cannot convey the flow of the language, its nuances of emphasis and delivery. As a senior language speaker and teacher, Roma Yibiyung Winmar provided invaluable advice and inspiration to the entire company throughout the adaptation, translation, and rehearsal of *Hecate*. As an additional step to support the cast to learn lines during the early rehearsal period, Kylie and I read and recorded audio of the script, sharing it with the company via an online filesharing platform. This audio of the spoken Noongar language was accessible on the actors' personal devices and acted as a reference point from which they honed their performances.

Towards the end of the rehearsal period, Kylie engaged voice and dialect coach Luzita Fereday to provide tailored feedback for the cast. Luzita had previously worked with many of the ensemble as a trusted coach and colleague, which assisted in maintaining the supportive environment established throughout *Hecate*'s development and production. She listened to the audio recordings of the script we had made for the cast and then listened to the actors performing while following the script, noting discrepancies. She discussed what sounds each cast member could focus on improving with Kylie and I, providing notes for us to edit. The three of us thought it better that the notes be delivered by a Noongar speaker who could voice pronunciation examples, so I conveyed these notes to the cast both individually and more generally in a group setting.

The main obstacles for the actors included articulating 'rt', the 'retroflex stop' (e.g. *kert-kert*, 'quickly'), which does not exist in Australian English, and the velar nasal 'ng' and the voiced palatal nasal 'ny' consonant, which can often be part of the same word (e.g. *ngany*, 'I'). These sounds require significant muscular action and flexibility in the tongue which can only be built with consistent practice. In addition, the near-open front unrounded vowel sound (æ) is not found in the Noongar language but is characteristic of Australian English and the varieties of Aboriginal English spoken by most Noongar people today. Excluding this exceedingly familiar and comfortable sound from deliveries of Noongar dialogue was a significant challenge. Throughout the process of learning to perform in Noongar for *Hecate*, the ensemble continually and courageously stepped outside of their comfort zones.

Throughout *Hecate*'s workshop and rehearsal phases, I developed four key Noongar language songs for the production inspired by reinterpreted Shakespearean text and the musical and poetic conventions of Noongar song. From 2017 onwards, before the final cast had been selected, actors participating in the workshops would learn, repeat, and perform a song I had created for the wounded sergeant (Act 1, Scene 2) and *Hecate*'s theme song 'Boodjar'. Group singing helped guard against the 'shame factor' often associated with learning one's endangered Aboriginal language.[11] Most of the ensemble considered the suite of *Hecate* songs as pivotal in their language journey. Even long after the production closed, many of the cast remembered and sang the songs. They still do today. Singing can often assist awareness of pronunciation and rhythms in language-learning contexts.[12] The *Hecate* songs assisted the performers to develop the specific vocal articulations required to perform in Noongar language, while also helping to lift the ensemble's confidence.

Given the significant importance of song in Noongar culture, learning the *Hecate* songs functioned on multiple levels. The shorter songs were able to be learned and repeated quickly, increasing confidence among performers to be able to memorise Noongar text. Once eventually mastered, the longer or more complex songs provided both a sense of accomplishment and a feeling of connection and continuity with Noongar singers of the past. Although some argue that a 'language cannot be saved by singing a few songs',[13] these outcomes demonstrate how the mnemonic qualities of song can assist in invigorating and sustaining language acquisition and they highlight the intrinsic value of singing in support of cultural and emotional wellbeing. In workshops and then later during rehearsals, group singing increased feelings of connectedness in the ensemble, so much so that in the premiere season, singing *Hecate*'s closing song, 'Bokidja', together became part the cast's private pre-show ritual.

Connection and reception

As director, Kylie ensured that Noongar cultural practice and broader goals of language revitalisation were core to the development and eventual presentation of *Hecate*. Anticipating the need for audience members to feel welcomed into, reassured by, and connected to the space, Kylie arranged for Wardarndi woman Mitchella Waljin Hutchins to host Hecate Kambarnap, a unique pre- and post-show gathering space celebrating Noongar people and the maintenance and care of the Noongar language. This was also a space for the cast to sit alongside audience members, particularly Noongar people, to share their language reclamation journey through *Hecate*. Waljin offered warmth and cleansing fire-smoke to all wanting to honour Noongar sounds, stories, and speakers, and more importantly to people with spiritual and emotional triggers relating to language loss.

Hecate's first preview was predominantly attended by Noongar community members and other Indigenous people. Bobbi Henry considers this first night in *Hecate*'s first season her personal highlight, explaining that 'with family members and Elders in the audience, we felt the love'. As only 3 per cent of the Noongar community identify as speakers of the Noongar language, establishing Kambarnap, a place to meet, share, and debrief, was key to the holistic power of the work. Kylie explains:

> I expressed to Perth Festival that *Hecate* will not happen successfully if there's no Kambarnap. This isn't about showing off that we have the language. We need a space, separate from the theatre foyer and the dressing rooms, to cry together as one and face the fact that our language is on the brink of extinction here in our country. While this world-first production is being celebrated for its innovation, it will also celebrate attempts at wiping the Noongar language out if we don't make space for the feelings of loss our audience members are carrying. We must simultaneously support and encourage our community's healing journey. It shouldn't just be about us presenting a work for non-Noongar people to celebrate, it needs to also be about celebrating the language being restored amongst its community in

> a way Noongar community members can identify comfortably – a ceremony setting, not just a show.

More than a collaboration between creatives and cast, *Hecate* was a collaboration with the Noongar, and even the broader, community.

In the lead-up to *Hecate*'s premiere, Kylie explained, 'Noongar words and philosophy are the true hero in our *Macbeth* adaptation *Hecate*. The way we communicate, signal, celebrate, sing and cry our language has always been, and will always be, powerful'.[14] Adapting a Shakespearean work in an endangered Indigenous language context was a risky and audacious endeavour. *Hecate*'s rigour and grounding in culture, community development, and care led to critical acclaim and a broadly warm reception among Noongar audiences. As Roma Winmar observes:

> You'll always get people that want to knock it in the head or look out for a failure, but they never found any failure in that...no. At the end of the day there couldn't be anything else but praise. Funny that, yeah.

After witnessing *Hecate*, senior Noongar language speaker Vivienne Binyarn Hansen – who participated in Noongar-only hours during *Hecate* development workshops – posted the following on social media:

> Last night I had the absolute pleasure of being at the final performance of Hecate as part of the Festival of Perth and performed by the cast of Yirra Yaakin. Words are hard to find to describe what I saw and heard, Shakespeare spoken in the language of our Noongar people, it made tears fall from my eyes, my heart so full of wonder and sent my spirit soaring to the skies full of happiness. Congratulations to all the cast and crew on a wonderful performance [...] I know it is only going to lead to even bigger and brighter achievements in the future. Gnung koort djerup djerup ni baalup waangening Noongar.[15]

Binyarn led celebratory dancing on the Kambarnap grounds alongside Waljin after *Hecate*'s closing performance. This was a significant act to the *Hecate* company, which confirmed that in the eyes and heart of this esteemed Noongar Elder, the processes we took in developing and showing *Hecate* were respectful and appropriate.

Former artistic director of Yirra Yaakin Theatre Company and the instigator of the whole *Hecate* endeavour, Kyle J. Morrison describes how:

> Noongar language speakers were so scared that we were going to ruin the language because it's hard to see any versions of it done right when there's no versions of it done right or wrong, so, if you're trying something for the first time, phwaor, just the community just went, put their hands up, took a few steps back and – and then, after *Hecate*, there was silence. I think a lot of the old fellas just went 'mm, mhm', and just sat back. They don't need to say anything more, they don't need to tell us that we're doing good. We're getting a lot of good feeling from the community. Shakespeare is my dream, but it allowed us to open the gates and now mob can do what they want with our language.

Maitland Schnaars had one of the most dramatic trajectories of the *Hecate* ensemble, eventually being cast as Macbeth after dedicatedly building his confidence and competence in Noongar language over years of development workshops. He underscores the importance of *Hecate* in supporting the future of Noongar language:

> I think it's really kicked off the rejuvenation of the Noongar language – and that's not taking away from language classes and courses that people were running beforehand, 'cause there have been some people that have been running language classes way before. But what *Hecate* did, it really brought it to the consciousness of a much broader community. And my other proudest moment of *Hecate* was having [my daughter] Cezera in it. It's the highlight of everything I've done. It's the culmination of the moment I set foot on this path.

Futures

Hecate is one of exceedingly few examples of theatre in Indigenous languages of Australia. The nation's gradual abandonment of assimilationist policies, the proliferation of local Indigenous cultural revitalisation programs, and recent calls to decolonise the performing arts[16] likely mean that endangered languages such as Noongar will increasingly find their way onto Australian – and even global – stages. Reflecting on the development and reception of *Hecate*, the following conclusions may be useful for guiding similar endangered Indigenous language theatre projects in the future:

1. Holistic success hinges on the large-scale involvement of relevant Indigenous peoples as not just advisers, but also as directors, creatives, and cast.
2. Learning to perform in one's endangered Indigenous language is not inherently safe and requires courage supported by the philosophy of brave spaces.
3. Development days and rehearsals need to be flexible, prioritising the energy in the room over strict schedules.
4. Oral learning and singing can effectively underpin endangered Indigenous language acquisition and strengthen felt connections between performers and ancestors.

As an arts intervention in the context of language endangerment, the development and staging of *Hecate* directly addresses multiple factors contributing to language vitality identified by the UNESCO Ad Hoc Expert Group on Endangered Languages,[17] including bolstering intergenerational language transmission, responding to new domains and media, and developing materials for language education and literacy. It nourished a new group of Noongar language speakers, activated the cultural domain of theatre for Noongar language, and, in the publication of this book, produced a legacy resource. As a complex work adapted from a vaunted settler-colonial text, *Hecate* challenges deficit attitudes towards Noongar and other Indigenous languages.

Shortly after *Hecate*'s first season, cast members Trevor Ryan, Kyle J. Morrison and Bobbi Henry commenced masters degrees in performance research. Bobbi Henry shares that:

> *Hecate* was one of the highlights of my career and my life because of the cultural significance of language and working with an amazing and talented group of artists. Being involved in *Hecate* has opened new opportunities for me to explore my language further and pass it on to the next generations, along with academic pursuits that I could not have thought possible.

Reflecting on his performance in *Hecate*, Trevor Ryan states:

> It made me feel complete as an Aboriginal man, father, and grandfather to stand with pride that was shared amongst the other cast members with a sense of unity as Noongar people representing ourselves and our families. We are part of an ensemble that is more like a family where we can trust each other, being vulnerable without a feeling of doubt of being judged. Each night before I walked out onto the stage, I would imagine my mother walking beside me. We would perform and speak our native tongue as one. *Hecate* has made me further develop myself as a language speaker. I can share my knowledge and experience as a performing artist working within the community amongst our people. I walk with pride knowing who I am as a Noongar.

Since its initial 2020 season, *Hecate* is yet to be remounted or toured. The COVID-19 pandemic led to decreased arts funding and performance opportunities in the ensuing years. Even in the wake of critical and audience acclaim for *Hecate*, theatre companies and festivals across Australia and internationally seem unsure of the profitability of staging a work completely in one Indigenous language of Australia. In avoiding programming *Hecate*, performing arts festivals and theatre companies in major centres such as Sydney, Melbourne, and Brisbane continue the longstanding tendency for institutions in the east of Australia to largely ignore groundbreaking Noongar work in the performing arts.[18]

Despite these challenges, the ensemble considers further productions of *Hecate* inevitable and critical to the maintenance of Noongar language. Cezera Critti-Schnaars explains, 'the thing that excites me the most about doing it again is really just being surrounded by language again 'cause the hardest bit for me is keeping it up'. Indigenous-led arts projects like *Hecate* provide an exceedingly rare opportunity for Indigenous artists to bravely nurture capacity in endangered languages. In April 2023, the *Hecate* cast reunited independently to present a reading of the play at the Perth Institute of Contemporary Arts. This invite-only reading was attended mostly by young Noongar people interested in their language, family of the ensemble, and performing arts colleagues. After the reading, members of the cast discussed a future in which they could see future generations of Noongar actors perform their roles in *Hecate*. Rubeun Yorkshire emphasises the enduring impact of the work:

> I would love to see it grow. I would love to see it transform and have a rebirth. With *Hecate*, I got so many ideas. It's really changed the way I perceive everyday life and our place in the community and how we honour that space by creating. It's so delicate, it's a different stream of energy and consciousness. It's like an awakening. It's like a conversation I haven't had for millennia. It's not bastardised or watered down to be tolerated by the masses. It's something I get to observe and cherish for its time, but it passes on for our next generation that they get to honour that and feel the warmth of that. It feels very elemental and transcends – you need that vibration to spark life.

3
On Noongar Language in Hecate

Clint Bracknell

Noongar of the southwest of Western Australia constitute one of Australia's largest Aboriginal cultural blocs, both in terms of population and a vast estate of lands and waters which includes the capital city of Perth, the city of Albany, and the town of Esperance. Noongar as a people share a common ancestral language with at least three regional dialects.[1] As the first Aboriginal group in Western Australia to experience sustained foreign contact and British invasion, Noongar bore the brunt of land theft, frontier violence, and the dislocation from homelands and family resulting from successive government policies of segregation and cultural assimilation.[2] Despite staggering odds, we Noongar find ways to continue to sing and speak in our endangered language.

Hecate is indebted to longstanding community efforts across generations to share and maintain Noongar language. Although it remains critically endangered, consecutive Australian Bureau of Statistics census surveys recorded Noongar as a language spoken at home by 167 people in 1996; 196 people in 2001; 240 people in 2006; 369 people in 2011; 475 people in 2016; and 1536 people in 2021.[3] While this census data does not account for fluency or frequency of use, it clearly demonstrates increasing identification with the language. Despite challenges to its vitality, Noongar people have continued to value Noongar language. Sustained and community-instigated language revitalisation activity since the 1980s reflects the importance of language to Noongar identity.[4]

At Marribank, also known as Carrolup, near the town of Katanning in the south of Western Australia, a 1985 Noongar language conference brought Noongar people interested in sustaining the language together with linguists including Wilf Douglas, Alan Dench, and Nicholas Thieberger. At that time, there was 'a clear interest among members of the Noongar community to record what was still known among the older people and to pass that knowledge to younger people'.[5] In 1990 senior language speakers including Cliff Humphries, Ned Mippy, Kathy Yarran, Hazel Winmar, and Peter Farmer Snr met at Wellington Mill Recreation Camp in between the towns of Bunbury and Collie. Working together with the support of linguists, they created a brief Noongar language resource booklet including sentences and songs. They also officially recognised Noongar as a single language with three mutually intelligible dialects.[6]

Two years later, many of the same senior people and the broader Noongar community attended a large meeting in Narrogin to reach agreement on a spelling system.[7] Gina Williams reported on the meeting for Golden West Network. Speaking about the senior language speakers involved, Williams explains:

> This was a time when everyone else thought Noongar language was dead. These people are still here – their voices resonate in this language and it is a privilege. These magnificent people were so generous with their knowledge.

Williams also recalls participants at the Narrogin meeting proposing more than a dozen different possible spellings for the word 'Noongar', explaining that 'the bulk of the time was spent on deciding how best to spell that single word'.[8] The compiler of the 1992 Noongar Dictionary, Rose Whitehurst, described Elders at the meeting wanting to avoid being confused with the 'Nunga' of South Australia, and recalling that 'Noongar' was the way missionaries originally wrote the word.[9] At a subsequent community meeting at Marribank in 1997 participants instead unanimously agreed on the spelling 'Nyoongar'. Today, while the Department of Education Western Australia and the South West

Aboriginal Land and Sea Council use 'Noongar', some community organisations use 'Nyungar' and a variety of other spellings too.

Diversity of opinion on how best to spell 'Noongar' and various other words reflects diversity in the understanding and use of Noongar language more generally. The developers of the *Noongar Our Way* language learning kit, Glenys Collard and Sandra Wooltorton, explain that:

> There are several identifiable Noongar dialects in existence at the present time. Each dialect varies slightly in the pronunciation of words, some suffixes, and sometimes in the word itself. Sometimes, some will say: 'That is wrong! That is not how you say it. You should say it like this...' We regard everyone who already knows it, who learned it from their own parents or grandparents, as right. They have simply learned another variation of the word. Be aware of this. It need not cause difficulty or confusion.[10]

After decades of keeping the Noongar language hidden from authorities, it can be challenging for senior Noongar and their families to speak openly about it and reach consensus on the finer details. The question of how to account for diversity in Noongar language use in the production of *Hecate* led to discussions with a range of senior Noongar speakers, with several visiting rehearsals and speaking with the cast and creative team – in Noongar. The fact that we as a group of Noongar with diverse regional affiliations could all share language and understand each other emphasises the underlying mutual intelligibility of Noongar language, despite dialectic differences.

Since the 1990s, a small number of committed teachers have provided Noongar language education at Western Australian primary schools, including Moorditj Noongar Community College. Noongar language classes are also offered by community organisations including Langford Aboriginal Association, and prisons. Books by Yelakitj Tom Bennell and Munyari Ralph Winmar prominently featured Noongar language, ushering in the publication of various illustrated story books in the twenty-first century.[11] Since 2010, Noongar Radio

100.9fm aired Noongar language segments originally hosted by Charmaine Bennell. The children's television program *Waabiny Time* also premiered in 2010 on the National Indigenous Television Network, promoting the language to a national audience.

While Noongar language is clearly visible across education and the arts today, it is nevertheless emerging from the devastation of an unjust settler-colonial history. Recent government policies implicitly denied fundamental human rights to Aboriginal people who used their languages in public, and many senior people literally had the language 'flogged out of them' as children.[12] Among the broader public of Western Australia, there has been a rapid movement from denigration and ignorance towards the Noongar language to an emergent interest, particularly as a means for non-Indigenous people to express allyship with Noongar people and explore concepts of identity and belonging. Increased appetite for Aboriginal languages to be taught in schools is welcome, but there is an initial need to develop a community of Noongar language speakers and resources that engage with the language at a deeper level.[13] Despite recent gains in awareness and visibility, the Noongar language itself remains largely unconsolidated, with no exhaustive dictionary or detailed technical grammar currently in publication. In this context, the challenge of a Noongar adaptation of *Macbeth* demanded detailed and unprecedented work with historical Noongar language materials.

Finding the words

Shakespeare used well over 20,000 unique English word forms in his poems and plays.[14] The most comprehensive dictionary produced in an Aboriginal language to date is for the Warlpiri language from the Northern Territory, which includes over 10,000 entries.[15] While children still grow up with Warlpiri as their first language today, more than a century of language suppression in the Noongar region has significantly diminished local vocabularies. Consequently, in the process of adapting *Macbeth* into *Hecate*, we could not exclusively rely on our own knowledge of the language and the memories of senior speakers.

Hecate huddles together a few hundred Noongar words and exclamations that float through the community, archival wordlists, and old audio recordings. A diverse range of Noongar words have been recorded since the early nineteenth century and demonstrate remarkable similarity to Noongar vocabulary spoken today. This language material also includes Noongar terms that have fallen out of use for various reasons, including fewer people conversing in Noongar as their first language.[16] The limited use of Noongar language in expressive culture and performing arts over the past hundred years has also adversely affected the retention and expansion of Noongar vocabulary.

There is a persistent myth that Shakespeare invented hundreds of new English words including 'bubble' and 'zany'. Rather than being a linguistic innovator, Shakespeare was 'a typical member of an artistic community' responding to and reflecting cutting-edge developments in the English language of the day to appeal to contemporary audiences.[17] As Professor of English Literature Jonathan Hope reminds us,

> Languages are collaborative, communal efforts – words come into being thanks to the morphological and phonetic resources of the language, and its cultural contacts, not because a few users are divinely gifted wordsmiths.[18]

While not necessarily provoking the invention of new words, *Hecate* provided us with the opportunity to reintroduce and revitalise archaic Noongar vocabulary. For example, the term 'kambarn' appears as 'gambarn: to associate' in John Brady's 1845 *Descriptive Vocabulary* and as 'kampern: gathering' and 'kaamp: meet' in C.G. von Brandenstein's 1970 field notes. Incorporation of this word into the script for *Hecate* led to the cast and creative team sharing it with a broader community of speakers. While our communal, collaborative effort facilitated the readoption of many old Noongar terms, this process began with comparing and discussing archival sources.

Among the various written records of Noongar language, British naturalist Robert Brown collected the earliest surviving wordlist in 1801 at Albany. The Swan River colony's appointed Protector of Aborigines, Charles Symmons, published the first grammatical description of the Noongar language in 1842.[19] Compiling the most voluminous collection of Noongar vocabulary, journalist and ethnographer Daisy Bates surveyed a large number of Noongar people across the southwest region in the early twentieth century.[20] American Gerhardt Laves became the first trained linguist to document Noongar as part of a broader study of Aboriginal languages when he visited Albany in 1931 and transcribed stories told by speakers of the southeastern Noongar dialect, Kurin.[21] After remaining in storage until the 1980s, Laves' unpublished work was deposited at the Australian Institute of Aboriginal and Torres Strait Islander Studies library (AIATSIS). Access to the Kurin material remains restricted on the instructions of Noongar people consulted in 2006.[22]

As possibly the first audio recording of Noongar language elicitation, linguist Ken Hale interviewed Tom Cowan and Tom Kickett at York, WA, in 1960.[23] Subsequently, audio field recordings were made by researchers Wilf Douglas in 1965 at Mount Barker, Gnowangerup, Narrogin, Brookton, and Merredin, and Carl Georg von Brandenstein in 1970 at Esperance.[24] This material is held at the AIATSIS archives and, together with less comprehensive material, comprises less than three hours of recorded Noongar speech before the 1980s. Douglas' significant 1960s fieldwork along with his continued collaboration with the Noongar community underpinned a series of published Noongar vocabularies.[25] Relying heavily on senior Noongar speaker Charlie Dabb, von Brandenstein combined his work at Esperance with historical sources in an attempt to 're-create' a 1500-word vocabulary, published as 'Nyungar Anew'.[26]

More recent recordings of Noongar conducted as part of language revitalisation projects are held at the AIATSIS archives and other institutions with conditional or restricted access conditions. Transcripts of anthropologist Tim McCabe's extensive 1995 recordings with senior Noongar speakers including Cliff Humphries significantly contributed to the 2006 Noongar native title determination.[27] Even if generally inaccessible, the existence of such recordings provides evidence of Noongar language's persistent presence. So too does the emergence of contemporary speakers like Kylie who initially learned the language orally from senior speakers, outside of formal education settings.

In working with a language no longer spoken by Indigenous people of the Californian coast, linguist Sylvia Broadbent employed a process of language 'reconstitution' involving the comparison of different versions of what various recorders of a language hear and transcribe.[28] To furnish *Hecate* with the necessary depth of vocabulary, we expanded this process by drawing on not just archival records but our collective memories of Noongar speech too. As a result, *Hecate* may include some Noongar words in forms never previously written down. The glossary at the end of this book matches each word in the script with relevant historical and community sources. In cases where we were not confident as to the meaning or origin of a term, we triangulated sources to build up a picture of its use and function.

This work was complicated by the fact that English-speaking surveyors and pastoralists without linguistic training compiled most of the accessible primary sources of historical Noongar vocabularies, employing a range of different, and somewhat inconsistent, spelling systems.[29] Noongar language includes a number of sounds not heard in English.[30] Like many Aboriginal Australian languages, the Noongar language includes voiced and un-voiced consonant sounds vocalised as either 'b' or 'p', 'd' or 't', and 'g' or 'k' interchangeably without altering the meaning of words. Hence, disagreement still exists among scholars and community members on the most appropriate orthography to use for writing Noongar language. The wide variety of spelling systems used across written accounts of Noongar language necessitates a flexible approach to word identification, in which various options are voiced, compared, and considered to arrive at deduced, if not authoritative, interpretations of form, meaning, and usage. Employing this method, we have identified and consolidated a few hundred Noongar terms for *Hecate*.

4
Hecate in Noongar with Director's Notes

Kylie Bracknell

As a young person, I was bestowed with a great responsibility, caring for people, nurturing them to heal from the loss of language. Pride holds a lot of Noongar people back from speaking their mother tongue. They will literally have trouble saying one or two words because they want to do it right the first time. I think that is due to society not allowing Aboriginal people to fail at anything – we must be correct instantaneously always. *Hecate* certainly freed us from holding back.

Kyle J. Morrison long had ambitions to do something amazing with Shakespeare and Noongar language. I almost fell over when he shared, 'we've got an opportunity to do a full work in Noongar language at the Globe in London'. I informed Kyle that we needed to invest time to reclaim our language within our community and alongside our community before we translated anything at all, especially Shakespeare.

It was agreed that the first step would be to translate a selection of sonnets for Kyle, Trevor Ryan and I to perform. Staging a community preview of the sonnets at home in Perth was far more daunting for us than performing to the masses at the Globe in London.

Amplifying sustained Noongar language to a small crowd of eighty people and a weeping sound that reverbed back at us.

Overwhelming waves of emotion as we shared our unjustly silenced language with our own community, particularly our Elders.

The wonderful bolt of lightning that went through us at that moment spurred us all to follow through and do a full work.

'Kyle' or 'Kylie' in Noongar both translate as boomerang, so we view our relationship as two boomerangs clashing – to either make music or noise. We did both in the years it took to get *Hecate* to the big stage. *Macbeth* was Kyle's choice to adapt. It is a dark piece, but *Hecate* is a healing journey and a call to reconnect to boodjar.

We could not have put *Hecate* together so successfully without the support of Bell Shakespeare. Kyle J. Morrison, Peter Evans, Kate Mulvany, and I read *Macbeth* together. We got to the scene of Hecate. It was at this point I realised that this spiritual queen, representing intuitive female strength within society and the creation of life, simply had to be our focus.

Following this inspiration, we boldly titled the whole production *Hecate*, naming it after a character rarely heard or seen on stage. Hecate is often omitted from productions of *Macbeth* and thought of as a latter addition to Shakespeare's script by writer Thomas Middleton.

Developing *Hecate* was a steady *dabakarn* dance between reverence for Shakespeare and going in a brave and previously unexplored direction. It began with me honouring the teaching that I had received from two grandmothers who are no longer with us. At the core of those teachings is that things go in the time they need to go in. I told Kyle that I would hold his hand and have his back but that he had to trust that things would go in the time that the language reclamation process would dictate.

Hecate was originally set to premiere in 2018 but was pushed back to 2020. This process had to go across eight full years rather than be rushed to fit festival and theatre company schedules. The reclamation of our endangered language should never happen in response to a non-Noongar work. Our process harnessed the creative arts as a vehicle for us to be together as an ensemble and develop our intellectual understandings and modes of engagement with language, a pillar of cultural identity.

We began by teaching sonnets in Noongar to the group. The first time we did that I had the urge to request that the group did not speak English for one full hour. During that time one of the actors, because quite upset and uncomfortable, left the room after only five minutes. The actor who left the room came back and ended up playing the role of Macbeth in *Hecate*. He had six years to work on the layers of trauma forced upon us through the decades upon decades of our Noongar language being supressed.

Fortunately for us, some wonderful trailblazers have kept the language alive long enough to carry on – orally and through documentation.

The *Hecate* process was an empowering chance for Noongar performers to reclaim their language among each other, so it became conversational. It was not just about one or two people learning to speak well. If you can speak your language and you have no one to talk to, you must question whether the language is really being kept alive. We had to reclaim the language together. Now we can walk down the street and talk in Noongar language at any time. We acknowledge the Noongar people before us who have opened doors. At the opening night for *Hecate* I did not mention Shakespeare but spoke of those Noongar trailblazers.

Yibiyung was mighty. She first came onboard to edit my interpretive translations of the sonnets. Her heart beamed and she would almost summon her mother and my grandmothers who used to speak together in Noongar language. She would honour them and say 'wouldn't it be lovely if they were still here today to see the work that you're all doing together to keep our language strong just the way they wanted to. They'd be so proud'. She is full of optimism and praise and possibility and 'yes you can' and that's the leadership that we need and have always had in Noongar Country.

Never once did she say 'not Shakespeare'. She is a wonderful artist, educator, mother, and grandmother. She has lived many lives. She is one of the main Elders who has supported *Hecate* because she sees opportunity. That shows a lot of trust within us. She can see that we as younger people are going to step in the process correctly and be respectful. Other members of the community who have been supportive of this include Jill Dewar, Vivienne Hansen, Judy Bone, and Richard Walley, who came into the room to speak Noongar with the ensemble for our 'Noongar-only hour'. We have had highly respected language custodians enter the space and that energy of reassurance was always a breath of fresh air for our ensemble and our entire Noongar team. A handing over of the baton to say, 'you have our trust, you have our support, go forth and be brilliant'.

We had a healthy Noongar audience at the first premiere. The response was overwhelming. After one performance a senior Noongar man looked at me and said, 'my gosh, that was brilliant – how do they remember all that?' That was all he said, and he kept shaking his head, overawed that our language has been on the brink of extinction, and he had just experienced eighty straight minutes of Noongar language onstage performed by an all-Noongar cast.

After the closing show, another senior Noongar man, my uncle, looked at me and cried. We held each other for about five minutes straight in the auditorium. To have somebody senior to you who you have respected all your life just look at you and cry and hold you and after five minutes of tears say just a few words, it is the tears you remember. It is the embrace you remember because you know it was felt.

When you work on a performance in your critically endangered language, you know for sure you are going to have senior Noongar people in the audience, and it does cause you to quake a little inside. My hope was that people would embrace the mammoth journey and task that we as a team had gone through to get to the point where actors didn't need to call for a line or break down in tears because they didn't understand a particular word from their mother tongue. It was quite an emotional journey and the response that we received still overwhelms us today.

Being so transparent about the length of the project's journey and the time we took to nurture the reclamation of language in the Noongar community and for the ensemble really captured people's hearts and attention. It drew them in. Once we reached our destination, I reminded the team that this production, where we have arrived at, is a celebration of the journey we have taken together. The fact that we have increased our Noongar language-speaking community by at least nine more people.

In terms of how our Noongar community received *Hecate*, I had lots of people, family and extended family approach me after seeing it to say excitedly, 'that was amazing'. It's hard to get Noongar people into the theatre because it is sometimes perceived as an exclusive or foreign space. Despite that, *Hecate* was received really well. My only wish is that the entire Noongar community could have seen it. I have high hopes that they will in the future.

At one of the post-show discussions that we held I reminded people that William Shakespeare was a playwright, not a novelist. He wrote words down on the page so they could be performed, shared, and amplified through the human voice so that human beings could feel them.

Our collaboration as a team of Noongar creatives has chiefly been about spending so much time with each other and talking through so much. It has also involved staying present in a highly alert state, the way that you would in the bush. We never lose that, even in the city we're constantly alert. Having that moment at the end of the play where the cast sit on the stage and sing is a massive gesture of gratitude to *boodjar*. Without her none of us survive. Travelling downwards to the ground and being comfortable connecting with her is important. We don't do it enough.

The depth of storytelling that we Noongar bring starts in *boodjar*, Country, and travels up through us. My bold call to completely forgo surtitles forced audiences into feeling this to the point that they would really experience it and simply tell other people 'you've got to go see this'. Experiencing time in Australia without the wash of English explaining everything, except for in the program, made *Hecate* memorable as a production.

Hecate opens with a monologue adapted from Ross' speech in *Macbeth*. 'Alas, poor country!' is a cry, a shriek, a feeling that Indigenous people have about Country every day since colonisation. 'Almost afraid to know itself' – we look around Country now and it is so different to how it used to be. It is not sure if it can be our mother anymore.

'Good men's lives expire before the flowers in their caps' reminded me so much of young people in Indigenous communities whose lives are cut short. The painful reverb of disconnection from Country. It is not just Country that is weeping, it is her children, all living things connected to Country, *boodjar*. It is so strongly connected to us as people that the Noongar word for conception and the first trimester is *boodj*, and the word for pregnant – full term – is *boodjari*. The language of *boodjar* and *boodjari* crystalises that connection between earth, the feminine, and creating life.

HECATE

Adapted from William Shakespeare's *Macbeth* by Kylie Bracknell

Presented by Yirra Yaakin Theatre Company
in association with Bell Shakespeare.
A Perth Festival commission.

Subiaco Arts Centre
5–16 Feb 2020

CAST

HECATE, LADY MACDUFF, SEYTON	Della Rae Morrison
DUNCAN, FIRST MURDERER, DOCTOR	Trevor Ryan
MISCHIEF MAKER 1, MALCOLM, THIRD MURDERER	Mark Nannup
MISCHIEF MAKER 2, LENNOX, SECOND MURDERER	Kyle J. Morrison
MISCHIEF MAKER 3, MACDUFF	Ian Wilkes
MACBETH	Maitland Schnaars
BANQUO, GENTLEPERSON	Rubeun Yorkshire
LADY MACBETH	Bobbi Henry
FLEANCE, SON	Cezera Critti-Schnaars

Translators: Clint Bracknell and Kylie Bracknell
Editor/Senior Language Consultant: Roma Yibiyung Winmar
Cultural Consultants: Judy Bone, Jill Dewar and Mitchella Waljin Hutchins
Songwriter/Composer/Musical Director/Sound Designer: Clint Bracknell
Lighting Designer: Mark Howett
Set & Costume Designer: Zoë Atkinson
Movement Director: Janine Oxenham
Dramaturg: Kate Mulvany
Stage Manager: Sue Fenty
Deputy Stage Manager: Jennifer Poh
Assistant Stage Manager: Levi Widnall
Bell Shakespeare Consultants and Associate Directors: James Evans and Peter Evans

Ngwirin

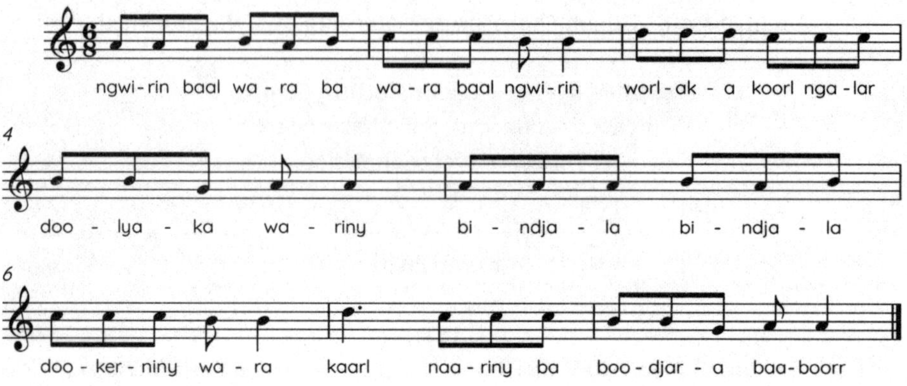

Boodjar

Nyornditj

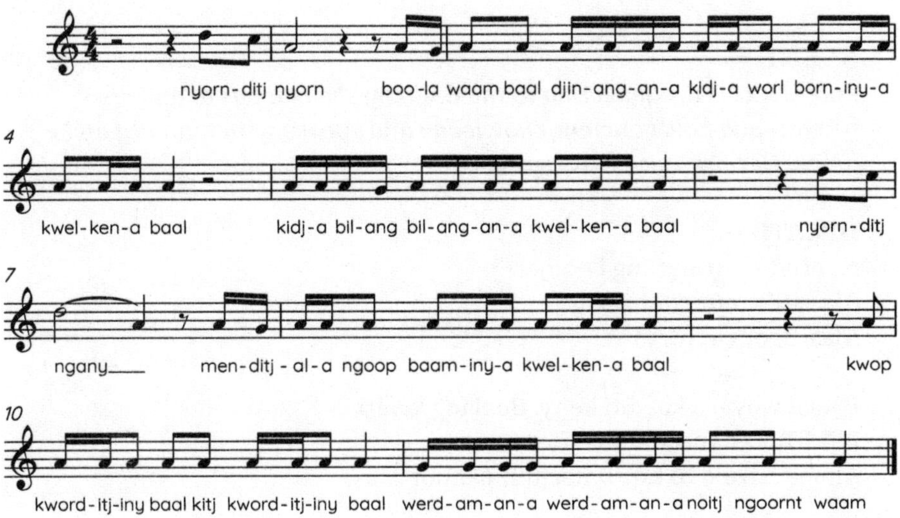

Bokidja

ACT I

SCENE I

Enter HECATE, connecting to the Country she belongs to and represents. She holds ancient knowledge and speaks with humility and grace. Her presence is everything.

HECATE
Nyornditj, ngalarang boodjar!
Alas-REL, our country!
Alas, poor country!

Baalal weyarn kaaditj keny. Baalang kwerl
It-ACT fear know alone. Her name
Almost afraid to know itself. It cannot

Yoowart 'ngaangk', yeyi baalang kwerl ngalarang bokal, nidjak,
Not mother, now her name our grave, here-LOC,
Be called our mother, but our grave, where nothing,

Nyoongara kaaditj-bt, kaawiny;
People don't-know, and laugh-CONT;
But who knows nothing, is once seen to smile;

Nitj maya waaliny worlak darabiny
Here voice cry-CONT sky-LOC dive-CONT
Where sighs and groans and shrieks that rend the air

Nyoongara dwongka-bt; nitj bakidiny koort-wera kabin
people deaf; here fight-CONT sorrow perhaps
Are made, not marked; where violent sorrow seems

Djoorabiny yeyi. Keny nyoongar noitj
Happy-CONT now. One person dead
A modern ecstasy. The dead man's knell

Baalitj kwerl kian, djoowakitj
He-REL name none, next-generation-REL
Is there scarce asked for who, and good men's lives

Wirndang noombit-mokiny,
Weary blossom-SIM,
Expire before the flowers in their caps,

Kert-kert noidjabiny.
Quick dying.
Dying or ere they sicken.

Boodjar, baal waaliny.
Land, it cry-CONT.
It weeps.

She touches the ground – boodjar – and suddenly we hear a fire crackling. The sound lingers. HECATE doesn't flinch. We see her strength. This story is hers – a tribute to the matriarchal energy of boodjar, life and order. She gazes forward into the future – 'the future in an instant'. She touches the ground again and the fire starts to burn.

All other cast become the MISCHIEF MAKERS and enter stage singing via auditorium, wading through the crowd towards the stage.

MISCHIEF MAKERS (song 1)
Ngwirin baal wara ba wara baal ngwirin:
Beautiful it bad and bad it beautiful:
Fair is foul, and foul is fair:

Worlaka koorl ngalar doolyaka wariny.
Sky-LOC travel we fog-LOC hanging.
Hover through the fog and filthy air.

Bindjala bindjala dookerniny wara;
Bubbles bubbles make-CONT bad;
Double, double toil and trouble;

Kaarl naariny ba boodjara baaboorr.
Fire burn-CONT and earth ripple.
Fire burn, and the earth bubble.

The MISCHIEF MAKERS reach the stage. They sing again.

Ngwirin baal wara ba wara baal Ngwirin:
Beautiful it bad and bad it beautiful:
Fair is foul, and foul is fair:

Worlaka koorl ngalar doolyaka wariny.
Sky-on travel we fog-LOC hanging.
Hover through the fog and filthy air.

Bindjala bindjala dookerniny wara;
Bubbles bubbles make-CONT bad;
Double, double toil and trouble;

Kaarl naariny ba boodjara baaboorr.
Fire burn-CONT and earth ripple.
Fire burn, and the earth bubble.

They assemble to worship HECATE and sing one more line.

Ngwirin baal wara ba wara baal Ngwirin:
Beautiful it bad and bad it beautiful:
Fair is foul, and foul is fair:

They halt and breathe in deep.

HECATE
Boola malkar dookern yeyi, yong yeyi:
Much magic make now, give now:
Great business must be wrought ere:

Benang ba, benang ba, benang
Tomorrow and, tomorrow and, tomorrow
To-morrow, and to-morrow, and to-morrow

Boodjar, baal waaliny.
Land, she cry-CONT.
It weeps.

HECATE flicks them away, so she is alone on stage.
She touches boodjar and the fire crackles some more.

SCENE II

Night. Stillness. Fire crackling.
Enter FLEANCE. HECATE watches her.

FLEANCE
Kidalak yaarn! Windji koorliny wa?
Night how! Where travel-CONT hey?
How now, night! Wither wander you?

Karam kidalak moornitj moorn, koondamal karni waangkang.
Yesterday night dark-REL dark, dream-ACT truly speak-PAST.
Thou thick night show'd me a truth last night.

FLEANCE sings part of an old song. HECATE just sang these very words. FLEANCE's father, BANQUO, taught her this song about humankind's duty of care to boodjar.

FLEANCE (song 2)
Boodjar baal waangkiny,
Land she speak-CONT,
All the world's a stage,

Boodjar baal waangkiny,
Land she speak-CONT,
All the world's a stage,

HECATE watches FLEANCE – her descendant. FLEANCE calls out to the night.

FLEANCE
Yeyi ngaitj kaaditj ngananginy benanginy biediny.
Now I-ACT know my-OBJ tomorrow-OBJ path-OBJ.
Mine destiny I do descry and know thy meaning.

FLEANCE, hoping for a reply, looks into the depth of the dark night sky just as HECATE did in her opening scene. She reaches down to boodjar and connects to it.
HECATE responds.

HECATE (song 2)
Boodjar baal waangkiny,
Land she speak-CONT,
All the world's a stage,

Boodjar baal waangkiny,
Land she speak-CONT,
All the world's a stage,

Maamangkara yokangkara kaadiny.
Man-PL woman-PL thinking.
And all the men and women merely players.

HECATE hears a loud noise. The fire is getting closer.

SCENE III

Darkness. Lights up.
The MISCHIEF MAKERS enter, cleverly camouflaged into the night.

MISCHIEF MAKER 1
Boordawan windji ngalar djinangalanginy?
Later where we see-LOC-ASS-CONT?
When shall we three meet again?

Malkar?
Thunder?
In thunder?

The MISCHIEF MAKERS mimic thunder, entertaining each other.

Bindari?
Lightning storm?
In lightning?

The MISCHIEF MAKERS mimic again.

Boroong?
Heavy rain?
Or in rain?

The MISCHIEF MAKERS mimic again.

MISCHIEF MAKER 2
Wirawoorliny baanal,
Whirlwind clear-LOC,
When the hurlyburly's done,

Waraitj kwopitj bakidjal.
Bad-REL good-REL fight-LOC.
When the battle's lost and won.

MISCHIEF MAKER 3
Kwadjat ngaangk dabat koorl.
Before sun fall travel.
That will be ere the set of sun.

MISCHIEF MAKER 1
Windjar?
Where?
Where the place?

Windjar?
Where?
Where the place?

MISCHIEF MAKER 2
Kwongkan boodjarak.
Sandplain land-LOC.
Upon the heath.

MISCHIEF MAKER 3
Bokidja, ngalarl Macbeth kambarn.
Afar, we-ACT Macbeth meet.
There to meet with Macbeth.

ALL (song 1)
Ngwirin baal wara ba wara baal ngwirin:
Beautiful it bad and bad it beautiful:
Fair is foul, and foul is fair:

Worlaka koorl ngalar doolyaka wariny.
Sky-LOC travel we fog-LOC hanging.
Hover through the fog and filthy air.

Exit MISCHIEF MAKER 1 & 2 – becoming MALCOLM and LENNOX alongside DUNCAN.
MISCHIEF MAKER 3 falls to the ground, becoming the wounded SERGEANT.

SCENE IV

Alarm within. Night. Indoors. Duncan's place of residence.
A wounded SERGEANT is on the ground in pain, bleeding from his side.
Enter DUNCAN, MALCOLM, LENNOX, with attendants, meeting the bleeding SERGEANT.

DUNCAN
Malcolm. Ngiyan baal ngoobalyong maam?
Malcolm. Who he bloody man?
Malcolm. What bloody man is that?

MALCOLM
Nidja baal, kidja-kadak
Here he hunter
This is the sergeant

Karam, baalitj moorditj
Yesterday he-REL strong
Who like a good and hardy soldier fought

Nganang barang-doordokanar. Bookor kobong!
My rescue-OCC. Brave friend!
'Gainst my captivity. Hail, brave friend!

Nyoona, biediyariny waangk yeyi:
You, boss-OBJ speak now:
Say to the king the knowledge of the broil

Bokidja bakidjap, djinangang natj?
Afar battleground, see-PAST what?
As thou didst leave it.

The SERGEANT, wounded, speaks carefully to DUNCAN.

SERGEANT
Yaakang kaaditj-bt;
Stand-PAST don't-know;
Doubtful it stood;

Koodjal wirndang kaep-waabar-mokiny, dit barang
Two weary water-play-OCC-SIM, together grasp
As two spent swimmers, that do cling together

woort-birniny.
Choke-CONT.
And choke their art.

The SERGEANT struggles to articulate his battlefield experience. It is painful.
The trauma envelops his face though he is elated to be alive – thanks to Macbeth. He sings a song to release the trauma within, conveying what he wittnessed.

SERGEANT (song 3)
Nyornditj nyorn
Alas-REL alas!

Boola waam baal djinangana
Many stranger he see

Kidja worl borninya
Spear sky cut-CONT

Kwelkena baal
Dodge he

Kidja bilang bilangana
Spear flash flash

Kwelkena baal
Dodge he

Nyornditj ngany
Alas-REL me

Mendidjala ngoop baaminya
Wound-LOC blood strike-CONT

Kwelkena baal
Dodge he

Kwop kwordidjiny baal
Good throw-CONT he

Kidja kwordidjiny baal
Spear throw-CONT he

Werdamana werdamana
Kill kill

Noitj ngoornt waam
Dead lie stranger

DUNCAN watches on, impressed.
The SERGEANT, with renewed energy, further praises MACBETH.

SERGEANT
Bwoar! Macbeth, baalang kwerl kwobitj kwop.
Wow! Macbeth his name good-REL good.
For brave Macbeth – well he deserves that name –

Kaawiny, bookor kidja-kadak,
Laughing, sharp spear-POSS,
Disdaining fortune, with his brandish'd steel,

Baalitj kidjak naariny,
His spear burn-CONT,
Which smoked with bloody execution,

Boordaoo kardaborn karang-kadakiny bilyak maadak,
Until cut-in-half enemy-OBJ navel-LOC leg-LOC,
Till he unseam'd him from the nave to the chaps,

Kaya kaadak yirangitj baam noort.
Yes head-INS up-REL put stench.
And fix'd his head upon our battlements.

The SERGEANT has exhausted his adrenaline. He is spent and loses his footing.

Ngany biedibap. Nganang mendidjal waaliny.
I'm tired. My wound-LOC cry-CONT.
But I am faint, my gashes cry for help.

DUNCAN
Nganang moort!
My family!
O valiant cousin!

Nyoonang maya ba ngoop dit kwop;
Your sound and blood together good;
So well thy words become thee as thy wounds;

Wardakadak-mokiny. (To Lennox) Boolyakadakak koorl!
Hero-SIM. Doctor-LOC go!
They smack of honour both. Go get him surgeons.

Exit SERGEANT, attended by LENNOX.
Enter a MESSENGER with a note – giving it to DUNCAN. The MESSENGER exits.
DUNCAN reads the note silently then expresses obvious cheer.

DUNCAN
Kayaritj kaya kwobitj kwop!
Yes-REL yes good-REL good!
Great happiness!

DUNCAN reads the rest of the note.
LENNOX returns. DUNCAN gives him an order to carry out.

DUNCAN
Boorda Cawdorap maam bardibiny yoowart
Soon Cawdor man deceive-CONT not
No more that thane of Cawdor shall deceive

(To Lennox) Ngwidam nitj: baal noidjabiny, wort koorl waangk,
Serious this: he-REL dead-TR, away travel speak,
Our bosom interest: go pronounce his present death,

Nyoondak baalang kwerl yong Macbeth.
You-ACT his title give Macbeth.
And with his former title greet Macbeth.

LENNOX
Kaya biediyar.
Yes boss.
I'll see it done.

DUNCAN
Cawdorap maamitj wirt. Macbeth moordidjabiny yeyi.
Cawdor-GEO man-REL weak. Macbeth strong-TR now.
What he hath lost noble Macbeth hath won.

Exit DUNCAN, MALCOLM, LENNOX, with attendants.

SCENE V

Night. Outdoors.
The MISCHIEF MAKERS return.

MISCHIEF MAKER 3
Windji nyoondak bara-koorl?
Where you-ACT go-astray?
Where hast thou been?

MISCHIEF MAKER 2
Mokoronginy.
Pig-OBJ.
Killing swine.

MISCHIEF MAKER 1
Natj nyoona?
What you?
Where thou?

MISCHIEF MAKER 3 makes shy harmless gestures to imply he has been on an amorous prowl. MISCHIEF MAKER 3 & MISCHIEF MAKER 2 laugh then stop when a loud drum is heard.

MISCHIEF MAKER 3
Ni, boorditj maya!
Hark, thump sound!
A drum, a drum!

We hear a loud drum sound.

Ni, boorditj maya!
Hark, thump sound!
A drum, a drum!

We hear a loud drum sound again.

Macbeth doth come.

MISCHIEF MAKER 1 & MISCHIEF MAKER 2 are confused and have no idea what the other MISCHIEF MAKER just said – they do not speak English.

MISCHIEF MAKER 2 & MISCHIEF MAKER 1
Natj?
What?
Huh?

MISCHIEF MAKER 3
Macbeth yoowarl koorliny.
Macbeth toward travel-CONT.
Macbeth doth come.

Macbeth yoowarl koorliny.
Macbeth toward travel-CONT.
Macbeth doth come.

The MISCHIEF MAKERS prepare to be seen.
Enter MACBETH and BANQUO.

MACBETH
Yeyi djart bardanginy nganang koort moornabiny.
Now sun jump-CONT my heart dark-TR.
So foul and fair a day I have not seen.

MACBETH and BANQUO notice the MISCHIEF MAKERS.
MACBETH is startled.

MACBETH
Ngiyan nyoondakat? Waangk ana?
Who you-PL? Speak yeah?
Speak, if you can: what are you?

MISCHIEF MAKER 1
Woola, Macbeth! Woola, nyoondalitj Glamisap maam!
Hooray, Macbeth! Hooray, you-REL Glamis-GEO man!
All hail, Macbeth! Hail to thee, thane of Glamis!

MISCHIEF MAKER 2
Woola, Macbeth! Woola, nyoondalitj Cawdorap maam!
Hooray, Macbeth! Hooray, you-REL Cawdor-GEO man!
All hail, Macbeth! Hail to thee, thane of Cawdor!

MISCHIEF MAKER 3
Woola, Macbeth! Woola, nyoondalitj biediyar boorda!
Hooray! Macbeth! Hooray, you-REL boss soon!
All hail, Macbeth, thou shalt be king hereafter!

The MISCHIEF MAKERS now turn their attention to BANQUO.

MISCHIEF MAKER 1
Kaya!
Yes!
Hail!

MISCHIEF MAKER 2
Kaya!
Yes!
Hail!

MISCHIEF MAKER 3
Kaya!
Yes!
Hail!

MISCHIEF MAKER 1
Nyoondalitj Macbeth-mokiny winyan ba, karni moordidjabiny.
You-REL Macbeth-SIM pitiful and, truly strong-TR.
You shall be lesser than Macbeth, and greater.

MISCHIEF MAKER 2
Djoorap-bt, yoran boolain.
Happy-NEG, alright more.
Not so happy, yet much happier.

MISCHIEF MAKER 3
Boordawan nyoonang djoowakitj biediyarabiny, nyoondalitj biediyar kwerl kian:
Later your next-generation-REL boss-TR, you-REL boss name without:
Thou shalt get kings, though thou be none:

Yeyi woola, Macbeth, woola Banquo!
Now hooray, Macbeth, hooray Banquo!
So all hail, Macbeth and Banquo!

ALL MISCHIEF MAKERS
Banquo Macbeth, woola!
Banquo Macbeth, hooray!
Banquo and Macbeth, all hail!

The MISCHIEF MAKERS angle to leave...they're stopped by MACBETH.

MACBETH
Yalak, koorart waangkarangkar, daa boolain:
Wait, short speak-OCC-PL, language more:
Stay, you imperfect speakers, tell me more:

Windji nyoondakat
Where you-PL
Say from whence

Kaadidjang nitj? Nadjal
Understand-PAST this? Why
You owe this strange intelligence? Or why

Nyoondakadal kwongkan boodjarak nyinang ngailak,
You-PL-ACT sandplain land-LOC sit-PAST we-EX-LOC,
Upon this blasted heath you stop our way,

Mila-waangk yongang?
Future-speak gave-PAST?
With such prophetic greeting?

The MISCHIEF MAKERS do not respond. They vanish.
MACBETH is left puzzled and deeply curious.

BANQUO
Boodjaritj bindjal-kadak, bilyaritj bindjal-kadak,
Earth-REL bubbles-POSS, river-REL bubbles-POSS,
The earth hath bubbles, as the water has,

Bindjal boola. Windji baalap balar?
Bubbles many. Where they-PL hidden?
And these are of them. Whither are they vanish'd?

MACBETH
Worlak koorl;
Sky-LOC travel;
Into the air;

Nyorndit j!
Alas-REL!
Would they had stay'd!

The prophetic information sinks in.
MACBETH gazes across at BANQUO and the same gaze is exchanged in return.

Boordawan nyoonang koolongitj biediyarabiny.
Later your child-REL boss-TR.
Your children shall be kings.

BANQUO
Boorda nyoondalitj biediyarabiny.
Soon you-REL boss-TR.
You shall be king.

MACBETH
Cawdorap maam: ana?
Cawdor-GEO man: right?
And thane of Cawdor too: went it not so?

BANQUO
Kora maya waangk.
Again sound speak.
To the self same tune and words.

HECATE is present.
BANQUO notices someone approaching.

BANQUO
Ngiyan nitj?
Who here?
Who's here?

LENNOX enters.

LENNOX
Biediyar Duncan baalang dwongk djoorabiny, Macbeth,
Boss Duncan his ear happy-CONT, Macbeth,
The king hath happily received, Macbeth,

Nyoonanginy wardainy kaaditj; Ngaitj nyoonak koorl
Your-OBJ renown-OBJ know; I-ACT you-LOC travel
The news of thy success; I am sent

Biediyarang daa yong;
Boss-POSS language speak;
To give thee from our royal master thanks;

Boorda nyoondak koorl biediyarak,
Soon you-ACT travel boss-LOC,
Only to herald thee into his sight,

Yeyi, milkar kwerl yong nyoonak,
Now, new name give you-LOC,
And, for an earnest of a greater honour,

Biediyarl waangk, nyoondalitj yeyi, Cawdorap maam:
Boss-ACT speak you-REL now Cawdor-GEO man:
He bade me, from him, call thee thane of Cawdor:

Yeyi, woola, Cawdorap maam!
Now, hooray! Cawdor-GEO man!
In which addition, hail, most worthy thane!

Kwerlitj nyoonalak.
Name-REL yours.
For it is thine.

BANQUO
(shocked) Natj?!
What?!
What?!

MACBETH
(in disbelief) Cawdorap maamitj doordok: nadjal
Cawdor-GEO man-REL alive: why
The thane of Cawdor lives: why do you dress me

Baalang kwoark nganyak yong?
His cloak me-LOC give?
In borrow'd robes?

LENNOX
Kaya karnarn doordok yeyi;
Yes true alive now;
Who was the thane lives yet;

Baalitj woolkar-kadak;
He-REL guilt-POSS;
But under heavy judgment bears that life;

Noidjabiny kert-kert.
Dying quick.
Which he deserves to lose.

Baalitj nyinang boodjarak winyanabiny;
He-REL be-PAST land-LOC pitiful-TR;
He labour'd in his country's wreck;

Karnarn, baalang dabadiny,
True, his fall-CONT,
But treasons capital, confess'd and proved,

Baalang koolyamang.
His lies-RES.
Have overthrown him.

BANQUO and MACBETH gaze at each other briefly, awkwardly. BANQUO approaches LENNOX to chat in private as MACBETH ponders upon the prophetic truth.

MACBETH
(Aside) Nidja wirnitj waangk
This haunted speak
This supernatural soliciting

Kwobitj wara, waraitj kwop
Good-REL bad, bad-REL good
Cannot be ill, cannot be good

Ngany Cawdorap maam
I Cawdor-GEO man
I am thane of Cawdor

Nidja kwop kabin, nadjal nganang malya koorонginy
This good perhaps, why my brain spin-CONT
If good, why do I yield to that suggestion

Nganang kaat djoombaral yira bardang
My head hair-ACT up jump
Whose horrid image doth unfix my hair

Nganang koordal baam ngarriliny: boorditj boorditj.
My heart-ACT hit ribs-OBJ: thump thump.
And make my seated heart knock at my ribs.

Weyarnitj milkar
Fear-REL fresh
Present fears

Koondamitj wara boolain.
Dream-REL bad more.
Are less than horrible imaginings.

Ngaitj waab mooriyak kaadiny,
I-ACT play murder thinking,
My thought, whose murder yet is but fantastical,

Widiwidang keny.
Shake alone.
Shake so my single state of man.

Ngany dabakarn,
I careful,
That function is smother'd in surmise,

Kian-kadak karnarn kaaditj.
Nothing-POSS true understand.
And nothing is but what is not.

BANQUO
Djinang, ngailang kobongitj miyalakeniny.
Look, our-EX friend-REL giddy.
Look, how our partner's rapt.

MACBETH
(Aside) Kabin ngany biediyarabiny, kaya,
Perhaps I boss-TR, yes,
If chance will have me king, why,

Kwerlitj biediyar nganalang, boorda.
Name-REL boss mine, soon.
Chance may crown me, without my stir.

Boordawan-boordaoo,
Sooner-or-later,
Come what come may,

Ngaangk yirabiny dabadiny dowirl.
Sun up-TR fall-CONT always.
Time and the hour runs through the roughest day.

LENNOX
Biediyaral boodjar yong
Boss-ACT land give
King Duncan withal established his estate upon

Nobak, baalitj Malcolm, yeyi Malcolmitj:
Son-LOC, he-REL Malcolm, now Malcolm-REL:
His eldest, Malcolm, whom he has named hereafter:

Cumberlandap biediyaritj koorart.
Cumberland-GEO boss-REL small.
The prince of Cumberland.

MACBETH
Malcolm. Cumberlandap biediyaritj koorart!
Malcolm. Cumberland-GEO boss-REL small!
Malcolm. The prince of Cumberland!

(Aside) Djindang, moornabiny;
Star-ASS, dark-TR;
Stars, hide your fires;

Ngananginy karanginy koordiny wara djinang.
My-OBJ wild-OBJ heart-OBJ fail-to see.
Let not light see my black and deep desires.

BANQUO
Djerang Macbeth, ngail kokon yaak.
Handsome Macbeth, we-EX wait stand.
Worthy Macbeth, we stay upon your leisure.

MACBETH
Kayaritj kaya
Yes-REL yes
Give me your favour

Ngalarl biediyarak koorl.
We-ACT boss-LOC travel.
Let us toward the king.

(Aside to BANQUO)
Ngoondan, kori kaaditj boolain, boordaoo,
Brother, just-now understand more, until,
Think upon what hath chanced, and, at more time,

Boordawan, ngali waangk
Later, we-FAM talk
The interim having weigh'd it, let us speak

Koorditj koodjalitj ngwidam.
Heart-REL pair-REL dignified.
Our free hearts each to other.

BANQUO
Kaya kwop.
Yes good.
Very gladly.

MACBETH
Kenyak yeyi. (To Banquo and Lennox) Kobongkar, ngalar wort koorl.
Enough now. Friend-PL, we away go.
Till then, enough. Come, friends.

They exit. The MISCHIEF MAKERS remain on stage.

SCENE VI

Night. Indoors. Macbeth's place of residence.
Enter LADY MACBETH, anticipating her husband's return. Enter FLEANCE delivering her a note – correspondence from MACBETH about the MISCHIEF MAKERS' prophecy and how he is now Cawdor-ap Maam. FLEANCE brushes her aunty's hair.

LADY MACBETH
(To Fleance) Kidalak biediyaral yoowarl koorliny.
Night boss-ACT toward travel -CONT.
The king comes here to-night.

(excitedly) Kaya, koorditj nganalang kongkitj nyoonalak: Macbeth kaarlak koorliny.
Yes, spouse-REL mine uncle-REL yours: Macbeth home travel -CONT.
So please you, it is true: our thane is coming too.

FLEANCE
(excitedly) Nganang maaman wa?
My father hey?
And my father?

FLEANCE remains on stage. LADY MACBETH exits reading the rest of the letter, confidently turning her focus to the spirits.

SCENE VII

FLEANCE anticipates her father BANQUO's return from battle, hoping he is still alive.

FLEANCE (song 2)
Boodjar baal waangkiny,
Land she talk-CONT,
All the world's a stage,

Boodjar baal waangkiny.
Land she talk-CONT.
All the world's a stage.

Enter BANQUO, joining in the song, surprising FLEANCE.

BANQUO (song 2)
Maamangkara yokangkara kaadiny.
Man-PL woman-PL thinking.
And all the men and women merely players.

FLEANCE is ecstatic to see her father again – he's alive!

FLEANCE
Maaman!
Dad!
Father

They embrace, reunited. HECATE observes, unseen.

HECATE
Boola malkar dookern yeyi, yong yeyi:
Much magic make now, give now:
Great business must be wrought ere:

Benang ba, benang ba, benang
Tomorrow and, tomorrow and, tomorrow
To-morrow, and to-morrow, and to-morrow

Boodjar, baal waangkiny.
Land, she talk-CONT.
All the world's a stage.

HECATE watches. BANQUO and FLEANCE hold their embrace.
Enter LADY MACBETH.

LADY MACBETH
(Aside) Yoowarl koorl, moorn moolarda
Toward travel, dark demons
Come, you spirits

HECATE exits, not wanting to be the subject of LADY MACBETH's calling.
BANQUO and FLEANCE exit too.

Dwongk boolaitj, yokanginy koordiny wort barang,
Listen much-REL, feminine-OBJ heart-OBJ away grasp,
That tend on mortal thoughts, unsex me here,

Nganyak yong boolain,
Me-LOC give more,
And fill me from the crown to the toe top-full

Ngoop moordidjabiny;
Blood strong-TR;
Make thick my blood;

Nganang yokang bibak koorl,
My feminine breast-LOC travel,
Come to my woman's breasts,

Doorrok djalam, doodjarangkar,
Drink bitter, murderer-PL,
And take my milk for gall, you murdering ministers,

Nyoondakaditj kokon balar nyininy,
You-PL-REL wait hidden sit-CONT,
Wherever in your sightless substances

Kidalak moorn, yoowarl koorl,
Night dark-LOC-CONT, toward travel,
Come, thick night,

Daabitj miyal-bt ngoobiny wara djinang,
Knife-REL blind blood-OBJ fail-to see,
Let my keen knife see not the wound it makes,

Demangkaral woordakal miyalak djinanginy,
Ancestors-ACT shade-LOC eyes-INS look-CONT,
Nor heaven peep through the blanket of the dark,

Baalabal waangk, 'Nanap, nanap!'...yoowart!
They-PL-ACT say 'Stop, stop!'...not!
To cry 'Hold, hold!'

Enter MACBETH. Greeting his wife. They embrace strongly – they've been apart for too long. He falls to his knees and tightly pulls her in pressing his cheek against her stomach where his child once flourished. Their love masks their pain from all.

Moorditj Glamisap! Cawdorap maam!
Strong Glamis-GEO! Cawdor-GEO man!
Great Glamis! Worthy Cawdor!

MACBETH
Mardangitj nganalang:
Love-REL mine:
My dearest love,

Kidalak biediyaral yoowarl koorliny.
Night boss-ACT toward travel-CONT.
Duncan comes here to-night.

LADY MACBETH
Baalal wort koorl boorda?
He-ACT away go soon?
And when goes hence?

MACBETH
Benang, baalang biet dalanginy.
Tomorrow, his path pursue-CONT.
To-morrow, as he purposes.

LADY MACBETH
Hor! benang baalitj
Oh tomorrow he-REL
O, never

Yoowart ngaangk djinang!
Not sun see!
Shall sun that morrow see!

Kwibil boola,
Stealthy much,
To beguile the time,

Nyoondalitj yoran-mokiny, miyal bilanginy,
You-REL innocent-SIM, eyes sparkle-CONT,
Look like the time; bear welcome in your eye,

Ngardangitj nornabiny.
Below-REL snake-TR.
But be the serpent under't.

MACBETH
Nganana boorda waangk.
We-SPO soon talk.
We will speak further.

LADY MACBETH
Ngaitj dookern.
I-ACT make.
Leave all the rest to me.

Exit.

SCENE VIII

Night. Macbeth's place of residence.
Enter DUNCAN, MALCOLM, BANQUO, FLEANCE and co.

DUNCAN
Kaarlap nitj kwobitj kwop;
Home here good-is good;
This castle hath a pleasant seat; the air

Maarritj milkar,
Air-REL fresh,
Nimbly and sweetly recommends itself

Nakal mooly naabiny.
Gentle nose adorn-CONT.
Unto our gentle senses.

BANQUO
Birokal djert,
Hot-season-LOC bird,
This guest of summer,

Yoran nyininy nitj, kaya.
Alright being here, yes,
The temple-haunting martlet, does approve,

Demakoombar
Great ancestors
Heaven's breath

Wowak nidjak: ali djerdal
breathe here-LOC: there bird-ACT
Smells wooingly here: this bid

Mai yirangitj baam:
Nest up-REL put:
Hath made his pendent bed and procreant cradle:

Djert boolarabiny, ngany wardar.
Bird multiplying, I observer.
Where they most breed and haunt, I have observed,

Kaya maarr karreba boola.
Yes air tenderness much.
The air is delicate.

Enter LADY MACBETH.

DUNCAN
Djinang djinang, ngalang ngwidam yok!
Look look, our dignified woman!
See, see, our honour'd hostess!

Ngailarl nidjak ngoorndiny kidalak.
We-EXC-ACT here-LOC lie-CNT night.
We are your guest to-night.

LADY MACBETH
Ngail yong boola,
We-EX give much,
All our service

Koodjalitj koodjal kwop boolain.
Double-REL double good more.
In every point twice done and then done double.

DUNCAN
Windji Macbeth?
Where Macbeth?
Where's the thane of Cawdor?

Ngailarl djinangang baaliny.
We-EX-ACT saw him-OBJ.
We coursed him at the heels, and had a purpose

Arwoon baalitj kert-kert: nyorn ngailaritj yakain-mokiny;
Wow he-REL quick: alas we-EX-REL turtle-SIM;
To be his purveyor: but he rides well;

Ngalarl Macbeth koorl ana: baalitj nganang koordal nyininy,
We-ACT Macbeth travel yeah: he-REL my heart-LOC be-CNT,
Conduct me to mine host: we love him highly,

Djoorap karnarn.
Happy true.
And shall continue our graces towards him.

They exit.

SCENE IX

Macbeth's place of residence.

MACBETH

Maaritj nganalang werdam, boorda
Hands-REL mine kill, soon
If it were done when 'tis done, then 'twere well

Kert-kert werdam.
Quick kill.
It were done quickly:

Duncan koort karnarn nyininy nitj;
Duncan heart true be-CNT here;
He's here in double trust;

Baalitj djoorabiny nganitj kobong nganitj Cawdorap maam,
He-REL happy-CONT I-REL friend I-REL Cawdor-GEO man,
I am his kinsman and his subject,

Kwerlitj moorditj koodjal boordaoo koolyawar;
Name-REL strong two until liar;
Strong both against the deed;

Enter LADY MACBETH.

MACBETH

Yaarn! Warda natj?
How! News what?
How now! What news?

LADY MACBETH

Duncan ngaarnang boorda: nadjal nyoondak wort nyininy?
Duncan eat-PAST soon: why you-ACT away be-CNT?
He has almost supp'd: why have you left?

MACBETH
Baalitj djoorabiny ngail waangk, wa?
He-REL happy-CONT we-EX talk, hey?
Hath he ask'd for me?

LADY MACBETH
Kayaritj kaya?
Yes-REL yes?
Know you not he has?

MACBETH
Nganana yoowart wara dookern:
We-SPO no bad make:
We will proceed no further in this business:

Baalal nganyak kwerl yongang; boola nyoongaral
He-ACT me-LOC title give-PAST; many people-ACT
He hath honour'd me of late; and I have bought

Bilanginy waangkiny ngany.
Sparkle-CONT talk-CONT me.
Golden opinions from all sorts of people,

Djoorabiny ngabanginy, kwerlitj kwop nganalang,
Happy-CONT wear-CONT, title-REL good mine,
Which would be worn now in their newest gloss,

Boorda wardak kworditj wara.
Soon renown-INS drop bad.
Not cast aside so soon.

LADY MACBETH
Natj! Nyoondak yowir ngoornda-djinanginy
What! You-ACT drunk dream-CONT
Is your hope drunk

Ngany kaadidjiny. Nyoonang koort weyarniny
I understand-CONT. Your heart fear-CONT
Such I account thy love. Art thou afeard

Nganana bookorabiny waab.
We-SPO brave-TR play.
To be the same in thine own act and valour

Natj nyoondak baranginy? Nyoondalitj waangk
What you-ACT grasp-CONT? You-REL talk
As thou art in desire? Wouldst thou have that

Boorda, boorda, biediyaranginy kwerliny barang wa?
Soon, soon, boss-POSS-OBJ title-OBJ grasp hey?
Which thou esteem'st the ornament of life?

MACBETH
Kenyak:
Enough:
Prithee, peace:

Nganitj kwop maam-mokiny;
I-REL good man-SIM;
I dare do all that may become a man;

LADY MACBETH
Nyoondalitj maam-mokiny, karnarn, nyoona maam yoowart;
You-REL man-SIM, true, you man not;
When you durst do it, then you were a man;

Ba, boolain bookorabiny, boorda
And, more brave-TR, soon
And, to be more than what you were, you would

Nyoondalitj koombarabiny maam.
You-REL large-TR man.
Be so much more the man.

Tensions are running high.
LADY MACBETH changes tactics and drives the dagger into Macbeth's lack of manhood by bringing up a painful recent reality – the loss of their child.

Ngaitj bibi yongang nidjak, ngany kaaditj
I-ACT breast give-PAST this-LOC, I know
I have given suck, and know

Koonyak koort:
Soft heart:
How tender 'tis to love the babe that milks me:

Kooniny kaaw, ngorlak-bt daa,
Baby laugh, toothless mouth,
I would, while it was smiling in my face,

Boordaoo ngaitj bibi wort barang,
Until I ACT breast away grasp,
Have pluck'd my nipple from his boneless gums,

Malyariny baam! Werdam! Nyoona kaaditj-bt
Brain-OBJ strike! Kill! You don't-know
And dash'd the brains out, had I so sworn as you

Natj nyoondak warnang nidjak.
What you do-PAST this-LOC.
Have done to this.

MACBETH
Nganana warabiny?
We-SPO failing?
If we should fail?

LADY MACBETH
Nganana warabiny!
We-SPO failing!
We fail!

Duncan nookerdal –
Duncan sleep-LOC –
When Duncan is asleep –

Nganana dookern boola
We-SPO make much
What cannot you and I perform upon

Duncan baan wa? Dookernitj dookern
Duncan exposed hey? make-REL make
The unguarded Duncan? What not put upon

Baalang koodjal babinitj, woolkar-kadak-mokiny
His two friend-REL, guilt-POSS-SIM
His spongy officers, who shall bear the guilt

Ngananaitj nakal yoran ana?
We-SPO-REL gentle innocent yeah?
Of our great quell?

MACBETH
Karnarnitj karnarn,
True-REL true,
Will it not be received,

Nyoondak ngoobak naap koodjal babinak
You-ACT blood-INS paint two pledged-friend-LOC
When we have mark'd with blood those sleepy two

Biediyariny baam baalabang koodjal daabak,
Boss-OBJ strike their-PL two knife-INS,
Of his own chamber and used their very daggers,

Boorda doodjara koodjal nyininy ana?
Soon murderer two be-CONT yeah?
That they have done't?

LADY MACBETH
Boorda nganana waaliny koombar
Soon we-SPO cry-CONT large
We shall make our griefs and clamour roar

Duncan noidjal.
Duncan dead-LOC.
Upon his death.

MACBETH
Nganitj bookor ba, miran
I-REL brave and, poise
I am settled, and bend up

Don-djinanginy yeyi.
Aim-CONT now.
Each corporal agent to this terrible feat.

Wort koorl, ngoonyongitj ngoonyong yong:
Away go, sweet-REL sweet give:
Away, and mock the time with fairest show:

Yoran nyin nyoonang kwibil koort ngarda ngoorndiny.
Innocent be your stealthy heart below lie-down-CNT.
False face must hide what the false heart doth know.

Exit.

ACT II

SCENE I

Macbeth's place of residence. Night.
Enter BANQUO, and FLEANCE bearing a torch before her. HECATE is there, somewhere.

BANQUO
Kidalak yaarn, koolong?
Night how, child?
How goes the night, my child?

FLEANCE
Yaawin ngoorndiny;
Moon lie-down-CONT;
The moon is down;

BANQUO becomes uneasy, sensing danger nearby.
Hecate watches on.

BANQUO
Yaawin ngoorndiny?
Moon lie-down-CONT?
The moon is down;

Worlitj moorn;
Sky-REL dark;
There's husbandry in heaven;

Boola djinda nookerdiny. Arwoon!
Many star sleep-CONT. Ha!
Their candles are all out.

Nganitj biedibap boya-mokiny.
I-REL tired stone-SIM.
A heavy summons lies like lead upon me.

BANQUO pre-empts danger and guards FLEANCE.
Enter MACBETH.

FLEANCE
Ngiyan alidja?
Who there?
Who's there?

MACBETH
Kongkan keny.
Uncle alone.
A friend.

BANQUO
Yaarn, nyoondalitj nookert kian wa? Biediyar korndal nookerdiny.
How, you-REL sleep none hey? Boss hut-LOC sleep-CONT.
What, sir, not yet at rest? The king's a-bed.

Karam kidalak, ngaitj ngoornda-djinangang mambara mardiny:
Yesterday night, I-ACT dream-PAST creature three:
I dreamt last night of the three weird sisters:

Baalabitj karni waangkang nyoonany.
They-PL-REL truly talk-PAST you-OBJ.
To you they have show'd some truth.

MACBETH
Dwongka-bt dwongka-bt:
Deaf deaf:
I think not of them:

Boordawan, ngali waangkiny nitj.
Later we-FAM talk-CONT this.
Yet, when we can entreat an hour to serve, we would spend it in some words upon that business,

Kwop ana.
Good yeah.
If you would grant the time.

BANQUO
Kayaritj kaya.
Yes-REL yes.
At your kind'st leisure.

MACBETH
Ngali dit yaak, kaya,
We-FAM together stand, yes,
If you shall cleave to my consent, when 'tis,

Nyoondalitj moordidjabiny boolain.
You-REL strong-TR more.
It shall make honour for you.

BANQUO simply nods – he'd rather keep reading MACBETH's body language because he knows him better than he knows himself. They have, after all, been in battle together.

MACBETH
Nookert yeyi wa!
Sleep now hey!
Good repose the while!

BANQUO
Kwop!
Good!
Good repose the while!

BANQUO and FLEANCE exit. HECATE follows them.

MACBETH
(To the dagger – internal thoughts) Daab wa,
Knife hey,
Is this a dagger which I see before me,

Nganang maaral daap maadiny djinang?
My hand-ACT knife handle-OBJ see?
The handle toward my hand?

Yoowarl koorl. Ngaitj barang.
Toward go. I-ACT grasp.
Come, let me clutch thee.

Nganitj daap kian, daap djinanginy.
I-REL knife none, knife see-CONT.
I have thee not, and yet I see thee still.

Ngany karang koorliny daabang;
I wild travel-CONT knife-RES;
Thou marshall'st me the way that I was going;

Ngoobal waangk
Blood-ACT talk
It is the bloody business which informs

Miyalak. Yeyi nyoongara nookerdiny
Eye-LOC. Now person-PL sleep-CONT
Thus to mine eyes. Now o'er the one halfworld

Boodjar noitj-mokiny, koondamal wara warn
Country dead-SIM, dream-ACT bad do
Nature seems dead, and wicked dreams abuse

Nookerdiny ngabang;
Sleep-OBJ cover;
The curtain'd sleep;

Ken ken, nganalang, maya-bt
Step step, mine, silent
Hear not my steps, which way they walk, for fear

Djen maya-kora weyarniny,
Foot echo fear-CONT,
Thy very stones prate of my whereabout,

Yeyi ngany doodjarabiny.
Now I murderer-TR.
And take the present horror from the time.

A sound is heard – what is it?
MACBETH exits.

SCENE II

The same. Enter LADY MACBETH. She is bold and fired up.

LADY MACBETH
Dat! Ni!
Quiet! Listen!
Hark! Peace

Macbeth dookerniny:
Macbeth make-CONT:
He is about it:

Duncan baan ngoorndiny; Baalang koodjal babin
Duncan exposed lie-down-CONT; His two pledged-friend
The doors are open; and the surfeited grooms

Yowir ngoorndiny: ngaitj yoomp dookernang,
Drunk lie-down-CONT: I-ACT poison fix-PST,
Do mock their charge with snores: I have drugg'd their possets,

Baalabitj noitj-mokiny, noidjabiny karnarn.
They-PL-REL dead-like, dying true.
That death and nature do contend about them, whether they live or die.

A sound is heard – the MISCHIEF MAKERS make noise. LADY MACBETH becomes agitated.

LADY MACBETH
Ni djinang wa.
Hark see hey.
He could not miss 'em.

Ngaitj daabak baamang baan;
I-ACT knife-INS put-PAST exposed;
I laid their daggers ready;

Enter MACBETH, much to LADY MACBETH's relief.

LADY MACBETH
Koort nganalang!
Spouse mine!
My husband!

MACBETH
Baal noitj. Natj nyoondak dwongk-kaadidjang?
He dead. What you-ACT hear-PAST?
I have done the deed. Didst thou not hear a noise?

LADY MACBETH
Kambanyitj waal djidilyitj miyalyan.
Owl-REL scream cricket-REL cry.
I heard the owl scream and the crickets cry.

Nyoondak waangkang wa?
You-ACT talk-PAST hey?
Did not you speak?

MACBETH
Windjar?
Where?
When?

LADY MACBETH
Yeyi.
Now.

MACBETH
Ni!
Hark!

Ngiyan alidja ngoorndiny?
Who there lie-down-CONT?
Who lies i' the second chamber?

LADY MACBETH
Malcolm.

MACBETH
Nidja woolkaritj wara.
This guilt-REL bad.
This is a sorry sight.

MACBETH looks at his hands.

LADY MACBETH
Balbit waangk, 'nidja wara'.
Foolish talk, 'this bad'.
A foolish thought, to say a sorry sight.

MACBETH begins to unravel, his state of mind becomes rocky.

MACBETH
Keny maam kaaw nookerdang, ba koodjal maam waal 'Mooriyak'!
First man laugh sleep-PST, and second man cry 'Murder'!
There's one did laugh in's sleep, and one cried 'Murder!'

Keny maam demangkariny waal ba 'Kenyak' koodjal maam waangkang;
First man ancestor-OBJ cry and 'Enough' second man talk-PST;
One cried 'God bless us!' and 'Amen' the other;

LADY MACBETH
Wara warnitj dwonkak
Bad do-REL ear-LOC
These deeds must not be thought

Ngat; kabin, nganana kaat-warabiny.
Repeatedly; likely, we-SPO mad-TR.
After these ways; so, it will make us mad.

MACBETH
Ngaitj dwongk-kaaditj maya waangk, 'yoowart nookert'!
I-ACT hear sound talk 'not sleep'!
Methought I heard a voice cry 'Sleep no more'!

Macbeth werdam nookerdiny.
Macbeth kill sleep-OBJ.
Macbeth does murder sleep.

LADY MACBETH
Natj nyoona waangkiny?
What you say-CONT?
What do you mean?

MACBETH
Maya waal, 'yoowart nookert'!
Sound cry 'not sleep'!
Still it cried 'Sleep no more!' to all the house:

'Glamisapal nookerdiny werdam, Cawdorapitj
'Glamis-GEO-ACT sleep-OBJ kill, Cawdor-GEO-REL
'Glamis hath murder'd sleep, and therefore Cawdor

Yoowart nookert yeyi. Macbeth yoowart nookert yeyi'.
Not sleep now. Macbeth not sleep now'.
Shall sleep no more; Macbeth shall sleep no more'.

LADY MACBETH
Kaep barang,
Water grasp,
Go get some water,

Ngoobalyong maariny kayebal baam.
Bloody hand-OBJ water-LOC put.
And wash this filthy witness from your hand.

Nadjal nyoondak daap kedang nidjak?
Why you-ACT knife carry-PAST here-LOC?
Why did you bring these daggers from the place?

Wort kworditj bokidja: Nyoondak naap
Away throw afar: You-ACT paint
They must lie there: go carry them; and smear

Biediyarang babingkariny ngoobak.
Boss-POSS pledged-friend-PL-OBJ blood-INS.
The sleepy grooms with blood.

MACBETH
Ngany yoowart koorliny.
I not travel-CNT.
I'll go no more:

Ngaitj weyarn kaadidjiny;
I-ACT fear understand-CONT.
I am afraid to think what I have done;

Nidja wirnitj, wara.
It evil, bad.
Look on't again I dare not.

LADY MACBETH
Weyak!
Coward!
Infirm of purpose!

Daap yong:
Knife give:
Give me the daggers:

Ngaitj babingkarang mirnidjiny naap.
I-ACT pledged-friend-PL-POSS face-OBJ paint.
I'll gild the faces of the grooms withal;

Ngoobitj ngoop baalap doodjara-mokiny boorda.
Blood REL blood they PL murderer-SIM soon.
For it must seem their guilt.

She exits, leaving MACBETH alone.
Knocking within.

MACBETH
Windji boornak baaminy?
Where wood-INS strike-CONT?
Whence is that knocking?

Knocking within. Aliwa MACBETH.

MACBETH
Windji boornak baaminy?
Where wood-INS strike-CONT?
Whence is that knocking?

Re-enter LADY MACBETH.

LADY MACBETH
Nganang maar mardar koodjal; kaanya
My hand red pair; shame
My hands are of your colour; but I shame

Nyoondalitj koort winyan djardar.
You-REL heart pitiful white.
To wear a heart so white.

Knocking within.

Ni!
Hark!
I hear a knocking

They begin to leave, then...another knocking within.

Ni! Kora maya baam.
Hark! Again sound hit.
Hark! More knocking.

Yoowart
Not
Be not lost

Winyan kaat waangk yeyi.
Pitiful head talk now.
So poorly in your thoughts.

MACBETH
Nganang warnangitj kaaditj, kabin kwop ngany waamabiny.
My do-PAST-REL know, perhaps good I stranger-TR.
To know my deed, 'twere best not know myself.

Knocking within again. MACBETH becomes more afraid.

Nidja maya baaminy! Duncan biyooabiny wa!
This sound striking! Duncan waking-up hey!
Wake Duncan with thy knocking! I would thou couldst!

LADY MACBETH leads him out. They exit.

SCENE III

The same. Knocking within. Enter HECATE, searching for the sound's location.

HECATE
Ni! Maya nidja!
Hark! Sound here!
Here's a sound indeed!

Knocking within.
HECATE listens to the sound. She follows it. She wants to describe its reason for being.

Ngiyan alidja?
Who there?
Who's there?

Knocking within.

Ngiyan alidja?
Who there?
Who's there?

Knocking within – is a ghost trying to break free?

Natj nyoona?
What you?
What are you?

HECATE listens and watches.
She waits. We hear the fire crackle. It draws her towards Macbeth.
She exits.

SCENE IV

The same. Enter MACDUFF, LENNOX and MACBETH.

LENNOX
Ben kwop, Cawdorap maam.
Daylight good, Cawdor-GEO man.
Good morrow, noble sir.

MACBETH
Kaya ben kwop, kobongkar.
Yes daylight good, friends.
Good morrow, both.

MACDUFF
Biediyar Duncan, biyoo wa?
Boss Duncan, awake hey?
Is the king stirring, worthy thane?

MACBETH
Yoowart.
No.
Not yet.

MACDUFF
Karamitj, baal waangkang kambarn yeyi:
Yesterday-REL, he say-PAST meet now:
He did command me to call timely on him:

Ngany kwadjat koorl.
I before travel.
I have almost slipp'd the hour.

MACBETH
Ngali dit koorl.
We-FAM together travel.
I'll bring you to him.

MACDUFF
Nyoondalitj djoorap warn boola
You-REL happy to do much
I know this is a joyful trouble to you.

Biedibab ana.
Tired yeah.
But yet 'tis one.

MACBETH
Ngany djoorabiny warniny ngat.
I happy-CONT do-CONT repeatedly.
The labour we delight in physics pain.

Koornt daa nitj.
Hut opening here.
This is the door.

MACDUFF
Ngaitj maya koombar,
I-ACT sound large,
I'll make so bold to call,

Nganitj babin.
I-is pledged-friend.
For 'tis my limited service.

MACDUFF exits to go greet KING DUNCAN good morning.

LENNOX
Biediyaral wort koorl boorda wa?
Boss-ACT away go soon hey?
Goes the king hence to-day?

MACBETH
Kaya: baal wort koorliny.
Yes: he away travel-CONT.
He does: he did appoint so.

LENNOX
Karam kidalakitj wara:
Yesterday night-REL bad:
The night has been unruly:

Mayaritj worlak wariny; Wirnitj.
Sound-REL sky-LOC hanging; haunted.
Lamentings heard i' the air; strange screams of death.

Wirlo
Curlew
The obscure bid

Waalang: nyoongaral waangk, boodjar
Cry-PAST: person-PL-ACT say, earth
Clamour'd the livelong night: some say, the earth

Naarang widiwidang.
Burn-PAST shake.
Was feverous and did shake.

MACBETH
Kaya karam kidalakitj wara.
Yes yesterday night-REL bad.
'Twas a rough night.

Re-enter MACDUFF, his miyal horrified.

MACDUFF
O wara, wara, wara! Daaliny koort
O bad, bad, bad! Tongue heart
O horror, horror, horror! Tongue nor heart

Yoowart waangk yeyi!
Not say now!
Cannot conceive nor name thee!

MACBETH / LENNOX
Yaarn natj?
How what?
What's the matter?

MACDUFF
Yeyi ngany karni kaaditj-bt karnarn!
Now I truly don't-know true!
Confusion now hath made his masterpiece!

MACBETH
Natj nyoondak waangk?
What you-ACT say?
What is't you say?

MACDUFF
Korndak darap koorl, nyoonang miyal werdam
Hut-LOC enter go, your eyes kill
Approach the chamber, and destroy your sight

Ngany daa-bt;
I mute;
With a new Gorgon: do not bid me speak;

Djinang yeyi, boorda waangk.
See now, soon talk.
See, and then speak yourselves.

Exit MACBETH and LENNOX to see for themselves the very thing MACDUFF cannot describe.

Biyoo, biyoo!
Awake, awake!
Awake, awake!

Maya baam. Mooriyak wara koombar!
Sound strike. Murder bad large!
Ring the alarm-bell. Murder and treason!

Banquo Malcolm! Biyoo yeyi!
Banquo Malcolm! Awake now!
Banquo and Malcolm! Awake!

Nookert bardang,
Sleep jump,
Shake off this downy sleep,

Nyoondakaditj noitj-mokiny.
You-PL-REL dead-SIM.
Death's counterfeit,

Djinang alidja noitj karnarn.
See there dead true.
And look on death itself! Up, up,

Djinang
See
And see

Wirnitj koombar!
Evil large!
The great doom's image!

O wara, wara!
O bad, bad!
O horror, horror!

Malcolm! Banquo!

Maya baam.
Sound strike.
Ring the bell.

Bell rings.
Enter LADY MACBETH.

LADY MACBETH
Natj nidja.
What here.
What's the business,

Nadjal dwongk baaminy
Why ear strike-CONT
That such a hideous trumpet calls to parley

Nookerdal? Waangk! Waangk!
Sleep-LOC? Talk! Talk!
The sleepers of the house? Speak, speak!

MACDUFF
O karreba yok,
O tenderness woman,
O gentle lady,

Nyoondalitj dwongka-bt nitj wirnitj waangk.
You-REL deaf this evil talk.
'Tis not for you to hear what I can speak.

Enter BANQUO.

O Banquo, Banquo,

Ngalarang biediyar noitj!
Our boss dead!
Our royal master's murder'd!

LADY MACBETH
Nyorn, wara!
Alas, bad!
Woe, alas!

Natj, ngalak kaarlal nitj?
What, our home here?
What, in our house?

BANQUO
Waraitj wara woorrar.
Bad-REL bad long-way.
Too cruel any where.

Macduff, ngaitj naakiny:
Macduff, I-ACT begging:
Dear Duff, I prithee, contradict thyself,

'Yoowart' waangk yeyi.
'No' say now.
And say it is not so.

Re-enter MACBETH and LENNOX.

MACBETH
Ngwidam yoowart:
Serious not:
There's nothing serious in mortality:

Nitj waab: warda biedi noitj.
This play: renown path dead.
All is but toys: renown and grace is dead.

Enter MALCOLM.

MALCOLM
Natj wa?
What hey?
What is amiss?

MACDUFF
Nyoonang maam noitj. Mooriyak.
Your father dead. Murder.
Your royal father's murder'd.

LENNOX
Baalang koodjal babinitj, kabin, warnang:
His pledged-friend-REL, likely, do-PAST:
Those of his chamber, as it seem'd, had done 't:

Baalabang mirnitj maar ngoobalyong;
Their-PL face hand bloody;
Their hands and faces were all badged with blood;

Koodjal daabitj mardar, djinang
Two knife-REL red, see
So were their daggers, which unwiped we found

Korndal nyinang:
Hut-LOC be-PST:
Upon their pillows:

Baalabitj miyal mookiyang, weyak; yoowart
They-PL-REL eye useless; coward
They stared, and were distracted; no man's life

Koort karnarn.
Heart true.
Was to be trusted with them.

MACBETH becomes deeply concerned and stages a form of grief.

MACBETH
O, nganitj karang nyinang wara,
O, I-REL angry be-PAST bad,
O, yet I do repent me of my fury,

Ngaitj baalabiny werdamang.
I-ACT them-PL-OBJ kill-PAST.
That I did kill them.

MACDUFF
Nadjal werdamang?
Why kill-PAST?
Wherefore did you so?

MACBETH
Ngiyan baalitj moorditj ba djoorabiny, dabakarn ba karang,
Who he-REL strong and happy-CONT, careful and angry,
Who can be wise, amazed, temperate and furious,

Karnarn ba yoran, dowirl? Nitj maam kian:
True and innocent, always? This man none:
Loyal and neutral, in a moment? No man:

Ngany karang koordang.
I wild heart-RES.
The expedition my violent love.

Kaaditj-bt, kaya. Nyornditj Duncan noitj ngoornt,
Don't-know, yes. Alas-REL Duncan dead lie-down,
Outrun the pauser, reason. Here lay Duncan,

Baalang maap bilanginy ngoobang;
His skin sparkle-CONT blood-RES;
His silver skin laced with his golden blood;

LADY MACBETH
Ngany biedibap, ni!
I tired, hark!
Help me hence, ho!

MACDUFF
Yok djinang.
Woman see.
Look to the lady.

They look to the lady. LADY MACBETH is carried out. Focus shifts back to the group.

BANQUO
Ngalar kambarn waangkitj ngoobalyong
We gather talk-REL bloody,
Let us meet and question this most bloody piece of work,

Kaaditj boolain. Ngalar weyarnabiny karangabiny: kaya ngalaritj
Know more. We afraid-TR angry-TR: yes we-REL
To know it further. Fears and scruples shake us: and thence

Kaaditj-bt, kenyak
Don't-know, enough
Against the undivulged pretence I fight

Ana.
Yeah.
Of treasonous malice.

MACDUFF
Kayaritj kaya.
Yes-REL yes.
And so do I.

ALL
Kaya.
Yes.
So all.

MACBETH
Ngalarl kwoarkak barang yeyi,
We-ACT cloak-INS grasp now,
Let's briefly put on manly readiness,

Kambarniny boorda.
Meet-CONT soon.
And meet i' the hall together.

MALCOLM is left alone on stage, crumbling beneath the surface of his skin, pondering this unexpected twist. His safety and future unsure.

MALCOLM
(Aside) Nadjal ngany daa-bt?
Why I mute?
Why do I hold my tongue?

Nadjal ngany daa-bt?
Why I mute?
Why do I hold my tongue?

MALCOLM is vulnerable. HECATE watches him. She hums then sings then hums while he comes to terms with the loss.

HECATE (song 2)
Boodjar baal waangkiny,
Land she say-CONT,
All the world's a stage,

Boodjar baal waangkiny,
Land she say-CONT,
All the world's a stage,

Maamangkara yokangkara kaadiny.
Man-PL woman-PL thinking.
And all the men and women merely players.

Baalap wongin yeyi boordawan noitj ba,
They-PL alive now later dead and,
They have their exits and their entrances,

Yoowarl-bili wort-bili biedi biedi koorliny,
This-way that-way hop path path travel-CONT,
And one man in his time plays many parts,

Boodjar baal waangkiny.
Land she say-CONT.
All the world's a stage.

MALCOLM takes a moment to grieve his father where he was murdered. He knows he will never have this moment again. He looks to the skies – the future in an instant – as FLEANCE did earlier.

MALCOLM
(To his father) Windji ngany koorliny? Nanap yoowart nitj:
Where I travel-CONT? Stop not here:
What will I do? I shan't not consort with them:

Yeyi, karreba kian.
Now, mercy none.
There's no mercy left.

MALCOLM exits, heading to a safer location away from the culprit.

SCENE V

Outside Macbeth's place of residence.
We hear a fire crackling. HECATE is still there, listening.
Enter MACDUFF and LENNOX, suspicious about the murder.

LENNOX
Woolkar-kadak ngiyan?
Guilt-POSS who?
Is't known who did this more than bloody deed?

MACDUFF
Baalabiny Macbeth werdamang.
Them-PL-OBJ Macbeth kill-PAST.
Those that Macbeth hath slain.

LENNOX
Yoran yoowart wa?
Innocent not hey?
What good could they pretend?

MACDUFF
Baalabitj boondongang:
They-PL-REL money-RES:
He was suborn'd:

Malcolm, biediyarang nop,
Malcolm, boss' son,
Malcolm, the king's son,

Woort-bardang; kaya
Away-fly; yes
Is stol'n away and fled; which puts upon him

Woolkar djarin baaliny ana?
Guilt accuse him-OBJ yeah?
Suspicion of the deed.

LENNOX
Wara!
Bad!
'Gainst nature still!

Balbit, baalal maamaniny baamang ba
Foolish, he-ACT father-OBJ strike-PAST and
Thriftless ambition, that wilt ravin up

Maat dakan! Boorda
Family-line break! Soon
Thine own life's means! Then 'tis most like

Macbeth biediyarabiny wa.
Macbeth boss-TR hey.
The sovereignty will fall upon Macbeth.

MACDUFF
Baalitj biediyar yeyi
He-REL boss now
He is already named, and gone

Karnarn.
True.
To be invested.

Exit MACDUFF and LENNOX.
HECATE now realises the MISCHIEF MAKERS have taken things into their own hands. She exits.

ACT III

SCENE I

Night. Indoors. Macbeth's place of residence.
Enter MACBETH, as king, LADY MACBETH, as queen, and FLEANCE preparing to sketch their portrait. Enter BANQUO reflecting upon the MISCHIEF MAKERS' prophecy and MACBETH's sudden rise to power.

BANQUO
Nyoondalitj yeyi: biediyar, Cawdorap, Glamisap, boola.
You-REL now: boss, Cawdor-GEO, Glamis-GEO, much,
Thou hast it now: king, Cawdor, Glamis, all,

Mambara mardiny karni waangkang,
Spirit-creature three truly say-PAST,
As the mischief makers promised,

Kabin boordawan
Perhaps later
Yet it was said

Nganitj maaman keny
I-REL father alone
That I should be the root and father

Boordawan nganang koolongkaritj biediyarabiny boola.
Later my child-PL-REL boss-TR many.
Of many kings.

MACBETH
Kobong kwop.
Friend good.
Here's our chief guest.

Kidalak ngalarl daatj ngaarn ngwidam,
This we-ACT meat eat serious,
To-night we hold a solemn supper sir,

Nyoondalitj alidja nyin kwop.
You-REL there be good.
And I'll request your presence.

BANQUO
Kaya biediyaral
Yes boss-ACT
Let your highness

Waangk; ngaitj warn
Say; I-ACT do
Command upon me; to the which my duties

Babinitj babin
Pledged-friend-REL, pledged-friend
Are with a most indissoluble tie

Dowirl.
Always.
For ever knit.

MACBETH
Nyoondak woorrar koorliny wa?
You-ACT long-way travel-CONT hey?
Is't far you ride?

BANQUO
Bokidja, biediyar, kabin
Afar, boss, likely
As far, my lord, as will fill up the time

Ngaitj korakoorl daadjak.
I-ACT return meat-PURP.
'Twixt this and supper:

MACBETH questions BANQUO's devotion to his new king.

MACBETH
Malcolm, ngoobalyong bokidja
Malcolm, bloody afar
We hear, our bloody cousin is bestow'd

Woorrar nyininy, daa-bt
Long-way be-CONT, mute
In England, not confessing

Baalitj bardip naakiny,
He-REL deceive begging,
His cruel parricide,

BANQUO simply nods in favour, sceptical of the truth.
A new tension builds.

Fleance dit koorliny nyoona?
Fleance together travel-CONT you?
Goes Fleance with you?

HECATE enters. She heard FLEANCE's name.

BANQUO
Kaya, biediyar: ngail wort koorl yeyi.
Yes, boss, we-EX away go now.
Ay, my good lord: our time does call upon 's.

BANQUO exits, breaking the tension. Or has he? HECATE watches MACBETH as he reflects upon the MISCHIEF MAKERS' prophecy for BANQUO.

MACBETH
(To himself) Boordawan nyoonang djoowakitj biediyarabiny.
Later your next-generation-REL boss-TR.
Thou shalt get kings.

An ATTENDANT brings in TWO MURDERERS then exits, leaving them to talk with Macbeth.

MACBETH
Nyoondakadal:
You-PL-ACT:
Both of you

Kaaditj Banquo karang-kadak ana?
Know Banquo enemy yeah?
Know Banquo was your enemy.

BOTH MURDERERS
Karnarn, biediyar.
True, boss.
True, my lord.

FIRST MURDERER
Ngail ngat–
We-EX repeatedly–
Though our lives–

MACBETH
(Interrupting him) Nyoondakadang miyalal ngoorr karnarn. Boorda
Your-PL eyes-LOC character true. Soon
Your spirits shine through you. Within this hour at most

Ngaitj waangk nyoondakadak biet;
I-ACT say you-PL-LOC path;
I will advise you where to plant yourselves;

Dwongk boolaitj,
Ear much-REL,
Acquaint you with the perfect spy o' the time,

Nidja kidalak; kaya,
This night; yes,
The moment on't; for't must be done to-night,

Bokidja bo; boorda
Afar far; soon
And something from the palace; always thought

Baan ana: baaliny
Clear yeah: him-OBJ
That I require a clearness: and with him –

Karni dookern –
Truly fix –
To leave no rubs nor botches in the work –

Fleance, baalang kowat,
Fleance, his daughter,
Fleance his son, that keeps him company,

Dit koorl
Together travel
Whose absence is no less material to me

Maamanang, biet dalanginy
Father-ASS, path pursue-CONT
Than is his father's, must embrace the fate

Moorn. Walak-walak yeyi:
Dark. Separate now:
Of that dark hour. Resolve yourselves apart:

Boorda waangk nyoondakadak.
Soon talk you-PL-LOC.
I'll come to you anon.

BOTH MURDERERS
Kaya, biediyar.
Yes, boss.
We are resolved, my lord.

MACBETH
Kwop: wort kokon yaak.
Good: away wait stand.
I'll call upon you straight: abide within.

Exit FIRST & SECOND MURDERERS.

Kenyak. Banquo, nyoonang koordoomit,
Enough. Banquo, your soul,
It is concluded. Banquo, thy soul's flight,

Yira koorliny kidalak nitj, karnarn.
Up travel-CONT night this, true.
If it find heaven, must find it out to-night.

A THIRD MURDERER steps out of the shadows. MACBETH signals to him that he must join the other two murderers to ensure that the daughter of BANQUO be murdered along with her father. There can be no mistakes. THIRD MURDERER acknowledges the task and exits, leaving MACBETH alone with his thoughts.

SCENE II

Night. Indoors. Macbeth's place of residence.
Enter LADY MACBETH. Her husband is in deep thought. She interrupts.

LADY MACBETH
Yaarn, biediyar! Nadjal nyoona keny nyininy,
How, boss! Why you alone be-CONT,
How now, my lord! Why do you keep alone,

Winyanitj winyan.
Pitiful-REL pitiful.
Of sorriest fancies.

Warnitj warnang.
Do-REL do-PAST.
What's done is done.

MACBETH
Ngananal norniny baamang, nornitj noitj yoowart:
We-SPO-ACT snake-OBJ strike-PAST, snake-REL dead not:
We have scotch'd the snake, not kill'd it:

Nganana ngaarn weyarniny nookert weyarniny
We-SPO eat fear-CONT sleep fear-CONT
Ere we will eat our meal in fear and sleep

Koondam weyarniny.
Dream fear-CONT.
In the affliction of these terrible dreams.

Duncan noitj bokalak ngoorndiny;
Duncan dead grave-LOC lie-down-CONT;
Duncan is in his grave;

Ngalak koolyam wara warnang.
Our lies bad do-PAST.
Treason has done his worst.

LADY MACBETH
Dabakarn nganang biediyar, mirnitj wa;
Careful my boss, face hey;
Gentle my lord, sleek o'er your rugged looks;

Kidalak nitj kobongkariny kambarn kaawiny.
Night this friend-PL-OBJ meet laugh-CONT.
Be bright and jovial among your guests to-night.

MACBETH
Kaya, mardang; ba, dit kaawiny, nyoondalitj:
Yes, love; and, together laugh-CONT, you-REL:
So shall I, love; and so, I pray, be you:

Boorda nyoondak Banquo kwop waangkiny;
Soon you-ACT Banquo good speak-CONT;
Let your remembrance apply to Banquo;

Nyoonang ngoorr ngwidam, miyal daaliny.
Your character dignified, eyes tongue.
Present him eminence, both with eye and tongue.

LADY MACBETH
Natj dookerniny?
What fix-CONT?
What's to be done?

MACBETH
Nyoondalitj yoran, mardang,
You-REL innocent, love,
Be innocent of the knowledge, dearest chuck,

Nyoondalitj yoran.
You-REL innocent.
Be innocent of the knowledge.

They embrace.
MACBETH looks to the night sky.

(To himself) Wara biet boolarabiny.
Bad path multiplying.
Things bad begun make strong themselves by ill.

They know their path is set – they cannot turn back. They exit together.

SCENE III

A park near the palace.
HECATE awaits, to protect her descendant, FLEANCE.
Enter THREE MURDERERS, clumsy.

FIRST MURDERER
Ngiyanal waangkang nyoonak?
Who-ACT say-PAST you-LOC?
But who did bid thee join with us?

THIRD MURDERER
Macbeth.

FIRST MURDERER and SECOND MURDERER gaze at each other, both disappointed in MACBETH's lack of trust. SECOND MURDERER begins to pace in frustration but is stopped by FIRST MURDERER.

FIRST MURDERER
Dat yaak.
Quiet stand.
Then stand with us.

Boorda baalabal yoowarl koorliny.
Soon they-PL-ACT toward travel-CONT.
Near approaches the subject of our watch.

THIRD MURDERER
Ni! Dwongk-kaadidjiny.
Hark! Hear-CONT.
Hark! I hear them.

Enter BANQUO and FLEANCE with a torch. HECATE close by.

FLEANCE
Boorda kaep boroonginy, maam.
Soon water heavy-rain-CONT, father.
It will rain to-night, father.

Nyoongaraitj moolyabiny ngat ngat werdaminy ana?
People-REL hateful repeatedly repeatedly kill-CONT yeah?
Do all men kill the things they do not love?

A djididjidi calls. BANQUO knows FLEANCE can see the future in an instant, yet he must protect her, so he does. HECATE keeps FLEANCE safeguarded while the MURDERERS ambush her father.

BANQUO
O, wara! Wort bardang, Fleance, Bard, bard, bard!
O, bad! Away fly, Fleance, go, go, go!
O, treachery! Fly, good Fleance, fly, fly, fly!

Bangal-baam. Doodjara!
Revenge. Murderer!
Thou mayst revenge. O slave!

BANQUO is murdered. A fire begins to crackle. The murderers' lights go out.
FLEANCE escapes, guided by HECATE.

THIRD MURDERER
Ngiyan kaarl baamang?
Who fire strike-PST?
Who did strike out the light?

It is dark. The MURDERERS exit. HECATE sings and as she does, BANQUO is placed into a grave. A soft torchlight flicks back on. FLEANCE has long fled. HECATE holds a burial ceremony for BANQUO. She sings.

SCENE IV

A party (pre-banquet drinks) at MACBETH's place of residence.
Enter King MACBETH, Queen LADY MACBETH, LENNOX, Lords and Attendants.
Enter HECATE, posing as a cocktail waitress, serving drinks.

LADY MACBETH
Waangk, biediyar, kobongkarak;
Say, boss, friends-LOC;
Pronounce it for me, sir, to all our friends;

Nganang koort djoorabiny baalabitj nidjak.
My heart happy-CONT they-PL-REL here-LOC.
For my heart speaks they are welcome.

FIRST MURDERER appears at the door. MACBETH is quick to divert.

MACBETH
Djinang, baalabitj yoran nyininy.
See, they-PL-REL alright be-CONT.
See, they encounter thee with their hearts' thanks.

MACBETH approaches the FIRST MURDERER at the door...

Ngoop nyoonang mirnidjak.
Blood your face-LOC.
There's blood on thy face.

FIRST MURDERER
Banquo ngoop.
Banquo blood.
'Tis Banquo's then.

MACBETH
Kwop baalitj ngoop kian.
Good he-REL blood without.
'Tis better thee without than he within.

Noitj yeyi?
Dead now?
Is he dispatch'd?

FIRST MURDERER
Biediyar, baalanginy woordiny bornang; ngaitj.
Boss, his-OBJ throat-OBJ born-PAST; I-ACT.
My lord, his throat is cut; that I did for him.

MACBETH
Nyoondalitj moorditj woort-bornar: kaya
You-REL strong throat-cut-OCC: yes
Thou art the best o' the cut-throats: yet he's good

Nyoondak Fleance dit warn: kabin,
You Fleance together do-PAST: perhaps,
That did the like for Fleance: if thou didst it,

Nyoondalitj wardakadak ana.
You-REL hero true yeah.
Thou art the nonpareil.

FIRST MURDERER
Biediyaritj Biediyar,
Boss-REL boss,
Most royal sir,

Fleance wort bardang.
Fleance away fly.
Fleance is 'scaped.

MACBETH finds it difficult to contain his frustration, physically displaying 'But now I am cabined, cribbed, confined, bound in to saucy doubts and fears'. He asks…

MACBETH
Banquo kenyak ana?
Banquo finished yeah?
But Banquo's safe?

FIRST MURDERER
Kaya, biediyar: Banquo ngarda boodjarak ngoorndiny.
Yes, boss: Banquo below earth-LOC lie-down-CONT.
Ay, my good lord: safe in a ditch he bides.

MACBETH gestures for the MURDERERS to exit.
LADY MACBETH enters.

LADY MACBETH
Nganang biediyar,
My boss,
My royal lord,

Nyoondalitj djoorap-bt: kobongkarl boondong yong ngarniny.
You-REL happy-NEG: friends money give eat-CONT.
You do not give the cheer: the feast is sold.

MACBETH
Kaya, mardang, ngany kaaditj!
Yes, love, I know!
Sweet remembrancer!

(To the guests) Korbol kwop ngoorr kwop,
Stomach good character good,
Now, good digestion wait on appetite,

Koodjal moorditj dowirl!
Both strong always!
And health on both!

The BANQUO'S GHOST enters MACBETH's place.

MACBETH
Boola nyoongara ngwidam nidjak,
Many people dignified here-LOC,
Here had we now our country's honour roof'd,

Banquo bara-koorl;
Banquo go-astray;
Were the graced person of our Banquo present;

Nyornditj nyorn.
Alas-REL alas.
Who I challenge for unkindness

LENNOX
Banquo yoowart nitj, biediyar,
Banquo not here, boss,
His absence, sir,

Baalitj babin dowirl. Ngalar djoorabiny
He-REL pledged-friend always. We happy-CONT
Lays blame upon his promise. Please't your highness

nyinalanginy.
Sit-LOC-ASS-CONT.
To grace us with your royal company.

MACBETH sees BANQUO'S GHOST and begins to freak out.

MACBETH
Natj! Ngiyan malkar dookernang?
What! Who magic make-PST?
Which of you have done this?

LENNOX
Natj, biediyar?
What, boss?
What, my good lord?

MACBETH
(To the Ghost) Ngany daap kian: yoowart yoowarl widiwidang
I knife none: not toward shake
Thou canst not say I did it: never shake

Nyoonang ngoobalyong djoombar.
Your bloody hair.
Thy gory locks at me.

LENNOX
Kobongkar wort koorl: biediyar menditj.
Friends away go: boss sick.
Gentlemen rise: his highness is not well.

LADY MACBETH
Yalak, kobongkar: biediyar yoran,
Wait, friends: boss alright,
Sit, worthy friends: my lord is often thus,

Dowirl: kaya, nyoondakat kokon nyin;
Always: yes, you-PL wait sit;
And hath been from his youth: pray you, keep seat;

Ngaarn, baal kwop. (To Macbeth) Nyoondalitj maam, wa?
Eat, he good. You-REL man, hey?
Feed, and regard him not. Are you a man?

MACBETH
Nyorn, djinang! Aliwa! Ni! Ni!
Alas, see! Beware! Hark! Hark!
Prithee, see there! Behold! Look! Lo!

Bokalal kworditj
Grave-ACT throw
If charnel-houses and our graves must send

Noitj baal nitj, boodjaritj
Dead him here, earth-REL
Those that we bury back, our monuments

djandoo-mokiny kandanginy.
Raptor-SIM vomit-CNT.
Shall be the maws of kites.

BANQUO'S GHOST vanishes.

LADY MACBETH
Ngiyan, balbit waangkiny?
Who, foolish talk-CONT?
What, quite unmann'd in folly?

MACBETH
Ngaitj karni yaakiny, karni djinanginy.
I-ACT truly stand-CONT, truly see-CONT.
If I stand here, I saw him.

LADY MACBETH
Koolyamitj, kaanya!
Lies, shame!
Fie, for shame!

MACBETH
Kooralang,
Long-ago-LOC-ASS,
The times have been,

Kaya, nyoongaritj malya kian, baalitj noitj,
Yes, person-REL brain none, he-REL dead,
That, when the brains were out, the man would die,

Yeyi baalitj yaakar booyang boolain,
Now he-REL stand-OCC strange more,
This is more strange

Mooriyakitj yoran.
Murder-REL alright.
Than such a murder is.

LADY MACBETH
Nganang biediyaritj biediyar,
My boss-REL boss,
My worthy lord,

Kobongkaritj biediyar-bt.
Friends-REL leaderless.
Your noble friends do lack you.

MACBETH
(To the guests) Yoowart bard-djinang ngany, nyoondakaditj kobong-karitj ngwidam
Not move-off-look me, you-PL-REL friends-PL-REL dignified
Do not muse at me, my most worthy friends

Ngany yoran nyininy, menditj yoowart
I alright be-CONT, sick not
I have a strange infirmity, which is nothing

Nyoondakadal ngany kaaditj (raises a toast). Kaya, ngalaritj moorditj ngoorr kwop;
You-PL-ACT me know. Yes, we-REL strong character good;
To those that know me. Come love and health to all;

Ngalarang kobongitj Banquo miyaliny, nyorn;
Our friend-REL Banquo wanting, alas;
And to our dear friend Banquo, whom we miss;

LORDS
Babin karnarn.
Pledged-friend true.
Our duties and the pledge.

They toast and cheer.
BANQUO'S GHOST re-enters.

MACBETH
Wara! Wort koorl! Boodjarak darap!
Bad! Away go! Earth-LOC enter!
Avaunt! And quit my sight! Let the earth hide thee!

Ni, malak wirnitj!
Hark, shadow evil!
Hence, horrible shadow!

Koolyamitj, nitj!
Lies-REL, this!
Unreal mockery, hence!

BANQUO'S GHOST vanishes. MACBETH is puzzled, looking for the ghost.

Nganang ngoorr booyangabiny nyoonang
My character strange-TR you-RES
You make me strange

Nidjak djinang ba nyoondalitj yoran
Here-LOC see and you-REL alright
Even to the disposition that I owe

Nganitj white-TR kabin bookor-bt.
I-REL djardarabiny maybe brave-NEG.
When now I think you can behold such sights.

LENNOX
Biediyar, natj nyoondak djinang?
Boss, what you-ACT see?
What sights my lord?

LADY MACBETH
Dat nyin; baal warabiny;
Quiet be; he failing;
I pray you, speak not; he grows worse and worse;

Biediyar karang mayarang. Yeyi, nookert koorl:
Boss angry voice-RES. Now, sleep go:
Question enrages him. At once, good night:

Boordawan djinang!
Later see!
A kind good night to all!

Exit all but MACBETH and LADY MACBETH.

MACBETH
Ngoobitj ngoop; baalap waangk, ngoobitj ngoop:
Blood-REL blood; they-PL say, blood-REL blood:
It will have blood; they say, blood will have blood:

Kidalakitj natj?
Night-REL what?
What is the night?

LADY MACBETH
Benang boorda.
Tomorrow soon.
Almost at odds with morning which is which.

MACBETH
Natj nyoondak kaaditj, Macduff kian
What you know, Macduff none
How say'st thou, that Macduff denies his person

Ngalarang koombar kambarnitj?
Our large meet-REL?
At our great bidding?

LADY MACBETH
Nyoondak waangkang baalak wa?
You-ACT speak-PAST him-LOC hey?
Did you send to him sir?

MACBETH
Ngany kaaditj wardaritj
I know watcher-REL
There's not a one of them but in his house

Balar baalang korndak. Benang ngaitj,
Hidden his hut-LOC. Tomorrow I-ACT,
I keep a servant fee'd. I will to-morrow,

Kardart, mambara mardiny koorliny:
Straight, spirit-creature three travel-CONT:
And betimes I will, to the weird sisters:

Boorda baalapal waangk boolain; yeyi ngaitj kaaditj dalanginy,
Soon they speak more; now I-ACT know pursue-CONT,
More shall they speak; for now I am bent to know,

Waraitj, wara.
Bad-REL, bad.
By the worst means, the worst.

LADY MACBETH
Nyoondalitj biet-bt biet-bt, nookert.
You-REL weak lost, sleep.
You lack the season of all natures, sleep.

MACBETH
Yoowarl koorl, nganana nookert. Nganang booyang baamang
Toward travel, we-SPO sleep. My strange strike-PST
Come, we'll to sleep. My strange and self-abuse

Ngoorr weyarn boolarabiny:
Character fear multiplying:
Is the initiate fear that wants hard use:

Ngananaitj doodjaraitj milkar.
We-SPO-REL murderer-REL fresh.
We are yet but young in deed.

They exit.

SCENE VI

Outdoors.
HECATE waits for ALL MISCHIEF MAKERS to enter. MISCHIEF MAKER 1 carries a bunch of branches. She uses her magic to draw them in before freezing them. She mentally retraces their steps, seeing their interaction with MACBETH and BANQUO. She unfreezes them. They try hugging HECATE but their arms dangle in the air like scarecrows.

MISCHIEF MAKER 1
Yaarn, natj, Hecate! Mirnitj karang wa?
How, what, Hecate! Face angry hey?
Why, how now, Hecate! You look angerly.

HECATE
Kaanya nyoondakadal
Shame you-PL-ACT
How did you dare

Wirnitj waangk yongang Macbeth
Haunted speak give-PAST Macbeth
To trade and traffic with Macbeth

Nyoondalitj daa bardanginy.
You-PL-REL tongue jump-CONT.
In riddles and affairs of death

Baalitj nobitj bara-koorlar,
He-REL boy-REL go-astray-OCC,
A wayward son,

Moolyabiny, baalitj, baalap-mokiny,
Hateful, he-REL, them-PL-SIM,
Spiteful and wrathful, who, as others do,

Woombabaan, waarlar.
Vain, carelessly.
Loves for his own ends, not for you.

The MISCHIEF MAKERS flop to the ground, forced downwards by HECATE. They look to each other for comfort. They must bow to boodjar. She means business.

Boodjaritj ngalarang biediyar.
Country-REL our boss.
If ever we are nature's

Boodjaral ngoop yong ngalarak, ngalariny dookern.
Country-ACT blood give us-LOC, us-OBJ make.
Our blood to us, this to our blood is born.

Boodjarang koot koombarmit, bibi koombarmit,
Earth-POSS womb large-INTS, breast large-INTS,
Whose womb unmeasurable, and infinite breast,

Boola, baalal doordok yong ngalarak;
Plenty, it-ACT life give us-LOC;
Teems, and feeds all;

Boola malkar dookern yeyi, yong yeyi.
Much magic make now, give now.
Great business must be wrought ere.

The MISCHIEF MAKERS are flicked off stage by HECATE. She waits. A fire is crackling. She exits.

ACT IV

SCENE I

Night.
Enter the MISCHIEF MAKERS circling the water-filled ngama where BANQUO'S GHOST will eventually rise.

ALL
Bindjala bindjala dookerniny wara;
Bubbles bubbles make-CONT bad;
Double, double toil and trouble;

Kaarl naariny ba boodjara baaboorr.
Fire burn-CONT and earth ripple.
Fire burn, and the earth bubble.

MISCHIEF MAKER 2
Maara-ngaangk djip-djip,
Thumb itchy,
By the pricking of my thumbs,

Waraitj wara yoowarl koorliny.
Bad-REL bad toward travel-CONT.
Something wicked this way comes.

MISCHIEF MAKER 1 distributes branches. They become trees. Enter MACBETH, searching for the MISCHIEF MAKERS. They circle him, never stationary.

MACBETH
Yaarn, balar, moorni mambara mardiny!
How, hidden, dark, spirit-creature three!
How now, you secret, black, and midnight hags!

Natj nyoondakadal dookern?
What you-PL-ACT fix?
What is't you do?

The MISCHIEF MAKERS mustn't speak to him – HECATE has forbidden it.

MACBETH
Kayaritj kaya, waangkitj waangk,
Yes-REL yes, speak-REL speak,
I conjure you, by that which you profess,

Nyoondakadal kwibil kaaditj, waangk nganyak:
You stealthy know, speak me-LOC:
How e'er you come to know it, answer me:

Nyoondakaditj wirawoorliny dookern ngarda baam boorniny;
You-PL-REL whirlwind make down strike tree-OBJ;
Though you untie the winds and trees blown down;

Nganyak yong
Me-LOC give
Answer me

Waangk nitj.
Speak this.
To what I ask you.

The MISCHIEF MAKERS look to each other. They're wobbly with excitement, each one desperate to break the speaking rule HECATE just placed on them.

Waangk nitj.
Speak this.
To what I ask you.

They launch into competitive disobedience.

MISCHIEF MAKER 1
Macbeth!

MISCHIEF MAKER 2
Macbeth!

MISCHIEF MAKER 3
Macbeth!

MACBETH
Ngany weyarn nyoondakadang
I fear you-PL-RES
Thou hast harp'd my fear

Waangk nganyak.
Speak me-LOC
O what I ask you.

MISCHIEF MAKER 1
Aliwa Macduff;
Beware Macduff;

MISCHIEF MAKER 2
Aliwa Macduff;
Beware Macduff;

MISCHIEF MAKER 3
Aliwa Macduff;
Beware Macduff;

The MISCHIEF MAKERS 'shush' each other – they've said too much. Again.

MISCHIEF MAKER 1
Macbeth!

MISCHIEF MAKER 1 disappears from MACBETH's vision but stands right in front of him, becoming a tree. The other MISCHIEF MAKERS hide behind MISCHIEF MAKER 1 and become invisible to MACBETH. They leap out at different times hitting MACBETH with branches. MACBETH suddenly hallucinates, only able to see the branches and nothing else. MACBETH is fighting off the 'forest of Dunsinane'.

MACBETH
Ngiyan malkar dookern, boorniny
Who magic make, tree-OBJ
Who can impress the forest, bid the tree

Boodjarak yira bardanginy?
ground-LOC up fly-CONT?
Unfix his earth-bound root?

MACBETH becomes angered and takes the bushes out of the air (MISCHIEF MAKERS' hands) and throws them into the ngama. MACBETH repeats himself.

Ngiyan malkar dookern, boorniny
Who magic make, tree-OBJ
Who can impress the forest, bid the tree

Boodjarak yira bardanginy?
ground-LOC up fly-CONT?
Unfix his earth-bound root?

As the branches land in the ngama the BANQUO'S GHOST rises from it. He sits on the edge. The MISCHIEF MAKERS cannot see BANQUO'S GHOST but they watch as MACBETH begins to hallucinate. MACBETH is desperate to know more from the MISCHIEF MAKERS.

Nganyak waangk, nyoondakat kaaditj
Me-LOC speak, you-PL know
Tell me, if your art

Mila: Banquo koolongitj
Future: Banquo child-REL
Can tell so much: shall Banquo's issue ever

Biediyarabiny nitj boodjarak wa?
Boss-TR this land-LOC hey?
Reign in this kingdom?

Nganyak waangk, nyoondakat kaaditj:
Me-LOC speak, you-PL know:
Tell me, if your art

MACBETH clocks BANQUO'S GHOST and trembles all over.

Wirnitj! Yeyi, djinanginy, karnarn;
Evil! Now, see-CONT, true;
Horrible sight! Now, I see, 'tis true;

The MISCHIEF MAKERS vanish.

Macbeth, paralysed, is afraid of BANQUO's GHOST – it's haunting him wherever he goes.

MACBETH
Windji baalap? Wort koorl?
Where they-PL? Away go?
Where are they? Gone?

Windji baalap? Wort koorl?!
Where they-PL? Away go?!
Where are they? Gone?!

Enter LENNOX, seeing MACBETH hallucinate again.

LENNOX
Biediyar natj nyoona miyaliny?
Boss what you wanting?
What's your grace's will?

MACBETH
Nyoondalitj mambara mardiny djinangang?
You-REL spirit-creature three see-PAST?
Saw you the mischief makers?

LENNOX
Yoowart, biediyar.
No, boss.
No, my lord.

MACBETH
Kori baalabal nyoonany boordook koorl wa?
Just-now they-PL-ACT you-OBJ close travel hey?
Came they not by you?

LENNOX
Biediyar, ngaitj waangk yong
Boss, I-ACT speak give
My lord, I bring you word

Macduff wort bardang.
Macduff away fly.
Macduff is fled.

MACBETH
Wort bardang!
Away fly!
Fled!

LENNOX
Kaya, biediyar.
Yes, boss.
Ay, my good lord.

MACBETH
Yeyi kaaditj
Now know
From this moment

Nganang koorditj karni-miyaliny
My heart-REL true-wanting
The very firstlings of my heart shall be

Nganang maaritj warn. Kori,
My hand-REL do. Just-now,
To the firstlings of my hand. And even now,

Biediyarang kaaditj koorl, kaadidjiny ba baaminy.
Boss-ASS know move, know-CONT and strike-CONT.
crown my thoughts with acts, be it thought and done.

LENNOX, perplexed, acknowledges MACBETH words.

LENNOX
Yeyi, maarritj booyang.
Now, air-REL strange.
Things have been strangely borne.

Duncan ngoorr kwop ngwidam
Duncan character good dignified
The gracious Duncan

Baal noidjal Macbeth waangkang 'nyoorn':
He dead-LOC Macbeth speak-PST 'alas':
Was pitied of Macbeth: marry, he was dead:

Bookor Banquo kidalak moornitj moorn bara-koorl;
Brave Banquo night dark-REL dark go-astray;
And the right-valiant Banquo walk'd too late;

Baaliny, arwoon, Fleance werdamang, wa?
He-OBJ, ha, Fleance kill-PST, hey?
Whom, you may say, if't please you, Fleance kill'd,

Kenyak! Kabin Macduff
Enough! Perhaps Macduff
But, peace! I hear Macduff

Nidja wirndang boodjarak yoowarl koorliny yeyi.
Here weary country-LOC toward travel-CONT now.
May soon return to this our suffering country

Kayaritj kaya. Kwopitj kwop –
Yes-REL yes. Good-REL good –
With a blessing. To ratify the work –

Kabin ngalar yoran boorda.
Perhaps we alright soon.
We may again receive free honors.

Nitj ngalar miyaliny boola. Kori waangkang
This we wanting much. Just-now talk-RES
All which we pine for now. And this report

Macbeth karang koombarmit
Macbeth angry large-INTS
Hath so exasperated the king that he

Baal waarlar bakitj dookerniny.
He carelessly fight make-CONT.
Prepares for some attempt of war.

They exit in different directions. LENNOX has an idea. BANQUO'S GHOST stands and follows MACBETH.

SCENE II

Macduff's place of residence.
Enter LADY MACDUFF and her SON. They're best friends.

LADY MACDUFF
Nadjal Macduff woorrar bardanginy?
Why Macduff long-way fly-CONT?
What had he done, to make him fly the land?

Ngany karang-bt yeyi, wa?
I angry-NEG now, hey?
Must I have patience?

She sits her SON down to make sure his hair is clean.

LADY MACDUFF
Baalal ngaliny mardang-bt.
He-ACT us-FAM-OBJ love-NEG.
He loves us not;

SON
Nganang maamanitj, woolkar-kadak wa?
My father-REL, guilt-POSS hey?
Was my father a traitor, mother?

LADY MACDUFF
Kaya, woolkar-kadak.
Yes, guilt-POSS.
Ay, that he was.

SON
Woolkar-kadakitj natj?
Guilt-POSS-REL what?
What is a traitor?

LADY MACDUFF
Arwoon, baalitj babinak bardip waangk.
Ha, he-REL pledged-friend-LOC deceive speak.
Why, one that swears and lies.

SON
Balbiditj babin balbiditj koolyawar ana?
Fool-REL pledged-friend liar yeah?
So liars and swearers are fools?

LADY MACDUFF
Winyan waangkar, nyoonang daa bardang!
Pitiful speak-OCC, your language jump!
Poor prattler, how thou talk'st!

Yeyi, nyornditj,
Now, alas-REL,
Now, God help thee,

Yaarn nyoondalitj maam-bt nyorn?
How you-REL fatherless alas?
How wilt thou do for a father?

Enter three MURDERERS.
LADY MACDUFF is startled, immediately uneasy.

LADY MACDUFF
Ngiyan mirnitj?
Who face?
What are these faces?

FIRST MURDERER
Nyoonang maam windjar?
Your man where?
Where is your husband?

LADY MACDUFF
Yoran, bokidja woorrar
Innocent, afar long-way
I hope, in no place so unsanctified

Nyoondak wara djinang baaliny.
You-ACT fail-to see him-OBJ.
Where such as thou mayst find him.

FIRST MURDERER
Baalitj woolkar-kadak.
He-REL guilt-POSS.
He's a traitor.

SON
Nyoondalitj bardip, karang-kadak!
You-REL deceive, enemy!
Thou liest, thou shag-haired villain!

FIRST MURDERER
(Grabbing him) Nop mookiyang!
Boy useless!
Young fry of treachery!

Two of the MURDERERS grab the SON and drag him away to kill him. The other holds LADY MACDUFF. The boy is stabbed and dies in front of his mother.

SON
Baalal ngany werdamang, ngaangk.
He-ACT me-OBJ kill-PAST, mother.
He has killed me, mother.

LADY MACDUFF escapes, running free.

LADY MACDUFF
Mooriyak!
Murder!
Murder!

The MURDERERS chase after and catch LADY MACDUFF. LADY MACDUFF is then killed too. We hear HECATE hum 'Boodjar'.

SCENE III

Before the King's palace.
Enter MALCOLM then MACDUFF. Both arranged to meet here, both wary of the other. MALCOLM is reluctant to speak. MACDUFF isn't sure where to begin.

MALCOLM
Macbeth, ngalarang daaliny menditj kwerliny waangkang,
Macbeth, our tongue sore name-OBJ speak-RES,
This tyrant, whose sole name blisters our tongues,

Koora baalitj yoran nyinang. Nyoondalitj babin baalang.
long-ago he-REL innocent be-PAST. You-REL pledged-friend his.
Was once thought honest. You have loved him well.

MACDUFF
Ngany koort karnarn.
I heart true.
I am not treacherous.

MALCOLM
Kaya Macbeth koort kian.
Yes Macbeth heart without.
But Macbeth is.

MALCOLM eyeballs MACDUFF, unsure if he can trust him with his life. Has MACDUFF been sent here to kill him? They are wary of each other, senses heightened. Both cautious yet determined to reach a resolution.

MACDUFF
Ngany wirndang biet-bt.
I weary lost.
I have lost my hopes.

Ngoop, ngoop, boodjar menditj!
Blood, blood, country sore!
Bleed, bleed, poor country!

MACDUFF, becoming hopeful, begins marking points of significance in the sky, revealing the history of their people and why DUNCAN was so revered. MACDUFF (aloud) recalls a song DUNCAN once shared with him.

(song 4)
Bokidja bo binar,
There far comet,
Soft light through yonder,

Karreba biet worlakal baaminy,
Tenderness path sky-LOC put-CONT,
Two of the fairest stars in all the heaven,

MACDUFF
Maamitj biediyaritj baalang nop kaadidjiny.
Father-REL path-REL his son know-CONT.
It is a wise father that knows his own child.

MACDUFF sings the song in full.
MALCOLM's natural response is to join in, singing the song his father taught him and MACDUFF.

MALCOLM/MACDUFF (song 4 – repeat once)
Bokidja bo binar
There far comet
Soft light through yonder,

Karreba biet worlakal baaminy,
Tenderness path sky-LOC put-CONT,
Two of the fairest stars in all the heaven,

Djinda baalap kanangkoor,
Star they-PL shine,
Twinkle in their spheres as daylight,

Kora maya waab,
Again sound play,
That birds would sing,

Mardanginy kwadjat mardang
Love-CONT in-front-of love.
Love goes toward love.

They embrace with strength, trust and hope.
MALCOLM is ready to return home.
Enter LENNOX.

LENNOX
Nyoongar, kwop.
Person, good.
Sir, amen.

MACDUFF
Nakal ngoondan, yoran nyin.
Gentle brother, alright be.
My ever-gentle cousin, welcome hither.

MALCOLM
Kori warda winyan natj?
Just-now news pitiful what?
What's the newest grief?

LENNOX is somewhat uneasy.

LENNOX
Waraitj wara waangkaritj woort bidjabiny:
Bad-REL bad speak-OCC-REL throat dry-TR:
That of an hour's age doth hiss the speaker:

Wirnitj warda boolarabiny.
Evil news multiplying.
Each minute teems a new one.

He remains uneasy turning to MACDUFF.

Ngany daa-kadak,
I language-POSS,
I have words,

Kabin ngaitj baanak waal,
Perhaps I-ACT plains-LOC cry,
That would be howl'd out in the desert air,

Baalitj dwongkiny wara barang.
It-REL Ear-OBJ fail-to grasp.
Where hearing should not latch them.

MACDUFF
Natj?
What?
What?

LENNOX
Nyoonang kornt; nyoonang yokiny nobiny
Your shelter; your woman-OBJ son-OBJ
Your castle is surprised; your wife and babes

Werdamang karang:
Killed angry:
Savagely slaughter'd:

MALCOLM
Waraitj wara!
Bad-REL bad!
Merciful heaven!

MACDUFF
Nganang nop?
My son?
My children too?

Nganang koort?
My spouse?
My wife kill'd too

Horrified silence envelops them. MACDUFF breaks down. LENNOX and MALCOLM offer their support. They give him all the time he needs.

MALCOLM
Nyoornditj nyoorn:
Alas-REL alas:
Be comforted:

Ngalar bangal-baam dookern,
We revenge make,
Let's make us medicines of our great revenge,

Walbarn koort-werainy.
Heal sorrow-OBJ.
To cure this deadly grief.

MACDUFF
Baalap ngwirin nganalang wa?
They pretty mine hey?
All my pretty ones?

Natj nyoondak waangk? Natj?!
What you-ACT speak? What?!
Did you say all? All?!

Noitj waarlar?
Dead carelessly?
All at one fell swoop?

MALCOLM rests his hand on MACDUFF's shoulders.
LENNOX urges MACDUFF to strength by singing a lyrically altered version of the sergeant's song. MALCOLM joins in.

LENNOX / MALCOLM (song 3)
Nyornditj nyorn
Alas-REL alas!

Boola moort ngaitj djinangana
Much family I see

Kidja worl borninya
Spear sky cut-CONT

Kwelkena baal
Dodge he

Kidja bilang bilangana
Spear flash flash

Kwelkena baal
Dodge he

MACDUFF is overcome with grief and lifts LENNOX off the ground in rage. MALCOLM takes up the song in full voice, grounding MACDUFF.

Moorditj ngany
Strong me

Mendidjala ngoop baaminya
Wound-LOC blood strike-CONT

Kwelkena baal
Dodge he

LENNOX recovers and resumes singing.

Kwop kwordidjiny baal
Good throw-CONT he

Kidja kwordidjiny baal
Spear throw-CONT he

Werdamana werdamana
Kill kill

Norniny baam
Snake strike

MACDUFF manages his grief, for now, and collects two branches from boodjar. He hands one to MALCOLM. He directs LENNOX to collect his own branch.

MACDUFF
Kardart koorl; ngalaritj moordidjabiny;
Straight travel; we-REL strong-TR;
Come; our power is ready;

Kidalakitj woorraritj wara djinang benanginy.
Night-REL long-way-REL fail-to see tomorrow-OBJ.
The night is long that never finds the day.

They exit together, united.

ACT V

SCENE I

A room at MACBETH's residence.
Enter a DOCTOR OF PHYSIC (Duncan's Ghost) and a WAITING-GENTLEPERSON (Banquo's Ghost).

DOCTOR (DUNCAN'S GHOST)
Baal biet-bt nyinang wa?
She weak sit-PAST hey?
When was it she last walked?

GENTLEPERSON (BANQUO'S GHOST)
Biediyar bakidjap koorlal.
Boss battleground travel-LOC.
Since his majesty went into the field.

Enter LADY MACBETH, with a taper (candle) – now constantly afraid of the dark.

DOCTOR (DUNCAN'S GHOST)
Nadjal baal kaarl-boorn-kadak?
Why she firestick-POSS?
How came she by that light?

GENTLEPERSON (BANQUO'S GHOST)
Kaarl-boornak ngat kediny.
Firestick-INS repeatedly carry-CONT.
She has light by her continually.

LADY MACBETH
Madooly nitj.
Filthy here.
Yet here's a spot.

Baan, madooly wara! Baan, yeyi!
Clear, filth bad! Clear, now!
Out, damned spot! Out, I say!

Ngiyan kaaditj mandjangitj ngoop-kadak boola.
Who know old-man-REL blood-POSS much.
Who would have thought the old man to have had so much blood in him.

DOCTOR (DUNCAN'S GHOST)
Ali nyoona djinang?
There you see?
Do you mark that?

LADY MACBETH
Noorditj ngoop ngat ngat
Stench-REL blood repeatedly repeatedly
Here's the smell of the blood still

Maar kayebal baam, maar kayebal baam.
Hand water-LOC put, hand water-LOC put.
Wash your hands, wash your hands.

DOCTOR (DUNCAN'S GHOST)
Menditj nidja ngany kaaditj-bt.
Sick this I don't-know.
This disease is beyond my practise.

A knock is heard.

LADY MACBETH
Dat nyin, ngoornt! Alidja Maya:
Quiet be, lie-down! There sound:
To bed, to bed! there's knocking at the gate:

Bard, bard, bard, bard, yoowarl maarak barang.
Go, go, go, go, toward hand-INS grasp.
Come, come, come, come, give me your hand.

Baal warnitj warn dowirl.
It do-is do always.
What's done cannot be undone.

Exit.

SCENE II
A room in MACBETH's place of residence.
Enter MACBETH. The DOCTOR (Duncan's Ghost) remains on stage.

MACBETH
Daa-bt yeyi; Warda worlak kworditj:
Mute now; deeds sky-LOC throw:
Bring me no more reports; let them fly all:

Mambaraitj kaaditj
Spirit-creature-REL know
The spirits that know

Boolaritj boola karni waangkang:
Much-REL much truly speak-PAST:
All mortal consequences have pronounced me thus:

'Aliwa Macduff'.
'Beware Macduff'.
'Beware Macduff'.

MACBETH contemplates. Does he still believe the MISCHIEF MAKERS' word?

Malyaitj koorditj nganalang
Brain-REL heart-REL mine
The mind I sway by and the heart I bear

Yoowart weyarn widiwidang.
Not fear shaking.
Shall never sag with doubt nor shake with fear.

HECATE enters as SEYTON.

Seyton! – Ngany koort menditj,
Seyton! – I heart sick,
Seyton! – I am sick at heart,

Djinanginy – Seyton, ngaitj waangk! – Bakidjal
See-CONT – Seyton, I speak! – Fight-LOC
When I behold – Seyton, I say! – This push

Ngany kaaw dowirl, kabin noitj boorda.
I laugh always, perhaps dead soon.
Will cheer me ever, or disseat me now.

SEYTON (HECATE) assesses MACBETH.

Ngaitj bakidjiny boolaritj boordaoo nganang kweidjitj daatj-bt bornang.
I-ACT fight-CONT much-REL until my bone-REL fleshless cut-RES.
I'll fight till from my bones my flesh be hack'd.

Kwoark nganyak yong.
Cloak me-LOC give.
Give me my armour.

SEYTON (HECATE)
Boorda.
Soon.
'Tis not needed yet.

MACBETH
Ngaitj ngabang.
I-ACT cover.
I'll put it on.

Kwoark nganyak yong.
Cloak me-LOC give.
Give me mine armour.

(To the Doctor) Boolyakadak, nganang yok yaarn?
Doctor, my woman how?
How does your patient, doctor?

DOCTOR (DUNCAN'S GHOST)
Baalitj menditj koondamang wirnidjang,
She-REL sick dream-RES haunted-RES,
She is troubled with thick coming fancies,

Nookert kian.
Sleep none.
That keep her from her rest.

MACBETH
Walbarn baaliny.
Heal her-OBJ.
Cure her of that.

Baalitj kaat menditj ana,
She-REL head sick yeah,
Canst thou not minister to a mind diseased,

Nyoondak birn barang malyak,
You-ACT dig grab brain-LOC,
Pluck from the memory,

Weyarniny koombariny koordak wa?
Fear-OBJ large-OBJ heart-LOC hey?
Which weighs upon the heart?

DOCTOR (DUNCAN'S GHOST)
Kaat monditj nyoongar
Head sick person
Therein the patient

Keny walbarniny.
Alone heal-CONT.
Must minister to himself.

MACBETH
Koolyam.
Lies.
I'll none of it.

(To Seyton) Moordiyap, kwoark nganyak yong.
Hurry, cloak me-LOC give.
Come, put mine armour on.

Ngany bookor weyarn-bt.
I brave fearless.
I will not be afraid of death.

DOCTOR (DUNCAN'S GHOST)
(Aside) Nganitj nidjak boondongang kabin benang ngany woorrar.
I-REL here-LOC money-RES likely tomorrow I long-way.
Profit again should hardly draw me here.

The DOCTOR exits.

SCENE III
Night.
Enter MALCOLM, MACDUFF, LENNOX marching the perimeter.

MALCOLM
Ngoondangkar, boordawan boordaoo
Brothers, sooner or later
Cousins, I hope the days are near at hand

Boodjar kwobabiny.
Land good-TR.
That chambers will be safe.

MACDUFF
Karnarnitj kanarn.
True-REL true.
We doubt it nothing.

LENNOX
Macbeth korndal, waarlar nyininy
Macbeth shelter-LOC, careless be-CONT
Macbeth keeps still in Dunsinane, and will endure

Ngalaritj kwadjat yaakiny
We-REL in-front-of stand-CONT:
Our setting down before 't:

Baalitj keny kobong kian
He-REL alone friend none
And none serve with him but constrained things

Koort kian.
Heart none.
Whose hearts are absent too.

They exit, marching.

SCENE IV

Night. Indoors. MACBETH's place of residence.
MACBETH is now armoured, SEYTON (HECATE) is still beside him.
Women begin to cry.

MACBETH
Maya natj?
Sound what?
What is that noise?

SEYTON (HECATE)
Yokangkar waaliny, biediyar Macbeth.
Women cry-CONT, boss Macbeth.
It is the cry of women, my good lord.

MACBETH
Ngaitj weyarniny bakanang kaaditj-bt-abiny;
I-ACT fear-OBJ taste don't-know-TR;
I have almost forgot the taste of fears;

Koora, nganitj winyan nyinang
Long-ago, I-REL pitiful be-PAST
The time has been, my senses would have cooled

Maya waal dwonk-baamang; kabin nganang
Sound cry ear-strike-PAST; likely my
To hear a night-shriek; and my fell of hair

Djoombaral yira bardang
Hair-ACT up jump
Would at a dismal treatise rouse and stir

Nganang miyalitj ngoop moorart;
My eyes-REL blood full;
I have supp'd full with horrors;

Weyarnitj, ngany kaaditj boola
Fear-REL, I know much
Direness, familiar to my slaughterous thoughts

Ngany kian-kadak yeyi.
I nothing-POSS now.
Cannot once start me.

Wailing is heard again. HECATE watches BANQUO'S GHOST and DUNCAN'S GHOST enter, walking towards her. She carefully restores the crown upon the head of DUNCAN'S GHOST as he passes. Both ghosts exit.

(To Seyton) Waaliny windjar?
Cry-CONT where?
Wherefore was that cry?

SEYTON (HECATE)
Nyoonang yok, biediyar, baalitj noitj.
Your woman, boss, she-REL dead.
The queen, my lord, is dead.

SEYTON (HECATE) exits.

MACBETH
Noitj boordawan kabin;
Dead later likely;
She should have died hereafter;

Nganana waangk.
We-SPO speak.
There would have been a time for such a word.

Benang ba, benang ba, benang
Tomorrow and, tomorrow and, tomorrow
To-morrow, and to-morrow, and to-morrow.

Baam, baam, kaarl kian!
Strike, strike, fire none!
Out, out, brief candle!

The wailing stops.

Ngalaritj malak koorliny.
We-REL shadow travel-CONT.
Life's but a walking shadow.

Danger is near and MACBETH braces for it.

SCENE V

Enter MACDUFF, ready to fight. He calls out to MACBETH. MALCOLM and LENNOX stand guard.

MACDUFF
Doodjar, mirnitj baan!
Murderer, face exposed!
Tyrant, show thy face!

Boordaoo ngaitj werdam nyoonany,
Until I-ACT kill you-OBJ,
If thou be'st slain and with no stroke of mine,

Nganang moort dowirl wirnitj wariny.
My family always haunted hanging.
My wife and children's ghosts will haunt me still.

MACBETH
Ngaitj kwelkenang nyoonany:
I-ACT dodge-PST you:
Of all men else I have avoided thee:

Wort koorl; nganang koordoomit moorart
Away travel; my soul full
But get thee back; my soul is too much charged

Ngoobang nyoonalak.
Blood-RES yours.
With blood of thine already.

MACDUFF
Daabitj nganang maya: nyoondalitj doodjaraitj ngoobalyong boolain
Knife-REL my sound: you-REL murderer-REL bloody more
My voice is in my sword: thou bloodier villain

Daa wirt!
Language empty!
Than terms can give thee out!

MACBETH and MACDUFF battle.

MACBETH
Moordiyap,
Hurry,
I will not yield,

Ngaitj yoowart bonyin ngarda boodjarak kwadjaditj nobang djen.
I-ACT not kiss down ground-LOC in-front-of-REL boy-POSS foot.
To kiss the ground before young Malcolm's feet.

Yoowarl koorl, Macduff,
Toward travel, Macduff,
Lay on, Macduff,

Baalitj mookiyangitj waangk, 'kenyak!'
He-REL useless-REL speak, 'enough!'
And damn'd be him that first cries, 'Hold, enough!'

They continue to battle until MACDUFF kills MACBETH.
MACBETH is decapitated. LENNOX holds the bag open for MACDUFF to deposit the head. They exit leaving MALCOLM alone.

SCENE VI

Night. Outdoors.
Enter FLEANCE, missing her father.
BANQUO'S GHOST is present, watching over his daughter.
DUNCAN'S GHOST is present, watching over his son.

FLEANCE
Nyornditj, ngalarang boodjar!
Alas-REL, our country!
Alas, poor country!

Baalal weyarn kaaditj keny. Baalang kwerl
It-ACT fear know alone. Her name
Almost afraid to know itself. It cannot

Yoowart 'ngaangk', yeyi baalang kwerl ngalarang bokal, nidjak,
Not mother, now her name our grave, here-LOC,
Be called our mother, but our grave, where nothing,

Nyoongara kaaditj-bt, kaawiny;
People don't-know, and laugh-CONT;
But who knows nothing, is once seen to smile;

Nitj maya waaliny worlak darabiny
Here voice cry-CONT sky-LOC dive-CONT
Where sighs and groans and shrieks that rend the air

Nyoongara dwongka-bt; nitj bakidiny koort-wera kabin
people deaf; here fight-CONT sorrow perhaps
Are made, not marked; where violent sorrow seems

Djoorabiny yeyi.
Happy-CONT now.
A modern ecstasy.

DUNCAN'S GHOST and BANQUO'S GHOST sing.
HECATE hovers, overseeing.

DUNCAN / BANQUO (song 4 – repeat once)
Bokidja bo binar
There far comet
Soft light through yonder,

Karreba biet worlakal baaminy,
Tenderness path sky-LOC put-CONT,
Two of the fairest stars in all the heaven,

Djinda baalap kanangkoor,
Star they-PL shine,
Twinkle in their spheres as daylight,

Kora maya waab,
Again sound play,
That birds would sing,

Mardanginy kwadjat mardang
Love-CONT in-front-of love.
Love goes toward love.

FLEANCE and MALCOLM are connected in spirit and song, for all time.
Enter LENNOX and MACDUFF with MALCOLM's crown.

MACDUFF
Woola, biediyar! Nidja kwop: yoran nyininy:
Hooray, boss! This good: alright be-CONT:
Hail, king! For so thou art: the time is free:

MALCOLM refuses the crown. MACDUFF places it on boodjar at his feet.

MACDUFF / LENNOX
Woola, biediyar Malcolm!
Hooray, boss Malcolm!
Hail, King!

HECATE approaches her descendant, FLEANCE. She transfers the spiritual crown to her.

SCENE VII

Night. Outdoors.
HECATE's job here is almost complete. She hums, then sings.
The fire ignites, lighting up boodjar. New life will grow.

HECATE (song 2)
Boodjar baal waangkiny,
Land she speak-CONT,
All the world's a stage,

Boodjar baal waangkiny,
Land she speak-CONT,
All the world's a stage,

Maamangkara yokangkara kaadiny.
Man-PL woman-PL thinking.
And all the men and women merely players.

Baalap wongin yeyi boordawan noitj ba,
They-PL alive now later dead and,
They have their exits and their entrances,

Yoowarl-bili wort-bili biedi biedi koorliny,
This-way that-way hop path path travel-CONT,
And one man in his time plays many parts,

Boodjar baal waangkiny.
Land she speak-CONT.
All the world's a stage.

All cast except LADY MACBETH and MACBETH join HECATE on stage – they sing 'Boodjar' in full, knowing their parts.
LADY MACBETH and MACBETH join the cast on stage for one more round of 'Boodjar' – they all gradually sit. HECATE stays standing.
All cast halt singing after 'Baalap wongin yeyi boordawan noitj ba,' and breathe inward… lights fade.

THE END.

5
Seven Sonnets in Noongar

Interpretive translation by Kylie Bracknell
Edited by Roma Yibiyung Winmar

Sonnet 18

Shall I compare thee to a summer's day?
birok kidala / ngany kaaditj nyoona?

Thou art more lovely and more temperate:
nyoondalitj kwop wa / djoorap kidala

Rough winds do shake the darling buds of May,
wara maarr-maarrang / baaminy boorn djilba

And summer's lease hath all too short a date;
djinang / birok wort koorl / baal ngoorndiny wa

Sometime too hot the eye of heaven shines,
worl miyal / kaarlangariny bilanginy

And often is his gold complexion dimm'd,
boorda djinang baal / baal yoornt / winyaarn wa

And every fair from fair sometime declines,
kwop-bt nyininy / baalap ngarda wirdiny

By chance or nature's changing course untrimm'd:
boodjarang kabin / kardart-koorl-bt wa

But thy eternal summer shall not fade,
boorda birok bo ngoordiny / nyoona kwobidja

Nor lose possession of that fair thou ow'st,
baranginy baal / nyoona kwop maadjidil

Nor shall Death brag thou wand'rest in his shade,
Nyoona koorl / kaarny wirnitj / miyal-bt wa

When in eternal lines to time thou grow'st.
boordawan ngaangk ngoorndiny / maladjiny koorl

So long as men can breathe or eyes can see,
kaaditj maaman wowak / miyal-djinang

So long lives this, and this gives life to thee.
baalitj wongin nidja / yonginy nyoonany.

Sonnet 44

If the dull substance of my flesh were thought,
nyoona kaaditj djinang / ngany daatj menditj

Injurious distance should not stop my way,
dat nyin wara / ngany koorl bokidja bo

For then despite of space I would be brought,
nyoona kaaditj / worl djinang ngany kaaditj

From limits far remote, where thou dost stay.
ngany djoorap / baal kaarlap alidja bo

No matter then although my foot did stand
koora / ngany djena ngoorndiny / nidja wa

Upon the farthest earth remov'd from thee,
nidja ngany nyin / nyoona bo bokidja

For nimble thought can jump both sea and land
ngany kaat koorl / bardang wardarn boodjara

As soon as think the place where he would be.
ngany kaadidjiny / nyoona nyin alidja

But ah, thought kills me that I am not thought,
ngany kaat-wara / miyaliny nyoona / kaat-bt

To leap large lengths of miles when thou art gone,
kaat miyaliny nyoona / nyoona boolyaka

But that, so much of earth and water wrought,
nyorn / ngany boodjar kaep nyininy / nyoona-bt

I must attend time's leisure with my moan,
boordawan djinang ngaangk / ngany winyan waangk

Receiving nought by elements so slow
barang-bt / boodjar dabakarn / wara

But heavy tears, badges of either's woe.
miyal midjaliny / ngalak koort weyarn

Sonnet 45

The other two, slight air and purging fire,
Bo koodjal / nakal maarra / kaarla yong

Are both with thee, where ever I abide;
baalap ngany nyininy wa / ngalak koorliny

The first my thought, the other my desire,
ngany maarra kaaditj / kaarla miyaliny / ngany

These present-absent with swift motion slide.
baalap nidja / nyorn baalap nyoona nyin

For when these quicker elements are gone
boorda / maarra kaarla boolyaka wa

In tender embassy of love to thee,
baalap djoorap nyin / nyoona boorn waangkiny

My life being made of four, with two alone
koodjal-koodjal ngany wongin / nyin koodjal

Sinks down to death, oppress'd with melancholy;
boodjara wirdiny / baal winyanabiny

Until life's composition be recured
ngany djoorap / koorliny wongin baranginy

By those swift messengers return'd from thee,
baal kooronginy koorl / nidja nganang nyin

Who even but now come back again, assured
baal kora yoowarl / nidja karnarn ngoorndiny

Of thy fair health, recounting it to me.
kaya baalap waangkiny / nyoona wongin wa

This told, I joy, but then no longer glad,
kaaditj djoorap / boorda djoorap-bt ngany

I send them back again and straight grow sad.
ngany baalap waangk / wort koorl / ngany weyarn warn

Sonnet 46

Mine eye and heart are at a mortal war,
ngany miyal ba koort / bakidjiny baaminy

How to divide the conquest of thy sight:
yaarn nganang miyal miyaliny djinanginy

Mine eye my heart thy picture's sight would bar,
miyal-bt wa / miyalak koort waangkiny

My heart mine eye the freedom of that right.
koortiny miyal waangk / yoowart djinanginy

My heart doth plead that thou in him dost lie
ngany koort miyaliny nidja / baalitj ngoorndiny

(A closet never pierc'd with crystal eyes),
miyal boodjara / yoowarditj koorliny

But the defendant doth that plea deny,
kaya alidja koorl / miyal waangkiny

And says in him thy fair appearance lies.
djoorap waangk / kwop djinanginy / baalap nyin

To 'cide this title is impanelled
miyal kaaditj djinang / karnarn waangkiny

A quest of thoughts, all tenants to the heart,
koort koorl / ngalak nyin / kaaditj koort ngoorndiny

And by their verdict is determined
baalap kwop waangkiny / karnarn kaadidjiny

The clear eye's moiety and the dear heart's part
miyal moorditj djinang / baal koort ngoorndiny

As thus: mine eye's due is thy outward part,
nidja mirnitj / ngany miyal djoorapiny

And my heart's right thy inward love of heart.
koort karnarn / ngany koort waangkiny / baranginy

Sonnet 71

No longer mourn for me when I am dead
nyoona dat nyin waaliny / ngany noidjang wa

Than you shall hear the surly sullen bell
maya baam / ni nyoona dwonka nyininy

Give warning to the world that I am fled
boola worl waangkiny / ngany boolyaka wa

From this vile world with vilest worms to dwell;
ngarda boodjar / ngany noitj / ninat ngoorndiny

Nay, if you read this line, remember not
yorlak djinanginy / yoowart kaadidjiny

The hand that writ it, for I love you so,
maara waangkiny / ngaltj nyoonany mardanginy

That I in your sweet thoughts would be forgot,
ngany nyoonang kwop kaat ngoorndiny / kian nyininy

If thinking on me then should make you woe.
nyoondak ngany kaaditj / nyorn winyanabiny

O, if (I say) you look upon this verse,
djinang nidjak / ngany maara waangkaniny

When I (perhaps) compounded am with clay,
boordawan ngany noitj / ba djardak ngoorndiny

Do not so much as my poor name rehearse,
ngany mokiyang / ngany kwerl nanap waangkiny

But let your love even with my life decay;
nyoona maardang-bt wa / ngany noitj wongin

Lest the wise world should look into your moan,
nyoona weyarn waal / baalap djinanginy

And mock you with me after I am gone.
ngany-bt / ngailal nyoonany wara waangkiny

Sonnet 127

In the old age black was not counted fair,
moorn koora / kwobidja-bt / djinanginy

Or if it were it bore not beauty's name;
moorn kwerl kwop-bt / baalap winyaan weyarn

But now is black beauty's successive heir,
aliwa ni / moornitj kwop baranginy

And beauty slander'd with a bastard shame,
baal djoorap-bt wa / kwobidja koorndany

For since each hand hath put on nature's power,
wilki boodjar barang / nidja maara

Fairing the foul with art's false borrow'd face,
wilki kwop baaminy / koolyamitj mirnitj

Sweet beauty hath no name, no holy bow'r,
kwop kwerl-bt / wortan koorl / baal boolyaka

But is profan'd, if not lives in disgrace.
baal wirnitj / baalap kaat kaanya wirdiny

Therefore my mistress' eyes are raven black,
djinang yok miyal moorn / wardongabiny

Her eyes so suited, and they mourners seem
baal kwop miyal / baalap weyarn miyaliny

At such who, not born fair, no beauty lack,
nidja baal kwobidja wa / djinanginy

Sland'ring creation with a false esteem:
djinang wilki kwobidja / kwop-bt mirnitj

Yet so they mourn, becoming of their woe,
winyaan mirnitj moort / wilki miyaliny wa

That every tongue says beauty should look so.
djaaliny-waangk / moorn mirnitj moorditj kaya

Sonnet 146

Poor soul, the centre of my sinful earth,
Winyan, koordoomit kard wirnitjap nyin,

[Hemm'd by] these rebel pow'rs that thee array,
Yoodan ngaitj nganang koordoomit bakitj,

Why dost thou pine within and suffer dearth,
Natj nyoona weyarn keny koort yoran kian,

Painting thy outward walls so costly gay?
Ba maapak wilki naabiny ngwirinitj?

Why so large cost, having so short a lease,
Natj, boondong boola, doordok koorat nyin,

Dost thou upon thy fading mansion spend?
Kornt noldjabiny yaarn yirangidja baam?

Shall worms, inheritors of this excess,
Ninat, nidja daatj biediyarabiny,

Eat up thy charge? Is this thy body's end?
Baalap ngaarn boordawan? Daadjitj noitjang?

Then, soul, live thou upon thy servant's loss,
Yeyi, koordoomit, nyoonang kornt korbol-wirt,

And let that pine to aggravate thy store;
Boorda baalang naaka waangkiny kwop ngaarn;

Buy terms divine in selling hours of dross;
Kooranap koorl kweidjabiny doordok-bt;

Within be fed, without be rich no more:
Koordoomit moorart, mereny-bt winyan:

So shall thou feed on Death, that feeds on men,
Kaya, noidjak ngaarn, baal nyoongar bakan,

And Death once dead, there's no more dying then.
Noidjitj noitj, kabin barang-doordokan.

Sonnets 2012–2013

L–R: Roma Winmar, Kyle J. Morrison, Kylie Bracknell, Trevor Ryan at Yirra Yaakin Theatre Company, Perth

Top: Trevor Ryan, Kylie Bracknell, Kyle J. Morrison at the Globe Theatre, London.

Bottom: Kylie Bracknell, Irma Woods, Kyle J. Morrison, Trevor Ryan, Ian Wilkes, Roma Winmar at Matilda Bay, Perth.

Early Development at Subiaco Arts Centre 2017–2018

Kylie Bracknell

Top: Kyle J. Morrison, Della Rae Morrison
Bottom: Cezera Critti-Schnaars, Maitland Schnaars
Opposite: Kylie Bracknell, Avery Bracknell

Above: Kyle J. Morrison

Opposite: Clint Bracknell

Later Development at Subiaco Arts Centre 2019

Above: The development room

Opposite top: Peter Evans, Kylie Bracknell, Kate Mulvany

Opposite bottom: Trevor Ryan, Rubeun Yorkshire, Mark Nannup

NOONGAR
91

Above: Della Rae Morrison, Jill Dewar, Janine Oxenham

Opposite: Mark Nannup, Trevor Ryan

Above: Maitland Schnaars and Bobbi Henry
Opposite: The cast

yirra yaakin

Above: Maitland Schnaars, Della Rae Morrison, Kyle J. Morrison, Ian Wilkes

Opposite: Cezera Critti-Schnaars, Della Rae Morrison

2017

Rehearsals at Subiaco Arts Centre 2020

Above: Begining with song

Opposite top: Smoke break

Opposite bottom: Janine Oxenham, Judy Bone, Cezera Critti-Schnaars

Above: Trevor Ryan, Kyle J. Morrison, Ian Wilkes, Mark Nannup

Opposite top: Bobbi Henry

Opposite bottom: Mark Nannup, Ian Wilkes, Kyle J. Morrison

HECATE

NOONGAR
91

Opposite top: Maitland Schnaars, Della Rae Morrison, Rubeun Yorkshire, Kylie Bracknell, Kyle J. Morrison

Opposite bottom: Maitland Schnaars, Trevor Ryan, Rubeun Yorkshire, Della Rae Morrison

Above: Happy rehearsal team

Above: Mitchella Hutchins, Avery and Clint Bracknell at Kambarnap

Opposite: The cast and director

THEATRE COMPANY

Onstage at Subiaco Arts Centre 2020

Images by Dana Weeks

Above: Hecate and mischief makers

Opposite: Three mischief makers

Above: King Duncan
Opposite top: Two murderers
Opposite bottom: Violence at Macduff's

Opposite top: Macduff sings

Opposite bottom: Doctor, Gentleperson, Lady Macbeth

Above: Three mischief makers

Reading Reunion at Perth Institute of Contemporary Arts 2023

Images by Marnie Richardson

Above: Active reading

Opposite: The team

Kylie Bracknell and audience

6
A Noongar Grammar and Glossary

Despite the oral origins of Noongar and most other Indigenous languages, literacy has been a key component of language revitalisation movements internationally.[1] The ability to write and read an endangered language expands the possible domains for language use, which can encourage renewed language vitality. Although very much a product of compromise between multiple families and individuals from different regions with different ideas, the phonetic Noongar spelling system that was developed and agreed upon at the 1992 meeting at Narrogin was used throughout the development of *Hecate* as advised by Roma Yibiyung Winmar. This consistent orthography supported the cast to learn and consistently pronounce words they may not have previously heard. In a way, it also means that all the old people who decided on that spelling system have had a hand in the creation of *Hecate*.

Consonants

b not as in English; closer to **p** as in s**p**it (at the beginning and middle of words)

d not as in English; closer to **t** as in s**t**all (at the beginning and middle of words)

dj as in ju**dge** (at the beginning and middle of words)

k as in s**k**ill

l as in **l**and or ni**l**

ly not as in English 'lee'; closer to bi**ll**ion
m as in **m**an
n as in **n**ight
ng as in si**ng** or si**ng**er (can also begin Noongar words)
ny not as in English 'nee'; closer to **n**uisance or o**n**ion
p as in s**p**it (only at end of words)
r as in **r**an
rd close to how some Americans say ha**rd**
rl close to how some Americans say ba**rl**ey
rn close to how some Americans say ba**rn**
rr close to a Scottish rolled 'r', as in spo**rr**an
t as in **t**ap (only at end of words)
tj as in ju**dge** (only at end of words)
w as in **w**ater
y as in **y**es

Vowels

a as in medi**a**
aa as in c**ar** or l**ar**ge
e as in t**e**n
i as in h**i**t
o as in l**aw** or c**our**t
oo as in b**oo**k

Noongar grammar and morphology is also significantly different to English. Linguists offer a variety of somewhat similar descriptions of how the Noongar language works, but the pressures of language shift and the scarcity of fluent speakers constrain efforts to fully document the Noongar language and its linguistic conventions.[2] As is the case with other Pama-Nyungan languages, the Nyungar language is agglutinative, meaning that its words can take on one or more word-endings (suffixes). Dependent on context, these suffixes, or word-endings, can function in various ways and may be slightly altered depending on the word they are attached to.[3] These word endings can mark who or what is doing something, who or what is being acted upon, and who is being talked about. While sentences in Noongar often follow a subject-object-verb structure, these word-endings allow word order to be flexible. Although it is by no means authoritative, we applied the following system in *Hecate* based on our analysis of existing literature including the works of Charles Symmons, Wilf Douglas, and C.G. von Brandenstein (indicated in the footnotes as appropriate) and our own personal experiences of speaking and hearing the Noongar language.

Suffixes for things (nouns)

ACT '-al' – subject/actor

To avoid ambiguity, the '-al' ending can be applied to the end of something (a noun) when it controls an action.[4]

Noongaral boorn barang	Nornal noongar bakan
Person-ACT stick grasp	Snake-ACT person bite
The person grasps the stick	The snake bites the person

OBJ '-iny' – object

For further clarity, the '-iny' suffix is sometimes applied to someone or something (noun) to indicate that an action is directed towards them. Depending on the context, the order of the words could change, and the sentence could retain the same meaning.[5]

Noongaral barang noorniny	Noornal bakan noongariny
Person-ACT grasp snake-OBJ	Snake-ACT bite person-OBJ
The person grasps the snake	The snake bites the person

LOC '-al' – location

This suffix can indicate the location of someone or something.

Noongar woordakal nyin	Noongar yaak kaepal
Person shade-LOC sit	Person stand water-LOC
The person sits in the shade	The person stands in the water

LOC '-ak' – location

The '-ak' ending can indicate where action is happening, or the location action is directed to.

Noongar boornak nyininy	Noongar korndak koorl	Nganyak kaep yong
Person tree-LOC sit-CONT	Person hut-LOC travel	Me-LOC water give
The person is sitting by a tree	The person goes to a hut	Give water to me

INS '-ak' – instrument

This ending can also specify an instrument someone is using to carry out an action.

Noongar baam koitjak	Noongar kidjak kworditj
Person axe-INS strike	Person spear-INS throw
The person strikes with an axe	The person throws a spear

PURP '-ak' – purpose

The '-ak' suffix can explain the purpose of an action too. Word order seems important here, with the purpose usually being stated after the action.

Noongar wort koorl daadjak	Noongar birn kaepak
Person away travel meat-PURP	Person dig water-PURP
The person goes out for meat	The person digs for water

POSS, ASS '-ang' – possession

The '-ang' ending can be used to indicate an association or possession.[6]

Yokang koot	Malak yowinang
Woman-POSS bag	Shadow moon-ASS
The woman's bag	The shadow of the moon

RES '-ang' – result, reason

Adding the '-ang' suffix can also indicate the reason for something.[7]

Noorn karang noongarang	Noornang noongar weyarn
Snake angry person-RES	Snake-RES person fearful
The snake is angry because of the person	The snake made the person fearful

POSS '-kadak' – possessor, possessing

The '-kadak' ending is also productively to create new words by referring to an item or skill someone or something has. For example, a boolyakadak is a sorcerer, not just someone who has boolya (magic). A wardakadak is a hero, not just someone who has warda (renown, fame, or others watching them). It seems like '-kadak' can sometimes generally be used to mean 'having' or 'possessing'. For example, if you had kian (nothing), you could say 'ngany kiankadak'.[8]

OCC 'ar' – occupation

The '-ar' ending can also be used productively to create a new word, associating someone or something with a proficiency or occupation.[9]

Biediyar	Maarr-waabar	Yongkar paanak waabar
Path/energy/ sinew-OCC	Cloud-play-OCC	Kangaroo plain-on play-OCC
Leader (knows the way)	Aeroplane (cloud player)	The kangaroo that plays on the plains

SIM '-mokiny' – like, similar to, simile

The '-mokiny' ending can be added to indicate that something is like something else.[10]

Noongar bardang yongkarmokiny	Nop birdiyarmokiny
Person jump kangaroo-SIM	Boy leader-SIM
The person jumps like a kangaroo	The boy is like a leader

PL '-kar' – plural, collective

'-kar' can be added to describe a collective or group of people. One could refer to a single koolong (child) or multiple koolongkar (child-PL). People from someone's home can be kaarlabkar (home-PL).[11]

NEG '-bt' – negative

The '-bt' ending is a negator and can also be used productively to create new words. For example, someone who does not listen is dwongka-bt (ear-NEG), and one who does not see is miyal-bt (eyes-NEG). Importantly for Macbeth, someone with insomnia is nookert-bt (sleep-NEG).[12]

GEO '-ap' – place of, geographical location

The '-ap' ending is associated with Noongar place names, for example 'yongkarap' (yongkar-GEO would be a place of yongkar (kangaroos).[13] Rather than simple 'place of fire', 'kaarlap' (fire-GEO) indicates home. It can describe the location of one's fire, familiarity with locations and local people, or one's homeland.

Suffixes for descriptions (adjectives)

TR '-abiny' – transforming, becoming, inchoative

The '-abiny' ending can indicate transformation, for example 'karangabiny' (angry-TR), becoming angry, and 'kweidjabiny' (thin/sharp-TR), becoming skinny or sharp.[14]

INTS '-mit' – intensifier

Adding 'mit' to the end of an adjective intensifies the meaning. Something that is very koombar (large) would be koombarmit (large-INTS). If someone is very karang (angry), they are karangmit (angry-INTS).[15]

Suffixes for actions (verbs)

CONT '-iny' – continuous
'iny' is added to the end of an action (verb) to indicate that it is not complete, or it is continuing.[16]

Noongaral biediyariny waangkiny	Nornal noongar bakaniny
Person-ACT boss-OBJ speak-CONT	Snake-ACT person bite-CONT
The person is speaking to the boss	The snake is biting the person

PST '-ang' – past tense
At the end of an action (verb), '-ang' can locate that action in the past.

Noongar nyinang.	Noongariny bakanang noornal
Person sit-PAST	Person-OBJ bite-PAST snake-ACT
The person was seated	The person was bitten by the snake

LOC '-al' – location in time
The '-al' word ending can also indicate that something is taking place after something has happened or been done (a verb).[17]

Koorlal nyoona nookert	Bakidjal ngany menditj
Travel-LOC you sleep	Fight-LOC I sore
After travelling, I sleep	After fighting, I am sore

REL '-itj' – relative clause
The '-itj' ending can be used to refer to a completed action (verb), thing (noun) or description (adjective) the speaker is talking about, or a time at which an action was completed.

Minyiditj bokitj nakalar waraitj	Kwopitj kwop	Karamitj waangk
Ants-REL there small-OCC bad-REL	Good-REL good	Yesterday-REL speak-REL
The ants which are over there are the little ones that are bad	What's good is good	What was said yesterday

In addition to using suffixes, a time focus can be indicated at the beginning of a sentence or as an afterthought, using terms including: koora (long ago), karam (yesterday), kori (just now), yeyi (now), boorda (soon), boordawan (later), benang (tomorrow), and mila (future).

Pronouns

The use of pronouns seems to vary among Noongar speakers, possibly because of dialectic differences. It is likely that what was once a complicated pronoun system has been conflated and streamlined over the past two hundred years of dramatic social and cultural change. Based again on comparing recorded sources and our own experiences as speakers, we have consistently employed the following system for *Hecate*

1st person

	Singular	Dual	Plural
Intransitive	Ngany	Ngal (inclusive) Ngail (EX exclusive) Ngali (FAM familial form, siblings, parents, children, and friends) Nganana (SPO spouse form)	Ngalar (inclusive) Ngailar (EX exclusive)
Active one ergative ACT	Ngaitj	Ngalal	Ngalarl
Acted on OBJ	Ngany	Ngalany	Ngalariny
With or belonging to POSS	Nganang	Ngalak	Ngalarang
Mine POSS	Nganalang	Ngalakada	Ngalarang
I/we who is/are – description REL	Nganitj	Ngalitj	Ngalaritj
Location (giving or going to) LOC	Nganyak	Ngalak	Ngalarak

2nd person

	2nd	2nd plural
Intransitive	Nyoona	Nyoondakat
Active one ergative ACT	Nyoondak	Nyoondakadal
Acted on OBJ	Nyoonany	Nyoondakadiny
With or belonging to POSS	Nyoonang	Nyoondakadang
Yours POSS	Nyoonalak	Nyoondakadang
You who is/are – description REL	Nyoondalitj	Nyoondakaditj
Location (giving or going to) LOC	Nyoonak	Nyoondakadak

3rd person

	3rd	3rd plural PL
Intransitive	Baal	Baalap Baalali (familial form) Baalain (spouse form)
Active one ergative ACT	Baalal	Baalabal
Acted on OBJ	Baaliny	Baalabiny
With or belonging to POSS	Baalang	Baalabang
They who is/are – description REL	Baalitj	Baalabitj
Location (giving or going to) LOC	Baalak	Baalabak

The Noongar Words in Hecate

This glossary gives the basic meaning of the Noongar words that appear in *Hecate*, drawing on the rich documentation of Noongar from when it was first written down in the early 1800s to contemporary Noongar publications.

The documentation shows how much variation there is in the way a spoken language can be written. Some of this variation is due to differences between speakers. In the same way that English is spoken with different accents and dialects, so too is Noongar spoken differently between Dongara and Esperance. In fact, Noongar is spoken across an area larger than England.

Some variation is due to the training and background of the explorer or linguist who was recording the language. For example, Carl Georg von Brandenstein (1909–2005) was a German anthropologist and had professional training in documenting languages. He used an idiosyncratic phonetic spelling system to write the Noongar words as they sound. By contrast, Rosendo Salvado (1814–1900) was a Spanish monk with no formal training in languages. The spelling system he used for Noongar is clearly influenced by Spanish, e.g. 'bocaggio' bokidja – 'over there'.

Just as some words don't have exact equivalents between Noongar and English, there are also some sounds which do not have exact equivalents. This adds another layer of variation to the spelling. For example, in Noongar the sounds 'p' and 'b', 't' and 'd', and 'k' and 'g' can largely be used interchangeably, and often sound somewhere between the two.

Every language is unique in the range of concepts and ideas that can be expressed by a single word and may have words for concepts that are unique to the culture. There are many words in Noongar that do not have exact equivalents in English. For example, the Noongar word 'kaaditj' can be translated into English as 'know' but also as 'understand' and 'listen' – in Noongar culture, the idea of 'understanding', 'knowing', and 'listening' go together. While the following glossary for *Hecate* is not authoritative, it considers the many ways each Noongar word has been translated differently by different explorers, linguists, and the Noongar speakers themselves.

Multiple sources for each Noongar word are given below, with their code.

Ad Adam, T. (1886). Vocabulary no.29, Two hundred miles north-east of Newcastle, pp.380–383 in E.M. Curr, *The Australian Race*, Vol.1.

Ar Armstrong, C.F. (1886). Vocabulary no.19, Perth, pp.334–335 in E.M. Curr, *The Australian Race*, Vol.1.

At Douglas, W.H. (1991). W.H. Atkins memorial Nyungar-English & English-Nyungar dictionary, [the author], Kalgoorlie.

Ba Barlee, F. (1886). Vocabulary no.24, Bunbury, pp.352–355 in E.M. Curr, *The Australian Race*, Vol.1.

Bd Bardil, documented in Bates, D.M. (c. 1910). Native Vocabulary – Williams. Section XII, 2B, 10.

Be Bennell, T. (Yelakitj) (1978). Personal recording. Battye Library, OH356. Transcribed by L. Collard.

Bi Tommy Bimbar, documented in Hope, J. (1916). Information hereunder supplied to Mr J. Hope by native Tommy Bimbar 15/5/1916, ms.

Bk Balbuk, documented in Bates, D.M. (c. 1910). Native Vocabulary – Woorurdup. Section XII, 2B, 15.

Bn Brown, Robert & Australian Joint Copying Project & National Library of Australia & State Library of New South Wales (1800). Papers and correspondence of Robert Brown (as filmed by the AJCP): [M1193, M2494-M2496], 1800–1855. Australian Joint Copying Project, Canberra.

Bo Boordenam, Beereenan, Boongong, Werdabirt, Bates documented in Bates, D.M. (c. 1910). Native Vocabulary – Albany. Section XII, 2B, 4.

Bt Baaburgurt (alias Bulyen/George Eliot), documented in Bates, D.M. (c. 1910). Native Vocabulary – Wonnerup (Vasse) and Capel Districts. Section XII, 2B, 13.

Bu Bussell, A.J. (193-). South-West Aboriginal language or dialect, ts.

By Brady, J. (1845). A descriptive vocabulary of the native language of Western Australia. Rome: S.C. de Propaganda Fide.

CK Tommy Cowan and Tommy Kickett, recorded in 1960 and documented in O'Grady, G.N., C.F. Voegelin and F.M. Voegelin (1966). 'Languages of the World: Indo-Pacific fascicle 6', pp.1–197 in Anthropological Linguistics, Vol.8, no.2.

Cr Chester, G. (1886). 'Vocabulary no.32, Kent District: Warrangoo tribe', pp.390–391 in E.M. Curr, *The Australian Race*, Vol.1.

Cy Chauncy, P. (1878). 'Appendix: Notes and Anecdotes of the Aborigines of Australia' in R. Smyth, The Aborigines of Victoria: with notes relating to the habits of the natives of other parts of Australia and Tasmania. Vol.1. J. Ferres, Government Printer.

Da Davis, J. (1969). A glossary of the Bibbulmum language, ts.

De Dench, Alan. (1994). 'Nyungar', pp. 173–192, in Macquarie Aboriginal Words, edited by Nicholas Thieberger and W McGregor. Sydney, NSW: The Macquarie Library.

Do Douglas, W.H. (1968). The Aboriginal languages of South-West Australia: speech forms in current use and a technical description of Njungar, Australian Aboriginal Studies no.14, Linguistic Series no.4, AIAS, Canberra.

Du Dumont D'Urville, M.J. (1834). Voyage de decouvertes de l'Astrolabe. Exécuté par ordre du Roi. Philology. Le Ministère de la Marine, Paris.

Dy Herbert Dyson, documented in Gilke, E. (n.d.) 24 words spoken by Herbert Dyson of Busselton, ts.

F Flinders, Matthew. (1814). A Voyage to Terra Australis.

Ga Goolaara, documented in Bates, D.M. (c. 1910). Native Vocabulary – Dandaragan. Section XII, 2B, 18.

Gi Gifford, E.F. (1886). Vocabulary no.26, Lower Blackwood: Peopleman tribe, pp.362–363 in E.M. Curr, *The Australian Race*, Vol.1.

Gl Glauert, L. (1950). 'Provisional list of Aboriginal placenames and their meanings', pp.83–86 in WA Historical Society Journal, Vol.4, no.2.

Gm Graham, W.H. (1886). Vocabulary no.23, Kojonup and Eticup, pp.348–351 in E.M. Curr, *The Australian Race*, Vol.1.

Go Goldsworthy, R.T. (1886). Vocabulary no.30, Mount Stirling: Kokar tribe, pp.384–385 in E.M. Curr, *The Australian Race*, Vol.1.

Gr Grey, G. (1839). Vocabulary of the Aboriginal language of Western Australia. C. Macfaull, Perth, WA.

Hc Hackett, D.E. (1886). Vocabulary no.21, York District: The Ballardong tribe, pp.344–345 in E.M. Curr, *The Australian Race*, Vol. 1.

He Hester, E.G. (1886). Vocabulary no.25, Blackwood District: Kardagur tribe, pp.360–361 in E.M. Curr, *The Australian Race*, Vol.1.

Hm Hammond, J.E. (1938). Vocabulary of South West Aborigines, ms. University of Sydney Archives, P130/11.

Hs Hassell, E.A. (1975) My dusky friends, C.W. Hassell, Fremantle.

Is Samuel Isaacs (likely), documented in Brockman, F.S. (nd). List of Native Names of the South–West Tribe compiled by F.S. Brockman, in Aboriginal Vocabularies, supplied by Old Settlers of WA. State Library of Western Australia, PR342.

J Joobaitch (alias Ngoorweel), documented in Bates, D.M. (c. 1910). Native Vocabulary – Guildford. Section XII, 2B, 14.

Jm Jakbam and Bumblefoot, documented in Bates, D.M. (c. 1910). Native Vocabulary – Albany and Denmark. Section XII, 2B, 3b.

K Kajaman, documented in Bates, D.M. (c. 1910). Native Vocabulary – Wer-ge-jan (Beverley). Section XII, 2B, 11.

Ka Kaiar and Wirijan, documented in Bates, D.M. (c. 1910). Native Vocabulary – Katanning. Section XII, 2B, 8b.

Ki King, P.P. (1827). Narrative of a Survey of the Intertropical and Western Coasts of Australia, performed between the years 1818 and 1822. Vol.2. Murray, London.

Kn Knight, W.E. (1886). Vocabulary no.19, Perth, pp.328–333 in E.M. Curr, *The Australian Race*, Vol.1.

Le Leake, B.W. (1938, April 26). 'Native names', The West Australian (Perth, WA: 1879–1954), p.9. http://nla.gov.au/nla.news-article41680219

Ly Lyon, R.M. (1833). 'A glance at the manners and language of the Aboriginal inhabitants of Western Australia, with a short vocabulary', pp.51–52 in the Perth Gazette, Vol.I, no.13, 30 March 1833; p.56, Vol.I, no.14, 6 April 1833; pp.59–60, Vol.I, no.15, 13 April 1833; pp.63–64, Vol.I, no.16, 20 April 1833.

MB Monnop, recorded in Bates, D.M. (c. 1910). Native Vocabulary – Victoria Plains. Section XII, 2B, 24.

MD Moore, G.F. and J. Drummond (1836). 'Native names' from the Perth Gazette, 21 May.

Mi Rooney, B. (2002). The Legacy of the Late Edward Mippy: An Ethnographic Biography. Doctoral dissertation: Curtin University of Technology.

Mo Moore, G.F (1842). A descriptive vocabulary of the language in common use amongst the natives of Western Australia, W.S. Orr & Co., London.

Mr Monger, H.J. (1886). Vocabulary no.17, Victoria Plains: Minnal Yungar tribe, pp.322–323 in E.M. Curr, *The Australian Race*, Vol.1.

Na Possible names for new Post Offices – supplied by the Native Affairs Department (date unknown). State Library of Western Australia.

Nga Ngalbaitch, documented in Bates, D.M. (c. 1910). Native Vocabulary – Korrlup (50 miles N.W. of Jerramungup). Section XII 2B, 7b.

Ngi Ngilgee, documented in Bates, D.M. (c. 1910). Native Vocabulary – Vassse. Section XII 2B, 12a.

Ngy Ngalyart, documented in Bates, D.M. (c. 1910). Native Vocabulary – Murray. Section XII 2B, 9.

Ni Nind, S. (1831). 'Description of the natives of King George Sound (Swan River Colony) and adjoining country', pp.21–51 in Journal of the Royal Geographical Society of London, Vol.1.

No Notum, Wirijan and Kaiar, documented in Bates, D.M. (c. 1910). Native Vocabulary – Katanning. Series XII 2B, 8a.

Ol Aboriginal Vocabularies, supplied by Old Settlers of WA. (1830s–ca.1968). State Library of Western Australia, PR342.

Rh Ranford, H.S. (1875). Wordlist, Stirling Range area, Field Book 8, p.146, Manuscript, Department of Land Administration Library, Midland, WA.

Ri Richards, Stan. (1994). The Bibbulmun: Land of Many Breasts. Northbridge, WA: Access Press.

Rw Rae, W. (1913). Native vocabulary, ts.

Sa Salvado, R. (1851). Two native dialects of the New Norcia district. Rome: S.C. de Propaganda Fide.

Sc Scott, R. (1886). Vocabulary no.22, Pinjarra, pp.346–347 in E.M. Curr, *The Australian Race*, Vol.1.

Sm Small, M.B (1886). Vocabulary no.24, Uduc, Harvey tribe, pp.358–359 in E.M. Curr, *The Australian Race*, Vol.1.

SHK Spencer, W.A., J.A. Hossell and W.A. Knight (1886). Vocabulary no.31, King George's Sound: Minung tribe, pp.386–389 in E.M. Curr, *The Australian Race*, Vol.1.

SW Serventy, D.L. and Whittell, H.M. (1967). Handbook of the birds of Western Australia. Perth: Lamb Publications.

Sy Symmons, C. (1842). Grammatical introduction to the study of the Aboriginal language of Western Australia. The Western Australian Almanack. C. Macfaull.

Ta Taylor, C. (1886). Vocabulary no.33, From Doubtful Bay to Israelite Bay, pp. 392–393 in E.M. Curr, *The Australian Race*, Vol.1.

TH Terry, F, and Hamersley, V. (n.d.). In Aboriginal Vocabularies, supplied by Old Settlers of WA. State Library of Western Australia, PR342.

Vb Brandenstein, C.G. von (1988). Nyungar Anew: phonology, text samples and etymological and historical 1500-word vocabulary of an artificially re-created Aboriginal language in the South-West of Australia, Pacific Linguistics, C-99, Canberra: ANU.

Wa Wainbret, documented in Helms, R. (1896). Anthropology, pp.237–332 in Transactions of the Royal Society of South Australia, Vol.16.

Wd Whitfield, G. (1886). Vocabulary no.18, Newcastle, pp. 324–327 in E.M. Curr, *The Australian Race*, Vol.1.

Wi Winmar, R.M. (1996). Walwalinj: The hill that cries, Nyungar language and culture. Manning, WA: Dorothy Winmar.

Wl Wall, J., documented in Bates D.M. (c. 1910). Native Vocabulary – Jerramungup. Series XII 2B, 50.

Wn Wirlomin Noongar Language and Stories Project. (2011). Mamang: An Old Story. Crawley, WA: UWA Publishing.

Wo Woolberr, documented in Bates, D.M. (c. 1910). Native Vocabulary – Gingin. Series XII 2B, 17.

Wt Whitehurst, R. (1992). Noongar dictionary. Bunbury: Noongar Language and Culture Centre.

ali, alidja	there	alla (Gr); alla (Mo); alli (By); alia (Sa); alla (Bt); alleea (MB); ale (Nga); alle (Ngi); alle (K); ally (Bu); alitj (At); alitj (Do); allee (Da); ali (Vb)
aliwa	beware!	alleea (MB); waw! (J); alle wa (K); aliwa (Do); allawah (Da); aliwa (Wt)
ana	yeah (exclamation or question)	an (By); ana (Wt); ana! (Mi)
arwoon	ha!, well how about that? (exclamation)	awoon (Wt)
ba	and	-bi, pa (Vb); be (Bu)
baaboorr	ripple (onomatopoeia)	baaburr, boora (Bt); paabur̃ (Vb)
baal	he, she, it	bal (Gr); bal (Mo); bal (Sy); bal (By); baal; bal (Sa); ball (Wa); bal (Bt); bal (Bk); bal (MB); bal (Nga); bal (Ngi); bal (J); bal (K); barl (Bu); bahrl (Hm); baal (CK); pal (Do); baal un (Da); paul (Vb); bal (At); baal (Wt); bal (Ri); baal (Mi)
baalang	their	bullallelang (Mo); bala (Bk); bolong (Nga); balla, balung (J); bala (K); barlartang (Bu); balang (At); balang, baloong (Wt)
baalabang	all of their	(see baalap); palapaŋ (Do)
baalap	they, them (duo or group)	balgup (Bt); balgup (Bk); balgup (MB); balgup (Ngi); balgup (J); balgup (K); paulap (Vb); balap (At)

baam	strike, put	boomak (Ly); boo-ma (Gr); buma (Mo); bu-ma (Sy); buma (By); baming (Sa); boma (Bt); bōm (Bk); bomain (J); baama (MB); bām (Nga); boma (Ngi); baaming (K); bomign (Bu); baaminy (CK); paminj (Do); barminy (Da); barminyiny (Be); puam (Vb); baminy (At); baaminy (Wt); bam, boma (De); baaminy (Mi)
baan	clear, exposed, the plains	ban-dak (Gr); barna (Mo); burnaija (Bt); burnaitch (Bk); boonan-boonan (J); burneej (K); barna (MB); barnaa (Ngi); paann (Vb); bandak (Wt); barnatj (De); burna (Na)
babin	pledged friend	bab een (Gr); babbin (Mo); babbin (By); babin (Sa); babbin (Hc); babin (Sc); babbin (Bt); babbin (Ngi); babbin, babbinguttuk (Bk); babbin (MB); babbin (K); babbin (J); babbin-yon (Hm); paabiny (Vb); babin (De); babbin (Ri)
bakan	bite	bak-kan (Gr); bakkan (Mo); bâk-kan (Sy); pacanin (Sa); bakkan (Bk); bakkaning (MB); baggan, bagan (Nga); bakkan (Ngi); bakkan, baggan (J); baggan, baggun (K); baakaniny (CK); barkanyin (Da); paaginy, paag, paagan (Vb); bakan, baakan (Wt); bakan (De); barganinj (Wi)
bakanang	taste	parkenong (Wl); baganang jinung (Nga); bacanan-an (Sa)
bakidjap	battleground	(see bakitj)
bakitj	fight	buk-ad-jee (Gr); băkadjin (Mo); bak-ad-ju (Sy); pachececuran (Sa); baajeejin (Bt); bakkajin (Bk); bakkajin (MB); bakkajin (Nga); baggeejin (Ngi); baggatch (J); baggajin (K); barkage (Bu); paagity (Vb); bagitj, balitj (At); bakadjoo (Wt); bakadjin (Ri)

balar	hidden	bal-lar (Gr); bal-lar-i-jow (Sy); ballar (Mo); bōleej (Bk); ballarin (Ngi); bwurla eejeen (MB); boleetch (J); boleej weej (K); paalär (Vb); ballah (Ri)
balbit	foolish	bal beit (Gr); balbyt (Mo); balbyt (By); balbaitch (Bt); balbit (Ri)
bangal-baam	revenge	băng-al (Mo); bang-al-buma (By); pongoticuia (Sa); boongo (Bt); boongoorang (Wt)
bara-koorl	go astray, become lost	barrabardo, barra (Mo); barrab-art (By); barraburrup (Bt); baragul (Bk); beragan gūl (Nga); barrai-yenning (Ngi); baragool (J); piir̃-e-quarn (Vb); barr, barra (De)
barang	grasp	bur-rang (Gr); bărrang (Mo); bâr-rang (Sy); barrangdedin (By); pocogn (Sa); burrong (Bt); burra yeerong (Bk); burrung (J); bulburrongur (K); burrong (MB); burrong (Nga); burrong (Ngi); burung (Bu); bee-rong (Hm); paṛaŋinj (Do); buranginy (Be); paaraŋ (Vb); barang (At); barang (Wt); barrang (De); barrang (Ri); barang-iny (Mi)
barang-doordokan	save, rescue	burrong dordagur (Bd); barraug dordakanan (By); Burrong dorda gun (J); Barrang dordakănăn (Mo).
bard	move off, go	bar-do (Gr); bardo (Mo); bardo (y); bardoo (Ly); bardo (Ri); paad(d) (Vb)
bardang	jump, fly	bar-dang-een (Gr); bărdanbardo (Mo); bâr-dang (Sy); bardang (By); par an (Sa); barding (Sm); burdong (Bk); burdong ngin (MB); bardong (Ngi); beela-burdong (J); burdong (K); biddung (Bu); paṭaŋinj (Do); paardaŋ (Vb); bardang (Wt); bardang (De); bardang (Ri)

bardip	deceive, make up a story	purtup (Ni); bar-ra lin (Gr); barrit (Mo); purt-up (By); bardip (Nga); bardee bin (Ngi); gin bardip (Bu); paardep (Vb); pardebin (At); bardap (De)
ben	light, daylight	ben, bennan (Ni); ben, bennan (Du); bina (Mo); pene (Sa); banna (Go); benung (Gm); pen, baneung (SHK); beenar (Kn); beenungur (Bt); bena (Bk); bena (MB); benna (J); benungan (K); piän, piänaŋ (Vb); bairnang, bernang (At); ben (Wt); ben (De); bin a (Ri)
benang	tomorrow	be-nung (Gr); binăng (Mo); bi-nâng (Sy); binang (By); benan (Sa); benang (Ba); beenang (Ar); bennung (Cr); beenang (Go); benong (Hc); benang (He); benning (Mr); benkurrulding (Ta); bēnong (Bk); benung (MB); bennim, bennung (Ngi); beningan (J); beningan (K); beenong (Ol); penaŋ (Do); benang (Be); piänaŋ-piänaŋ (Vb); bairnang, bernang (At); benang (Wt); benang (De); binang (Ri)
bibi	breast, milk	bpep (F); be-ep (Ki); peep (Ni); bibee (Ly); bee-bee (Gr); bibi (Mo); bi bi (Sy); bibi; pipi (Sa); biba (Ba); bibbee (Ar); pip (Cr); peba (Gi); pip (Gm); biba (Hc); bebe (He); pip (SHK); baba (Sc); pip (Ta); bibbie (Wd); beeba (Bt); beeba (Bk); beeba (MB); beeb (Nga); beeba (Ngi); bibba (J); beeb (K); beeba (Bu); bee-bee nal-goo (Hm); pip (Do); piip (Vb); bib, bibi (At); bibi, biib, bib (Wt); biba (De); bibbi (Ri); bibi (Mi)
bitj	dry	tda-bitch (Gr); piity (Vb)

biedi, biet	path, energy	peet (Ni); beedy (Ly); pit (Du); bee-dee (Gr); bidi (Mo); bi-di (Sy); bidi (By); beeda (Bt); beeda (Bk); beeda (MB); beet (Nga); beeda (Ngi); beeda (J); beida (Bu); piṛit (Do); beert (Da); piert (Vb); birt, birit (At); bidi (Wt); biroa (De)
biedibap	tired, lazy, weak, unwell, useless	bidibaba, babba, bidibabba (Mo); babba, bidi-baba (By); bandapiti (Sa); beedee bab', beet bab', beedee babba (Bk); beedabab (MB); beeteebabba, beetababba (Ngi); peetabup, beetabub (J); beeda bab, beed bab, beetabab (K); piert-paap (Vb); bidababa, bidabap (De)
biediyar	boss, leader	beerdyat (Ly); bee-dee-eer (Gr); batiri (Mo); battage bearda (Ba); biadera (Cr); badare (He); baddeeja, biderr (Bt); biderr (MB); beederr (Ngi); barder, batteetch (J); bedare (Bu); piṭiya (Do); bridarra (Da); pierteyiar (Vb); bidair (At); birdiya, boordiya (Wt); beerdiair (Wi); bridiya (Mi)
biediyar-bt	leaderless	(see biediyar)
biet-bt	lost, weak	(see biet)
bilang	flash, sparkle	balbarngighn (Bu); piärlaŋ (Vb)
bily	river, navel	be-il (Ki); peerle (Ni); bil, biil (Du); be-loe (Gr); bilo (Mo); bi-lo (Sy); bilo (By); bille; billo (Sa); beela (Bt); beeloo (Bk); beela (MB); beel (Nga); beela (Ngi); bee-la (Is); beeia (J); beela (K); pillyi (Ra); beelagur (Bi); bealyer (Bu); becler (Ol); piḷ (Do); beely (Da); bierl (Be); piily (Vb); bila, birla (At); bily (Wt); bila (De); bily (Mi); beelagur (Na)
binar	comet	bin-nar (Gr); binnar (Mo); bin-nar (Sy); binar (Wt)

bindari	lightning storm	pindare (Sa); binari (Nga); bindardee (Ngi); pinderi (At); binar (Wt); bindarri (De)
bindjal	bubbles	bindjəl (Wn)
birn	dig, scratch, pinch	be-an (Gr); bian (Mo); bi-an (Sy); bian (By); benbenan-in (Sa); binjeega (Bt); beena (Bk); bēning (K); been (MB); been (Nga); beean, bee-en (Ngi); beena (J); bean (Bu); peninj (Do); piiän (Vb); beniny (At); benanginy (Wt); bin, ben (De); bi an (Ri)
birok	hot season, summer, Birak	beruc (Ni); be-roke (Gr); birok (Mo); bi-rok (Sy); piroc (Sa); beeruk, doolbera (Bt); beerok, beeruk (Bk); beeruk (MB); bīrak (Nga); beeruk (Ngi); beeruk (J); beeruk (K); bearuck (Bu); beeruk (Da); birak (De); birok (Ri)
biyoo	awake	piyu ŋuṇṭinj (Do); biyu (At); biyoo (Wt)
bo	far	(see bokidja); bo (Da)
bokal	grave, mound, lower back	bo-gal, bo kal (Gr); bogal (Mo); bo-gal (Sy); bogal (By); bocal, batbal (Sa); boogal (Bt); bookal (Ngi); bookal, boogal (Bk); bugal, bukal (Nga); bookarla (Bu); pukaḷ (Do); puaggall, puagal (Vb); bookarl, bookal (Wt); bukal, bukala (De); bagal (Ri); bookal, bookoo (Mi); bokal, bogal (Gl)
bokidja, bokitj	there (further away)	bocun (Ni); bokoun (Du); bo·ko-jee (Gr); bokojo (Mo); bo-ko, bo-ko-ja (Sy); po-ko (By); bocaggio (Sa); bookoo (Bt); bokoya (Bk); bokoja (MB); bōkoja gūl (Nga); booga-ja, boko-ja (J); bookable (Bu); pukutj (Do); bo (Da); puagadyity (Vb); bugitj (At); bokadja, bookitj (Wt); bookartyen (Wi); bokadja (Mi)

bonyin	kiss	boonjin (Ngi); bonyininga (Nga); bunyan (J); bonyen (K); bunyan (De)
boodjar	land, earth	pendjer (Du); bood·joor (Gr); budjor (Mo); bud-jor (Sy); budjor (By); buggiar (Sa); booga (Ba); boodjoor (Ar); budger (Gi); boodjar (Go); poodjer (Gm); boodjer (Hc); boogjure (He); boocha (SHK); boodger (Kn); buga (Mr); booger (Sc); boojar (Sm); boocha (Ta); boojar (Wd); pudyar (Wa); boojar (Bt); boojoor (Bk); boojur (MB); boojer (Nga); barrja (Ngi); bood-ja-ra (Is); boojar (J); boojar, boojur (K); budja-bucha (Rw); boodja nooda (Bu); bouj-ardi (Hm); boodjer (CK); putjur (Do); boojarra (Da); boodjar (Be); puadyär̃ (Vb); badjarr (At); boodjar, boodjera (Wt); budjar (De); budjor (Ri); badja (Mi)
bookor	brave	boo·goore (Gr); bugor (Mo); bugor (Cy); boogera (Bt); boogur (Bk); boogur (J); boogur (K); buggero (Ol); pugarra (At)
boola	much, plenty	poole (Ni); boola (Ly); poul (Du); bel-uk-a (Gr); belăk (Mo); bel-âk (Sy); bellack (By); bulla (Sa); boola (Ba); boola (Ar); boolar (Gi); boolarong (Go); poola (Gm); boola (Hc); boolar (He); boola, boomba (SHK); bulla (Mr); boola (Sc); boola (Sm); boola (Wd); boola (Bk); boola (J); boolarrung (K); bulla (MB); bulārăng (Nga); balling-a-ngarrungin (Ngi); boolanger (Bu); boola (CK); pulaṛaŋ (Do); boolah, bullah (Hs); boollara (Be); pual (Vb); bula bularang (At); balang, boola, (Wt); bul (De); boulah (Ri)
boolain	more	(see boola); boolain (Ngy)

boolya	magic	boylya, boyl-ya (Mo); boolya, boolooja (Bt); boylya, bolya (Bk); boolya, bulya (MB); boyiya, boyl-ya, boylya (Nga); boylya (J); boylya (K); pulj, puḷ (Do); boolya (Da); booliah (Hs); püäly (Vb); boyl ya (Ri)
boolyaka	evacuate, flee	bul-lo-co (Ki); bulloco (Ni); bulgooleetch, bulyakool (K); boolyaka (Mi)
boolyakadak	sorcerer, doctor	boyl-ya (Gr); boyl-ya-gadăk (Mo); boyla-gadar (By); boglia (Sa); bulya-gadak (Cy); bulya (MB); boolya-duk (Da); bulyakarrak (De)
boondong	money	bundong (Cr); puntuŋ (Do); boorndi (Da); boorndoong (Wt)
boorda	soon	poordel (Ni); poro (Sa); burder (Ba); boorda (Ar); booda (Cr); burdar (Gi); booda (Go); boordo (Gm); boorda (Hc); boorder (He); poort, boordook (SHK); booda (Kn); booda (Mr); bardamal (Sc); borda-borda (Wd); boorda (MB); boordo (Nga); boorda yooal (J); boorda (K); puṭa (Do); boorda (Bo); puaert (Vb), burda burdawan (At); boorda (Mi)
boordaoo	until	purdau (Vb)
boordawan	later	burda burdawan (At); putawan (Do); boorda wanja (Bt); burdawan, pudawan (Do); purdaun, purdalaan, purdawaall (Vb)
boordawan-boordaoo	sooner or later	purdaun purdau (Vb); burda burdawan (Do)
boorditj	thump (onomatopoeia)	(boorditj)

boordook	close	bardook, barduk (Bt); borduck (Bu); barduk, borduk, bordok (Bk); barduk (By); borduck (Bu); barduk, bordak (De); bar-dook, per-dook (Gr); borduk (K); barduk (Mo); borduk (Nga); bardook (Ngy); boorduk (Ngi); bordock (Rh); ba-duk (Sy); puarduq (Vb); bardook (Wt); bar-dook (Gr); barduk (Mo); ba-duk (Sy); barduk (By); bardook (Ngi); bardoogut yooga (Bt); barduk, borduk (Bk); bordock (Rh); barduk (De).
boorn	tree, wood, stick	poorne (Ni); boornoo (Ly); boor-noo (Gr); burnu (Mo); bur-nu (Sy); pono (Sa); boona (Ba); boornoo (Ar); booan (Cr); bonner (Gi); bono (Go); poorn (Gm); boona (Hc); boonna (He); boon (SHK); boona (Kn); burna (Mr); boorna (Sc); boona (Sm); boon (Ta); bonna (Wd); buna (Wa); boorna (Bt); boorna (Bk); boorna (K); boorna (MB); boorn (Nga); boorna (Ngi); boorna (J); boonark (Bu); boona (Ol); puṇ (Do); boorn (Da); puurn (Vb); burn (At); boorn (Wt); burn (De); bonu (Ri); boorna (Mi)
booyang	strange, unknown	bo-yung, boyang (Gr); bo-yăng (Mo); booyunga, booyunger, booyungur (Bk); booyungur (MB); booyung, būyăng (Nga); booyung, booyungur (Ngi); booyung (J); booyung, booyungur (K); boorung (Bu); puiyaŋ (Vb)

booyi	smoke	boo-yoo (Gr); bu-yu gerik (Mo); buyu (By); boio; puio (Sa); boyer (Ba); buyer (Gi); poohey (Gm); booi (SHK); brara (Mr); booya (Sc); bwoya (Sm); pooi (Ta); boyea (Wd); puya (Wa); booyoo (Bk); booyee (Nga); kareek booya (Ngi); booyoo (J); karl booya (K); booyer (Bu); boush-yah (Hm); buliu (Ol); puy, puyi, kaḷ puy (Do); puay (Vb); buy, buyi (At); karl boyi (Wt); buya (De)
born	cut	borne (Gr); bohrn (Mo); karda-born (By); bondagan; poone (Sa); boorn burrong (Bt); borna (J); boning (MB); bornanya (Ngi); poṇinj (Do); paurn (Vb); borniny (Wt)
boroong	heavy rain	boroy (Ba); borong (Gi); gab-borungin (Hc); gab borongin (Bk); bor-ong (Is); gab borongin (K); borung (Bu); boroong (Wt)
boya	stone	pooye (Ni); poie, boiel, pouoi (Du); bo-ye (Gr); bu-yi billanăk (Mo); bu-yi (Sy); poa (Sa); boya (Ba); booyee (Ar); boyer (Gi); booye (Go); booy (Gm); boya (Hc); boey (He); booi (SHK); booya (Kn); boyer (Mr); boyeya (Sc); booye (Sm); bwoon (Ta); boya (Wd); poi (Wa); booya (Bt); bwaia (Bk); boya (MB); boya balart (Nga); boya (Ngi); boy-a (Is); bwaia (J); bwaia (K); bui, buyi (Rw); boyangoora (Bi); bouyer (Bu); boydine (Ol); boya (Gl); boya (CK); poy (Do); boy (Da); boy (Be); puiy (Vb); boy, boya (At); boya (Wt); boy (De); boya (Ri); boya (Mi)

daa	mouth, language, opening	taa (Bn); tar (Ki); taa (Ni); dya (Ly); taa (Du); dta (Gr); dta (Mo); dta (Sy); da (By); da (Sa); dah (Rh); da (Ba); dta, daa (Ar); dow (Gi); ta (Go); ta (Gm); daa (Hc); dar (He); taa (SHK); dar (Kn); dawar (Mr); daw (Sc); da (Sm); ta (Ta); dar (Wd); tā (Wa); daa (Bt); daa (Bk); taa (MB); tā (Nga); da-a (Ngi); daa (J); daa (K); ta (Rw); dar (Bu); yam-ar-tar (Hm); tayer (Ol); tja (Do); dar (Da); taa (Vb); daa, dja (At); djaa (Wt); dhaa (De); da (Ri); daa (Mi)
daa-bt	mute	(see daa)
daaliny	tongue	dar-lin, tha-lib (Ki); tarlin (Ni); dallang (Ly); da-kon-dail (Gr); dtallăng; dtakundyl (Mo); dtal-lâng (Sy); dallar (By); talagn (Sa); dalling (Ba); dallyne (Ar); tallong (Go); talling (Gm); tooling (Hc); darline (He); tarling, taaling (SHK); dallan (Kn); talling (Mr); dalin (Sc); daline (Sm); daling (Ta); dallang (Wd); daaling (Bt); dālain, daalin (Bk); daalin (MB); kaal daaling (Nga); ta-aling, daaling (Ngi); talang, talain, dalain (J); daaling (K); d-alygn (Bu); darlinging (Ol); tjaḷinj (Do); dulong (Da); tarling (Hs); djaaliny (At); daaliny (Wt); dhalany (De); daalang (Mi)
daap	knife	ta-ap (Ki); taap (Ni); taap (Du); dtabba (Gr); dtarh-ra (Mo); dtab-ba (Sy); dabba (By); tabba (Sa); boorna dabbin (Bt); dabba (Bk); dabba (MB); dāp (Nga); dabba (Ngi); dabba (J); dab (K); dapper (Bu); dab-bah (Hm); darp (Da); tap (Hs); taap, tääp (Vb); darp, daap (At); darp (Wt); dhaap (De); dtabba (Ri); daap (Mi)

daatj	meat, flesh	dadya (Ly); dad-ja (Gr); dad-ja (Sy); dadja (Mo); dadja (By); dade (Sa); daag-aa (Ar); dadger (Gi); taitch (Gm); daaja (Bt); daaja (Bk); daaja (MB); taaj, dāj (Nga); daaja (Ngi); taaja, daaja (J); daaja (K); taij, taich (Rw); dadger (Bu); tatj (Do); Dytch (Da); dartch (Be); taaty, taaity (Vb); daadja (Wt); dhadja, dhatj (De); dadja (Mi)
daatj-bt	fleshless	(see daatj)
dabakarn	slow, careful	dtub-buk (Gr); dtabbăk (Mo); dâb-bâk (Sy); tup-put (By); tapa can (Sa); dabbukan gool (Bk); dabbagun kool (MB); dabăgan (Nga); daabbal-un-gunja (Ngi); dabbuk (J); dabboolan gool (K); dubbakinn (Rw); d-arbalger (Bu); dubakiny (Da); taa-paagany (Vb); dabakany (At); dabakan, doobakiny (Wt); dhabalkan (De); dabakan (Mi)
dabat	fall	tabea (Ly); dab-but (Gr); dtabbat (Mo); tab-burt (By); dab at (Sa); dabbat (Bk); dabbat (MB); tabbut, dabbut (J); dabbat (K); dab-bee-yet (Hm); dhabat (De)
dakan	break	dákan (Gr); dargangăn (Mo); tak-kan (Sy); dargangan (By); tacancura (Sa); dakkarn (Bk); daganyung (K); dagganing (MB); been daggurning (Nga); dogarn ginjee (Ngi); dackarn (Bu); darkanyin (Be); taagg-, teegg- (Vb); djakaroong (Wt); dhakarn (De); dargeninj (Wi)
dalang	pursue	dtallăngiritch (Mo); daalung-at-gool (MB); dālăng bărong (Nga); dālăng bărong (Nga); dularng (Bu); taalaŋ (Vb); dalanginy (Wt)

darap	dive, enter	derboween (Ly); der-bow (Gr); dărbow (Mo); darbow (By); tarpacul, tarpauicico (Sa); gebaladarbain (Bt); taar̃b (Vb); djarbiny (Wt); darbow (Ri); tarpiny, tapalaṛinj (Do)
dat	quiet	daht (Gr); daht (Mo); daht (By); dat e nyinan (MB); dad nyin (K)
demakoombar	great ancestors	(see demangkar, koombar); demma goomber (Bt)
deman	ancestors, grandparents	tammin (Mo); daaman (Cr); demman (Wa); dimma (Bt); demma (Bk); demman (MB); dem (Nga); demma (Ngi); demma (J); demman (K); deemer (Bu); tem (Do); deman (Be); täim, täin (Vb); dem (At); deman (Wt); dhem(an) (De)
dit	together	te-ta (J); deet-gwart-gur (Gr); dit-guling (Ka)
djalam	bitter	djallam : Bitter (By); djalum (De); djal-lum (Gr); tallam (J); jallum (MB); djallam (Mo); jellam (Ngy); cialan (Sa); djal-lam (Sy)
djandoo	raptor, kite	tandu (Vb); jandu (Mo); jandoo, darndoo (Ba); Dtan-do (Gr)
djarin	accuse	gee-rin (Gr); djirin, woolgar djirin (Mo); jarrabin (Ngi); djaat (Wt)
djardar, djardak	light-coloured, white pipeclay	(see djaat); dardăk; daddar (Mo); dardaknabow, dardak (By); dardarr, dardara, dondeer (Bt); dardarr (Bk); dardar (MB); dardar, dardarr, dardaara (Ngi); darrar (J); dardarr, dardar, dardakup ye, dardara (K); djardak (Wt); dhurnda (De); dardar (Ri); tyiurtt (Vb); tdur duck (Gr); dâr-dâk (Sy)

djart	sun, light-coloured	djaāt (F); djaat (Ki); chaat (Ni); dtaat (Ly); tyiurtt (Vb); djatj, dhatj (De); djart (Wt); tiat, tchaat (Du); djaat (Gr)
djen	foot	jaān (F); jaan (Ki); chen (Ni); geena (Ly); jee-na (Gr); jinna (Mo); ji-na (Sy); jinna (By); chiena; dena (Sa); gin (Rh); jenna (Ba); djeena, jeena (Ar); genar (Gi); ginnur (Go); jean (Gm); gina-ngut (Hc); jenna (He); chen (SHK); jenna (Kn); jenna (Mr); jenna (Sc); jenna (Sm); chen (Ta); jenna (Wd); yen (Wa); jeena (Bt); jenaa (Bk); jinna (J); tcheena (K); jenna (MB); jen (Nga); jenna (Ngi); ginner (TH); chenn, jinn (Rw); chenn (Ra); jenner (Bu); jan-nah (Hm); tjen, tjin (Do); tyiän (Vb); djen, djin (At); djen, djin (Wt); djen (De); jina (Ri); djena (Mi)
djerang	handsome, fat, grease	cheerung (Ni); chiran; ciran (Sa); jerrung (Cr); geerong (Go); cheerung (Gm); jerragumba (Hc); jerrung (He); cheerung (SHK); jerring (Mr); cherrunge (Ta); gerang (Wd); jeeragumba (K); jeerung (MB); jeerungur (Nga), jeerang (J); jeerung (Da); tyieraŋ (Vb); djirung (At); djeroong, djirang (Wt); djira:ng (De); djerang (Mi)
djert	bird	keard (Ni); dyeeda (Ly); kierd (Du); jee-da (Gr); jida (Mo); ji-da (Sy); chert (SHK); jeeda (Bt); jēda (Bk); jerda (MB); jert (Nga); jēda (Ngi); jē-da (J); jerda (K); chirt, chert (Rw); tyiärt (Vb); tjert, djairt (At); djet (De); jee-da (SW); cheit (Na)

djididjidi	willie wagtail	jiddee-jiddee (Bk); jittee jittee (Da); tjiti-tjiti (Do); djidi-djidi (At); jiddeejiddee (J); jiti-jiti (Ka); jittee jittee (K); djidi-djidi (Mi); jittee jittee (MB); jiti-jiti (Nga); jiti-jiti (Ngi); jittee jittee (No); tyitti-tyitti (Vb); djidi-djidi (Wt)
djidily	cricket	kiddal (Mo); jet-tyl (Sy); jittal (Bk); jittail (MB); jitil (Nga); jittal (J); jēdil (K); tjitilj (Do); tyiidily (Vb); djidil (At); djidily (Wt); djidaly (De)
djilba	spring, green grass	dul-bar, jilba (Gr); jilba (Mo); jilba (Sy); jilba (By); chielba (Sa); jelba (MB); jelup (Nga); jilba (Nga); jilba (Ngi); jilba (J); jilba (K); jilba (Ri)
djinang	see, look	djin-nung (Gr); djinnăng (Mo); djin-nâng (Sy); cienan (Sa); jinanying (Ba); ginnung (Cr); ginnung (Go); ginnung (Hc); jinning (He); chirrung (SHK); jenning (Mr); jenong (Sm); chinnung (Ta); gennang (Wd); jummingin (Wa); jinnong (Bk); jennong (J); jinnung (MB); jinangin (Nga); jinnong (Ngi); jinnung (K); jinburange (Bu); geen-ong (Hm); djinang (CK); tjinaŋinj (Do); kuttajinoong (Da); tyiännaaŋ (Vb); djinang (At); djinang (Wt); djinang-iny (Mi)
djinangalanginy	all seeing each other here	(see djinang)

djinda	star	chindy (Ni); kindy (Ly); tchindai (Du); djin gun (Gr); tiendi (Mo); ti-on-dee (By); chin dan (Sa); gendong (Ba); ginde (Gi); tean (Go); chindung (Gm); teen (Hc); jindang (He); chindi (SHK); jimdang (Sm); deen (Wd); jindongin (Bt); jindong (Bk); jindung (MB); jindung (Nga); jendang (Ngi); teean (K); jundarng (Bu); gin-darng (Ol); tjintaŋ (Do); gindie (Hs); tyierndaŋ (Vb); djiindong (At); djinda, djindang (Wt); djindang (De)
djip-djip	itch (onomatopoeia)	jipjip, djubodtan (Mo); cipcip (Sa); jooba meerung (Bt); joob don (Bk); jeejar dungin (MB); jeeren jeeran (Ngi); jeeta gur doning (K); jip-jip, jit-jittemburra (J); tyiip-tyiip (Vb); djip-djip (Mi)
djoombar	hair	dju (Mo); joombar (Nga); chumber (Rw); kat tjumpuṛ (Do); djumbur (At); djoombar (Wt); djumbar (De)
djoorap	happy	joorabin (K); tjuṛapinj, tjuṛupinj (Do); djurubiny (At); djerabiny (Wt); djooroopiny (Mi)
djoowak	the next generation	tjuwak (Do); djoowak (Wt)
don	pierce, penetrate, thrust	don, dorn (Bk); don (Bd); taan, torn (By); dhan, dhorn (De); dtan, taan (Gr); dorna (J) don (K); dtan. (Mo); doning (Nga); dan'il (Ngy); dön; dôn (Ngi)
don-djinang	aim	(see don, djinang); don jinungin, donjinăngin (Ngi)
doodjar	murderer, culprit	doojar (Bt); doojar (Ngi)

dookern	make, cook	tokenor (Ni); toknor (Du); dook-koon (Gr); dukun (Mo); du-kun (Sy); too-koon (By); ducanan (Sa); dookern (Gm); daaja dookurn (Bk); dookan (J); doongurn (K); doogurn (MB); doogurn (Nga); dookurn (Ngi); dookarn (Bu); dooken (CK); tukuṇinj (Do); dookaniny (Be); tugul (Vb); dukurn (At); djookoorniny (Wt); dhukarn (De); dukun (Ri)
dooly	mist	dool-ya (Gr); dul-ya (Mo); dul-ya (Sy); duoglie (Sa); dolya (Bt); dwalya (Bk); dwalya (MB); duel (Nga); dolya (Ngi); dwalya (J); doolyert (K); tuäly (Vb); dooly (Wt); dhulya (De)
doordok	alive	toortock (Ni); dor-duk (Gr); dordăk (Mo); darda goonining (Bt); doordok, dordok (Bk); dordok (MB); dordok (Nga); dorduk (Ngi); dordok (J); dordok (K); tiurddaqq (Vb); turdok (At)
doorrok	drink, gulp	doorgat, doordguree (Ly); dew-er-ing (Wl)
dowirl	always, lasting	dow-eer (Gr); dow-ir (Sy); dower (Mo); tauwil (Vb); uotominan (Sa); wotel (Do)
dwongk	ear	twang (Bn); du-ong (F); duong (Ki); twank (Ni); dunga (Ly); toan, touank (Du); tonga (Mo); ton-ga (Sy); ton-ga (By); tuonga tagu (Sa); dwonga (Ba); donga (Ar); dwank (Gi); awank (Go); twonk (Gm); dwonga (Hc); dwanga (He); twonk (SHK); dwonga (Kn); tooka (Mr); dwanka (Sc); dwonga (Sm); dwanga (Wd); dwunga (Wa); dwonga (Bt); dwonga (Bk); dwonga (MB); dwonk (Nga); dwangaluk (Ngi); dwonga (J); dwonga (K); twonnk (Rw); dwanger (Bu); tong-gah (Hm); dwank (Ol); toŋka, twaŋk, twoŋk (Do); tuaangaqq qaattity (Vb); dwangkiny (At); dwank (Wt); dhungka (De); tongah (Ri); dwongk, dwonga (Mi)

dwongka-bt	deaf, not listening	twank a toot (Ni); touank atout (Du); tongaburapo (Sa); dwonger bult (Ba); dwongaburt (Hc); dwonga burt (Bk); dwonga burt (MB); dwongabărt (Nga); dwonga burt (Ngi); dwonga werra butting (J); dwong burt (K); dougerbut (Bu); twaŋk puṭ, twaŋkapuṭ (Do); dwankabut (Da); tuaanq-a-tuut (Vb); dwongkaburt (At); dwankaboort (Wt); dhwongka-bart (De); dwongaboort (Mi)
dwongk-kaaditj	hear, listen	(see dwongk, kaaditj)
kaadiny	thinking	kaadiny, kaadaniny (Wt); katinj (Do)
kaaditj	know, understand	kat-tidge (Gr); barra-kattidj (Mo); kat-tidj (Sy); barrakattidj (By); kaht (Gm); kárdidyin (Wa); koorija kuttikinji (Bt); kuttee-yan (MB); katitch (Nga); kuttitch (Ngi); kuttaitch (J); kuttig (K); cartage (Bu); kahta (Hm); dwankitj (CK); katitjinj (Do); kutich (Da); qaattity (Vb); kadadjiny (At); djaliny, kaadining, kadadjiny, kadidjiny (Wt); kadatj (De); kahta (Ri); kaditj, kadidjiny (Mi)
kaaditj-bt	don't know	(see kaaditj)
kaanya	shame	kanni (He); ganya, kaanya (Bt); kanya (Bk); kaanya (MB); kaanya baaba (Nga); kaanya burdanga (Ngi); ganya, kaanya (J); kanja (Do); kinya (Da); qaanya (Vb); kaanya (At); djoo, kaanya, kanya (Wt); kaanya, keny (De)

kaarl	fire	carle (Ni); cyala (Ly); cal, karl (Du); kal-la (Gr); kalla (Mo); kal-la (Sy); kalla (By); cala (Sa); karla (Ba); kalla (Ar); karlar (Gi); kalla (Go); kahrl (Gm); kalla (Hc); kalla (He); karl (SHK); karla (Kn); karla (Mr); koila (Sc); karla (Sm); karl (Ta); kalla (Wd); karla (Wa); kala (Bt); kala (Bk); kala (J); kala (MB); kaal (Nga); kala (Ngi); kala, kalla (K); kal (Rw); carler (Bu); kahla (Hm); calla-gutharrah (TH); kaḷ, kaḷa, watjan (Do); karla-murruny (Da); carl (Hs); qaall (Vb); kar(l) (At); karl (Wt); kalla (Ri)
kaarl-boorn	firestick	kal boorn (Nga); kalbūrn, kala boorna (J); kalboorn (K); boorna karla (Da); puurn-qaall (Vb); karl boorn (Wt)
kaarlap, kaarlal kaarlak	home, camp	kallip, kallabudjor (Mo); kal-leep (Gr); kallip (By); karla (Ba); kalla (Ar); karlar (Gi); kolla (Go); kahrl, kaunt (Gm); kata (Mr); kulal (Sc); kulall (Ta); kalla (Wd); kalal (Bt); yungaroo kala (MB); kāl (Nga); nyungarung kala (Ngi); kalleep (Ol); kaḷa kuḷinj (Do); karluk (Da); karla (Be); karla kurl (At); kalil, koolark (Wt); karla (De); karlil (Mr);
kaarlang	hot	galanynee (Ly); karlok (Du); kdl-lar-uk (Gr); kallăk; kallarăk (Mo); kal-lâng (Sy); kallang (By); calanaran (Sa); kalong (Ba); kulahr (Gm); kallanga (He); kullar (SHK); kallora (Kn); kolanger (Sc); yekla carrang (Wa); kalungur (Bt); kalaruk (Bk); kallarruk (MB); kalungur (Ngi); kallar (K); karinger (Bu); kaḷaŋ (Do); karlawooliny (Da); karlang (At); karla woorliny (Wt); karlarak (De); kal lang (Ri)

kaat	head, mountain	cat (Bn); kaāt (F); kaat (Ki); kaat (Ni); kaat (Ly); kat, kaat (Du); cata-mourda-mokine (MD); kat-ta (Gr); katta (Mo); kat-ta (Sy); katta (By); catta (Sa); kart (Rh); karta (Ba); katta (Ar); kater (Gi); katta (Go); kaht (Gm); karta (Hc); karta, kaat (He); kaat (SHK); karter (Kn); karta (Mr); kutta (Sc); kata (Sm); katta (Wd); kad (Wa); katta (Bt); katta (Bk); kat (K); katta (MB); kaat (Nga); katta (Ngi); kar-ta (Is); katta (J); kat (Rw); carter (Bu); kar-tar (Hm); carter (Ol); katta (Gl); kat, kata (Do); cart (Da); cart (Hs); qaatt (Vb); karda (At); kaat (Wt); kaat (De); kaat (Mi)
kaat-wara	mad	katta werra (Bk); katta wadde (MB); karainji (Nga); katta waggain (Ngi); katt a warra (K); cart-warra (Bu); kat waṛa (Do); kart warrah (Da); qaatt-waara, qaddawaa (Vb); kat wara (At); kaal wara (Wt); kaat wara (Mi)
kaaw	laugh	cowker (Ni); goaaween (Ly); kaoner, kauker (Du); go-a (Gr); goa (Mo); go-a (Sy); goa (By); caua; cauin, caulgn (Sa); goo-aga (Bt); Kowa (Bk); kowain (MB); gwert gauain (Nga); kowa (Ngi); kowwa (J); kowa (K); cowie (Bu); kawinj (Do); ka (Da); qaau (Vb); kawiny (At); kawiny (Wt); kawin (De); goa (Ri)
kabin	perhaps, likely	kubbain (Bk); gab-byne (Gr); gabbyn (Mo); kubbain (J); kubbain (MB); kubbain (Ngi); gab-byn (Sy)
kadak	possess, have (suffix)	ga duk (Gr); gădăk (Mo); gadak (By); guttuk (Ngi); cuttuck (Bu); -qaadaq (Vb); kadak (Mi)

kaep	water	kyp (Ly); kep oun aan (Du); gab-by (Gr); gabbi; kypbi (Mo); gab-bi (Sy); gabbi (By); cape; capi (Sa); gab (Rh); gabba (Ba); gabbee (Ar); gab (Cr); gab (Gi); kaba (Go); keip (Gm); gab (Hc); gabbee, gab (He); kaip (SHK); gabby (Kn); gabba (Mr); kaba (Sc); gabba (Sm); gabby (Wd); kepi (abb kep, gep) (Wa); geba (Bt); gabba (Bk); gabba (MB); gabba, gebba (Ngi); gabba (J); gabba (K); gep (Ra); gabbie, gabba (Bu); gahp-bi (Hm); cabadine (Ol); kayep (CK); kep (Do); keape (Da); kierp (Be); kep (At); kabi (Wt); kaba (De); gahpbi (Ri); yeba (Dy)
kambany	owl	gambigorn (Mo); kambeegur (Bt); kumbegur (Bk); kumbagur (MB); kămbain (Nga); kumbegor (J); kambeegur (K); cumbinger (Bu); cubine (Hs); kambany (Wt); kambigur (De); kambikoora (Mi); cumbine (SW)
kambarn	meet	gambarn (By); qaambärn (Vb); gum-bam (Gr)
kanangkoor	shining, glittering	kanungur (Mo); kanangoor (Wt); kan-an-gur (Gr); kanerroo (Ad)
kandang	vomit, bring up	kan-dang (Gr); kandang (Mo); kardil (Ka); kan-dang (By); candac (Sa); qaandaŋ (Vb)
karam	yesterday	kurrum (Cr); karrum (Go); koram (Gm); karron (Hc); kairum (Mr); kurrum (Ta); kooritch (Bt); karram (K); kurrum (Da); karram (At); kooroom (Wt); karram (De); kurrum (Wi)

karang	angry, wild	go-ran (Gr); garrang (Mo); gâr-rang (Sy); garrang (By); carancata; carancumbarupo (Sa); gaarung (Bk); garrung (MB); gaarung gaarung (Nga); gaara garrung (Ngi); karanga (TH); kaarung (J); garrung (K); carung (Bu); karangmit (CK); kaṛanjininj (Do); karrung (Da); carrungupiny (Be); qaaraŋ (Vb); karang (At); karang (Wt); karrang (De); garrang (Ri); kaarang (Mi)
karang-kadak	enemy, villain	karrung guttuk (MB); garrung guttuk (Ngy)
kardart	straight	katurt (Bk); katart goola, katurt (J); katurt : katurt (MB); karart (No)
kardaborn	cut in half	gur-rab-ár-rá, kar-da-bur-ran (Gr); kurdaburra (MB); qaart-paurn (Vb); kart burndongin (K)
karni, karnan	true, truly	ka na (Gr); karnajil; karnayul (Mo); kannagil (By); kurnijel (Bk); kurnijel gwabbaduk (MB); kurnigel (J); kurnijil (K); kaṇanj (Do); kunarn (Da); qaur-naa? (Vb); karni, karnany (At); karni, karnitj, (Wt); kanna? (Ri); kanan, kanandjil (Mi)
karreba	mercy, good conduct, tenderness	karra (Mo); karra, karragwabba (By); capari (Sa)
kart	middle	kar-da (Gr); kardăgor (Mo); kardagor (By); kardagul (Bt); kardagurl (MB); karda (Bk); karda (J); kardan (K); kardagur, kardagăr (Ngi); qaart (Vb)

kaya	yes, hi	ky, quaco (Ni); kaia, kai (Du); kwa, ky, koa, kya (Mo); qua (Sy); gwa (By); caia, caiatigi (Sa); kia (Ba); gwa (Ar); kiar (Gi); kiar (Go); kiya (Gm); kia (Hc); kia (He); kia (SHK); kire (Kn); kia (Mr); kya (Sc); koo (Sm); yar (Ta); kia, qua (Wd); ko go (Bt); kaia (Bk); kaia (MB); kaia (Nga); kaia (Ngi); kea, kaia (J); kaia (K); kaia (Rw); kyer (Bu); kayaṛ (Do); kia (Da); qaayaar̃ (Vb); kaiya (At); kaya (Wt); kaya, kay, kwa (De); gwa (Ri); kaya (Mi)
ken	step, dance	kool-ke-kan, gan-now, kan-now (Gr); gannow (Mo); gan-now (Sy); gannow (By); canaan, canatico, canaleu (Sa); gēninin, genening (Bt); kening, kēning, gēning (Bk); kening, goolganan (MB); kening, gening (Nga); gē-nin, kēning, gē-na mungoordeja (Ngi); kanna, kaana kaaning, ganna, ge-nar-ding (J); kening, ken wabbin (K); gehna (Bu); qäinn (Vb)
keny	one, alone, first	kain (Ni); gaen (Ly); ken (Du); gyne, kain (Gr); gyn (Mo); gyn (Sy); gain, kain, gyne (By); chegn (Sa); cane (Rh); kain (Ba); gyne (Ar); kane (Gi); kane (Go); kehn (Gm); kein (Hc); kean (He); kain (SHK); kain (Kn); kain (Mr); kain (Sm); kain (Wd); kein (Wa); geeyening, geeyening (Bt); gēn (Bk); gen (MB); gen (Nga); gen (Ngi); gen (J); gēn (K); gaingel (Bu); kaen (Hm); kane (Ol); keny (CK); kenj (Do); kaen (Da); caine (Hs); ken (Be); qääyün (Vb); kenong (At); kany, keny, keyiny (Wt); kany, keny (De)

kenyak	enough, satisfied, sufficient	ganyak (Ly); kin-nyok (Gr); gyne-yuk (Gr); gyngăk (Mo); gyn-yak (By); cagno (Sa); cagnac (Sa); cagno (Sa); kenyuk (Kn); kanyuk (Ngi); kanyuk, kenyuk (Bk); kenyuk (K); kanyuk, kenyuk, kenyak (MB); kenyuk, genyuk, ganyuk (J); kainyuk, kenyuk, kenyuk (K); kenjak (Do); qiänyaq yiäy (Vb); kanyiny, kendak, kenyak (Wt)
kert-kert	quick	gid-gid (MD); gate (Gr); getget (Mo); get-get (Sy); getget (By); ket-iangul (Rh); kirt-kirt (Gm); get-get (Kn); beeyagurt (Bt); gert gert (Bk); gert gert (MB); kait (Nga); gert gert (Ngi); gert kert (J); gert gert (K); kitt-kitt (Ra); keṭ (Do); keert arniny (Da); qüert-qüert (Vb); kataming (Wt); kert-kert (De); kil kit (Ri)
ket	carry	get koorl (MB); katte (Mo); cattaculo (Sa)
kidala	day	Ge-da-la gedala (Mo); gedalgup (Ba); gil-tah (Hm); kil-tah (Hm); kedala (Wt); qiadeeqq-quarn (Vb)
kidalak	night	kartiac (Ni); kartiak (Du); gidalget (Ba); katank (Cr); kidal (Gi); kittyuk (Gm); kuttik (SHK); kitlook (Sc); jidaluk (Sm); geetalgup (Bt); geedaluk (Bk); keedaluk (MB); gēdaluk (Nga); geedaluk (Ngi); gedaluck (Bu); qiadeeqq (Vb); kadiyak (De); kitiupcowa (Hs)
kidja-kadak	hunter	(see kitj)
kian	without, nothing	kian (Gr); kyan (Mo); kian (Ta); kaian, gī-en (Nga); kinj (Do); qiäny, qiäyäny (Vb); kiny (Wt)
kian-kadak	one who has nothing	(see kian, kadak) qeenqaadaq (Vb)

kitj	spear	keit (Ni); gidyal (Ly); keit (Du); gidjiboryl (Mo); gid-ji (Sy); gidji (By); caci (Sa); gidgee (Ba); gegee, gidgee (Go); gidgee (Hc); gidigi (He); kigge (SHK); gidgey (Kn); jiggi (Mr); giga (Sc); gigee (Sm); keech (Ta); burral-gigee (Wd); kedji (Wa); gijee mulyedegur (Bt); geejee, geej (Bk); geejee (MB); gij (Nga); geeja (Ngi); geejee (J); geej bening (K); borigle gidgie (Bu); gid-yee (Hm); koojedda (TH); kitj (Do); ceech (Da); geize (Hs); kedjal (Be); qiity quardityinyä (Vb); ketj, kitj (At); ketj, kitj (Wt); kidja (De); gidgee (Ri); kidji (Mi)
kobong	friend	guababan (Sa); kūbong (Nga); koobong (Ngi); coobarng (Bu); couburne (Hs); quabuŋ (Vb); kupurn (At); kubang (De); koobong (Bt); koobong (Bk); koobong (J); kobong (Ka); koobong (Ngi); kobong (Ngy); quabuŋ (Vb)
kokon	wait	kok-kon (MB); kogang-nginnow (Mo)
kongk, kongkan	uncle	kan-go (Gr); kangun (Mo); kan-gun (Sy); can-oni (Sa); concon (Sa); kongan (Bk); kongan (MB); kongan (Ngi); kongan (J); kongan (K); kong-ga (Ol); koŋan, koŋk (Do); conk (Da); konk (Be); qauŋq (Vb); kongk (Wt); kangan (Ri); kongk, kangku, kongka (De); kongk (Mi)

koodjal	two, pair, double, second	cojine (Ni); kadjen (Du); good-jail, good-djall (Gr); gudjal (Mo); gudjal (Sy); good-jal, good-dgal (By); guggial (Sa); cudjal (Rh); goojal (Ba); goodjal (Ar); kugal (Gi); goodjal (Go); kootchal (Gm); kojal (Hc); goojal (He); koochal (SHK); goodjal (Kn); kujal (Mr); gugal (Sc); goojal (Sm); goochal (Wd); kudjin (Wa); koojal (Bk); koojal (MB); koojal (Nga); koojal (Ngi); koojal (J); koojal (K); coojal (Bu); kod-gal (Hm); ku-jarl (Ol); koodjal (CK); kutjal (Do); koojal (Da); coogal (Hs); koodjal (Be); quüdyiny/ŋy (Vb); kudjal (At); koodjal (Wt); kudjal (De); koodjal (Mi)
koolong	child	koulon (Du); goo-lang-gur-ra (Gr); gulang-găra (Mo); gulang ara (By); goolanggurra (Ar); kullung boola (Cr); koolonger (Go); koolangarra (He); kullangkarry (Mr); goolangar (Sc); kulungarer (Ta); koolongur (Bk); koolongur wa (Nga); coolang (Bu); koolangoor (CK); coorlinga (Da); koorlongka (Be); koorlongka (Wt); gulangara (Ri); koolangka (Mi)
koolyam	lies	ko-lain (Gr); gul-yăm (Mo); guli (By); koolyum (Bk); koolyum (MB); koolyumin (Ngi); koolyum (J); koolyum (K); kuljumitj, kulumitj (Do); koolya mut (Da); quulyam (Vb); kulyumitj (At); koolymitj (Wt); kulyam (De); koolyi (Mi)
koolyawar	liar	(see koolyam); koolyawa (Da); gul-yambar (By); quuly-waer (Vb)

koombar	large, big, great	goom-bar (Gr); gumbar (Mo); gumbar (By); cum bar (Sa); goombar (Cy); kormon (Ba); goombar (Go); goombar (Gm); goombar (Hc); koombow (SHK); gumba (Mr); gombat (Wd); gumbar (Wa); goombar (Bk); goombar (MB); goombar (Nga); goombar (J); goombar (K); coumbarker (Bu); kumpaṛ (Do); koomba (Da); coombar (Hs); koombar (Be); quumpaar (Vb); kumbar (At); koobarniny, koomba (Wt); kumbar (De); koombar (Wi); koombar (Mi); cooma (Na)
koondam	dream	koon-dum (Gr); kundămm, kundăm-ngwundow (Mo); koondamma (Bt); goondam (Ngi); koondarm (Wt); koondam (Wo); gooin (No)
kooniny	baby, child, small, young	kooning (Cr); kwanyart (Ngi); goonain, gunain, guninyer (Nga); kurning, kuning (Rw); quanyurt (Bu); kuninj (Do); kwooninyga (Da); quuniny (Vb); kooniny (Wt)
koonyak	soft	goon-yack (Gr); gunyak (Mo); gun-yâk (Sy); goonyok (Bt); goonyok (Bk); goonyuk (MB); goonuk (Nga); goonya (Ngi); goonyok (J); goonyuk (K); counyup (Bu); kunyak (De)
koora	long ago	go-rah (Gr); gorah (Mo); go-rah (Sy); gorah, guragor (By); caran, curacura, cura (Sa); kooraa (Bk); koora (MB); kurā (Nga); koor-ra, koorarree, koorraa (Ngi); goorraa (J); koorarr (K); kuṛa (Do); kura (Be); quaraa (Vb); koora, kooralang (Wt); gora (Ri); kura (Wi)
kooranap	afterlife, creation place	kooranup, koorannup (Bk); koorannup (Ngi); koorannup (J); koordannup (K)

koorart	short, small	korert (Ni); goor-at, go-re-á d á, go-rad (Gr); gorad; gorada, goradan (Mo); go-rad, go-rad-da (Sy); gurad, guradan, gorada (By); koorert, koorart (Bk); kwoorurt (MB); koorurt (Ngi); koorat, koorut (J); kweyert (K); koorart (Bu); quarat (Vb); koorart, korad (Wt); kurarda, kurart, kwerart (De)
koordoomit	soul	gurdumit (Mo); gurdumit (By); quurtmiitt (Vb)
koorl	travel, go	gool-bang (Gr); gulbang (Mo); kol-bar-do (Sy); gulbang (By); caliacolin (Sa); gooley (Hc); koola (Kn); koorala (Mr); gulling (Ta); baragul (Bk); kooling (K); bokoja kool (MB); bokoja gool (Nga); baragool (J); goolin (Le); koorliny (CK); kuḷinj (Do); koorliny (Da); koorl koorliny (Be); quull (Vb); kulling, kurlinj (At); koorliny (Wt); kurl (De); koorl-iny (Mi)
koorndany	shy, bashful	gurndap (Nga); kurntany (Do); kurndany (At); kurnda (Ka); kurnda (No); koorndany (Mi)
koorong	twist, spin, weave	go-rang-ween (Gr); gorang (Mo); gurdin (By); corancin (Sa); goorago (Bt); koorungun (Bk); goordang (J); koorangan, gorangin (MB); kooragainga, koorongin, koorong (Ngi); goorong (J); quar̃aŋ, quar̃aŋ-quar̃anan (Vb); kooranginy, korang (Wt)
koort	heart, spouse	goor-doo (Gr); gurdu (By); cot; cut (Sa); gu-urt (Cy); koort (Gm); koort, yorkkoort (SHK); kurd (Wa); koordada (Bt); koort, goort (Bk); koord (MB); gūrt (Nga); goort (Ngi); koora (J); goort (K); kurnt, kuut, kut (Rw); coode (Le); kuṭ (Do); coort (Da); quurt (Vb); kurt (At); koort (Wt); kardu (De); guardar (Ri); koordada (Mi); koorooda (Na)

koort-wera	sorrow	goort werra (Bk); goort werra (MB); goort werra, goort welinya, goort wēdē, gūrt wē-dē, gūrt wera (Nga); goort werra (K); gurt werra (Ka); kood-warra (Bu); gurt were (No)
koot	bag, womb	choota (Ri); gweta (K); goota (Bt); goota, koota (Bk); goot (Bd); goto (By); gooter (Bu); kut, kudu, kuda (De); ko-to, go-to (Gr); coot (Hs); goota (MB); cuttu (Sa); quut (Vb)
kora	again	gar-ro (Gr); gar-ro (Sy); garro (By); karo (Bt); kor gool (Bk); kor (MB); kora yenna (Ngi); koragool (K); koṛ kuḷ (Do); qaur (Vb); korl (Wt); korr (De)
korakoorl	return	kar-ro-yool, garro-yool (Gr); garro yuăl (Mo); garro-yul (By); coroculo (Sa); korgooling (K); korgool (MB); koragool (Nga); koree-yenning (Ngi); koṛ kuḷ (Do)
korbol	stomach	ko-bül (F); cob-bul (Ki); corpul (Ni); caburla (Ly); kopell (Du); kob-ul-lo (Gr); kobbălo (Mo); kob-bâ-lo (Sy); gabbarn (By); cobol; cobul; copol (Sa); gobbel (Ba); kabool (Ar); gobbel (Gi); gobal (Go); korble (Gm); gobbal (Hc); gobel (He); korpal (SHK); gobble (Kn); gabbel (Mr); goble (Sc); gawbool (Sm); quikorple (Ta); gobble (Wd); kurpul (Wa); gabbula (Bt); gobbul (Bk); gobbel (MB); gobbel (Nga); gobbel (Ngi); gobbel (J); gobul (K); kobbi, kawbl, gobbi (Rw); cobble (Bu); kob-bel (Hm); kor-bel (Ol); kapuḷ, kopuḷ (Do); kobal (Da); cobal (Hs); koboorl (Be); quabül (Vb); kobril, kwobril (At); kaboorl, koboorl (Wt); kaburla (De); kobool (Mi)

korbol-wirt	hungry	(see wirt); werat (Go); weerat (Go); weerat (Hc); weerat (Kn); koobar (Sc); goober (Sc); korpleweret (Ta); weerurt (Bk); weer-rart (J); weerert (MB); weerurt-yoolap (Ngi); werrert, werrart (J); korbol wirt (CK); kopuḷ wiṭ (Do); kobble weert (Da); quabül-puutt (Vb); koboorl win, wirt (Wt); wirrart (De); kobool wirt (Mi); kopurl wirt (At)
kori	just now, just recently	goo-ree (Gr); gori (Sy); gori (Mo); gori (By); gori (Ri); quari (Vb)
kornt	shelter, hut	kaunt (Gm); kont (Nga); kornt (CK); kont (Do); kant (Da); quant (Vb); kawnt (At); kwont (Wt)
kowat	daughter	gwar-rut (Gr); gwoy-rat (Mo); gwoy-rat (Sy); kowat (Ar); jouka kowat (He); kowat (Sm); quarrut chook (Ta); kowat (Bk); kwerrurt (MB); kwerărt (Nga); kwarrert (Ngi); kowat (J); cowart (Bu); kowat (De)
kwadjat	in front of, before	gwad-jut (Gr); gwytch (Mo); gwytch-ang-ât (Sy); gwytich (By); quagget (Go); quadjet-goolie (Hc); quochat bennang (Wd); koorijenna (Bt); kwajjingat gool (Bk); kweja-ga (J); kaj-al-de (K); kwejjungat gool (MB); kwejăngat gūl (Nga); kwejat (Ngi); quadgartger (Bu); kutjukat (Do); quadyaŋ (Vb); kwadjal (De); quadjert (Wi)

kweitj	bone, sharp, thin	queet (Ni); goodye (Ly); kouit (Du); kotiay (Gr); kotyedak, kotyelara (Mo); kot-ye (Sy); kardidi (By); quega (Ba); goodjee (Ar); auage (Gi); gwage (Go); quaitch (Gm); gidgee (Hc); quage (He); queech (SHK); quatcha (Kn); quage (Mr); gwega (Sc); quegi (Sm); quach (Ta); quegie (Wd); gweejalur (Bt); kweejalur (Bk); kweejela (J); kweejalur (MB); kwej (Nga); gweeja (Ngi); queagie (Bu); kwetj (Do); quity (Vb); kwedj (At); kwetj (Wt); kudji (De); katye (Ri); koodji (Mi)
kwelka	hip bone	kől-ga (Gr); kool ke (Gr); querluk (Gm); kwelja (Bt); kwelga, kwēja (Bk); kwelga (MB); gwelga (MB); kweluk, kwelak (Nga); gwilga, kwilka (Ngi); gwelga, kwelga (J); weluk (K); kwelokk (Rw); kwelak, kwolak (Do); querlaq (Vb); koolgi, kwelak, kwilk (Wt); kwalak, kulka, kwelka (De); kwilk (Mi)
kwelken	dodge	gwel-gan-now (Gr); gwelgannow (Mo); quel-kain (By); quilkarn (Bu); querlq-qäinn (Vb)
kwerl	name, title	go-lee (Gr); kole; quele (Mo); kole (By); kwela (Bt); kwela (Bk); kwela (MB); kwel (Nga); kwela (Ngi); kwela (J); wela (K); quaial, queal (Bu); quaal (Vb); kwel (At); kwely (De)
kwibil	stealthy	quypul (Ni); kouaipoul (Du); quippal (Mo); qua-ul (By); kwibble (Hm); kwibidji (Wt)
kwoark	a man's kangaroo skin cloak	kwark (Da); quark (Hs); quarq (Vb)

kwongkan	sandplain	goon-gan (Gr); gongan (Mo); awongan (Rh); boojoor kwongan (Bk); kwongan (MB); kwongan (Nga); kwangan (Ngi); boojoor gwongan (J); gwongan (K); kwoŋkan (Do); quayaraŋqaann (Vb); kwongan (At); kwongkan (Wt); kwongkan (De)
kwop	good	quaup (Ni); kouaup (Du); gwab-ba (Gr); gwabba (Mo); gwab-ba (Sy); gwabba (By); guaba (Sa); quab (Rh); quabba (Ba); gwabba (Ar); quab (Cr); quaber (Gi); quabba (Go); quob (Gm); quobba (Hc); guabba (He); quab (SHK); quabba (Kn); quaba (Sc); quabba (Sm); quabba (Wd); gwabba (Bt); gwab (Bk); gwab (K); gwabba (MB); gwap (Nga); gwabba (Ngi); gwabba (J); kwob, kwawb (Rw); kwobbrup (Ra); quab (Bu); kwob-bah (Hm); kwabidak (CK); kwop (Do); quobaduk (Be); qwaap (Vb); gwop (At); koobidak (Wt); kwaba (De); kwabba (Ri); kwoba (Mi)
kworditj	throw, drop	gwar-do (Gr); gidjigwart (Mo); gwar-do (Sy), gwardo (By); kwert don, gwert don (Bk); kwarditch (MB); geej gwerda longin (Nga); kwerdin (Ngi); gwerda (J); wardij winj (K); kuṭitjinj (Do); quard (Vb); koordidjiny (Wt); kwert (De)
maadjidil	magic, magic stone	(see maadjit); maad-jit-teeyl (Gr); madjitil (Wt)
maadjit	Powerful shark or water snake ancestor	maar-tyiürtt (Vb); maad-jit, mad-jin-da (Gr); majinda (Mo); martiat (Ni); madjit (Do); marghet (Hs)

maam, maaman	man, father	maam (Ni); mamerupt (Ly); maam (Du); mam me-rup (Gr); mammăl (Mo); mam-mâ râp (Sy); mamman (By); mama (Sa); mamer (Ba); mamum (Ar); mann (Cr); mammon (Gi); mammon (Go); mam (Gm); maman (Hc); mamma, mam (He); mam (SHK); mamman (Kn); mamman (Mr); maman (Sc); mammon (Sm); marm (Ta); mammon (Wd); mammau (Wa); mamman (Bt); mamman (Bk); mamman (MB); maam (Nga); mamman, maam (Ngi); mamman, maan (J); mamman (K); mam (Rw); maman (Ol); maam (CK); mam (Do); maam (Vb); maam, maan (At); maaman, maan (Wt); maam (De); mamman (Ri); maman (Mi)
maambakoort	ocean	mammord (Ni); mammart (Mo); mum-mung-gup (Is); mampakuṭ (Do); maernbagart (Vb); mamangrnt, mamawrunt (At); mambakoort (Wt); mamart (De); mammart (Ri); mamagurt (No); mamagart, mamangart (Ka); mumboyet (At)
maap	skin, body	mawp (Ni); ma-bo (Gr); mabo (Mo); maap (Mo); ma-bo (Sy); mandu (Sa); mapo, mopo (Sa); mopa (Ba); moorpa (Ba); mabboo (Ar); mober (Gi); mawp (Gm); moot, mawp (He); morpe (Ta); mauba (Wd); mopa (Sc); moba (Sc); Boonda, mobba (Bt); mobba (Bk); moba (MB); moba mullong (Ngi); moba (J); morba (Bu); morber (Bu); morba (Bu); maup (Vb); maap, marp (Wt); mop (De); mabu (De); moba (De); maap (Mi)

maar	hand	ma (Rw); maar (Hs); maar (Wt); maara (Bk); mahr (Gm); mar (Nga); mar (No); mar (Rh); mar (Ta); mar-ra (Is); mar, mara, marr (At); maṛ, maṛa, mayaṛ (Do); mara (Bt); mara (K); mara (Mi); mara (MB); mara (Ngy); mara (Ngi); mara (Sa); mara (Wd); marh-ra (Sy); marh-ra (Mo); marhra (Ri); marr (Cr); marr (SHK); marr (Ni); marra (Ad); marra (Ba); marra (Gi); marra (Go); marra (J); marra (Wo); marra, mar (He); marta (Hc); murra (Kn); murra (Sc); myrha (Ar); mahra (Hm); mara, marra, maar (De)
maara-ngaangk	thumb	marh-ra-ngan-ga (Sy); mara ngaia (Bt); maara nganga (Bk); mara nganga (MB); mār ngank (Nga); mar ngank (Nga); mara mammal (Ngi); mara nganga (J); mara nganga (K); ŋaŋkaṇ (Do); maar-ŋaaŋq (Vb); ngangka (Wt); mar ngangk, mara ngangka, mar kayang (De)
maarr	wind, atmosphere	maar (Ar); maar (Sc); mahr (Gm); mar (He); mar (SHK); mar (Is); mar (No); mar (Ri); mar (Sa); mar (Sm); mar (Mo); marerrr (Ta); mari (At); marl (Cr); marr (Bu); marr (Go); marra (Kn); marra (Wd); mar (Sy); marr (Ngi); maar̃ (Vb); mārr (Wa); marr : cloud (Wt); marr (Wo)
maarr-maarrang	strong wind	(see maarr)
maat	leg, family-line, kinship affiliation, path	matt (Bn); maăt (F); maat (Ki); maat (Ni); matta (Ly); mat-ta (Gr); matta (Mo); mat-ta (Sy); matta (By); mata (Sa); mart (Rh); marta (Ba); mate (Gi); maater (Go); marta (Mr); matta (Wd); marta (Wa); mata (Bt); maata (Bk); mata (MB); maata, maat, māt (Nga); mata (Ngi); mata (J); mat, mata (K); marter, mart-warra (Bu); mah-ta (Hm); mat, maṭa kitj (Do); mart (Be); maatt (Vb); mart, maat (Wt); maat, mada (De); maat, mada (Mi)

madooly	dirty, filthy	matuyl (Bk); maat dily (Mi); madily (Wt); moyndeeya (J); min-udo (Gr); min-yudo (Mo)
mai	nest, structure, bed	(Ngi); mai, maih (Ki); mya (Ly); my-a, jee-da mya (Gr); mya, jidamya (Mo); my-a (Sy); my-a (By); mire (Ba); my-ya (Hc); mia (SHK); mya (Wd); maia, jēda maia (Bt); maia, jēda maia (Bk); mai-ak, jeda mai (J); mai (K); maa (MB); maia (Ngi); miah (Bu); mya-mya (Hm); myera (Ol); maaya (CK); may (Do); mia (Hs); maay (Vb); maia, maia-maia (At); maya, miya (Wt); may (De); mia mia (Ri); maya (Mi)
malatj	grow	ma-lá-gow (Gr); ma-iá-jin (Gr); malaj (Mo); mēlajin (K); maalady- (Vb)
malak	shade, shadow	mal-ya ruck, ma-lo, ma-li-gee, malli-gee (Gr); mal-yâr-râk (Sy); mal-yarâk, mallo, malliji (Mo); molla, ma-loo, malloo (Bt); molla (Bk); malga (K); mulyaruk, molla (MB); mōlăk, moluk, mālăk (Nga); molla (Ngi); molla (J); mol (K); moller (Bu); mooldup (Ol); malkakum (Do); marlak (Wt); malak, maalak (Wt); malu, murdak, mol, mola (De)
malkar	magic, thunder	mulgarradock (Ni); mulgar guttuk (Bt); mulgar (MB); mulgan (Nga); mulgar (Ngi); mulga-rarri (TH); mulgar cuttauck (Bu); malaṛ (Do); mulga (Hs); mulgariny (Be); maalqaar (Vb); malkar (At); malka mooditj (Wt); malka(r) karrak (De)
malya	brain	mal-ya (Mo); mal-ya (Sy); maaly (Vb); mung-jar-ree (Hm)
mambara	spirit creature	mamaṛa (Do); mamari, mambara (Wt); mamarap (De)

mandi	young woman	mun-dig-a-ra (Gr); mân-dig-gâ-ra (Sy); măndigăra (Mo); mandi (Sa); moonditch (Hc); mondey (Mr); mandeegur (Ngi); mandeegur (Bk); mandee (MB); mandeegur (J); mandeegur, mandur (K); mandeger, mandegar, mandakin (Bu); maŋa (Do); maandiy (Vb); maandi (De)
mandjang	old man, old woman	manjahly (Ni); mun-jang (Gr); mandju, mănjang, măndjalla, (Mo); manjang (He); manjung (Sc); minjung, maanyung, manjăng (Nga); munjung, manjung, munjung (K); manjugoordup (Bi); manjtjaŋ (Do); mandjang (Wt); mandjang (De); mandjang (Mi); mandjar (Gl)
mardang	love, sweetheart	mardok burning (J); mardong (Wt); mardang-iny (Mi)
mardar	red, red ochre	mărdar, murdar (Nga); murrda (Rw); mardar̃ (Vb); madarr-madarr (At); mardaa (Wt); mardarr (De); mirda (Do); mardar (K); murder (No)
mardiny	three	mardain (Bd); mirdine, merdine (Ba); murdign (Bu); merdine (Cr); mardany (De); maṭinj (Do); mardine (Gi); mirting (Gm); mur-tden (Gr); murr-dyn (Hm); merding (Hs); mardine (He); merting (SHK); marding (Ka); murtden (Mo); marding, murding (Nga); mardain, marding (Ngi); marding (No); Mud-dinge (Ol); murdine (Sc); mardine (Sm); merting (Ta); mäerdiŋ (Vb); marding (Wa)
maya	voice, sound	mya (Gr); mya (Mo); mya (By); mai-anba wangee-maia (Bk); maia wângin (Nga); maia wangee (K); maay (Vb); may wangkiny (At)

maya-kora	echo	mya kowá (Gr); myakowa (Mo); mya-akowa (By); maiauagagnitin (Sa); maian (Bt); mai koordonjoyn (Nga); maian (Ngi); maia kor kooling (K); maay-qaur-quulliny (Vb)
menditj	sick, wound, sore	mendeit (Ni); men-dyke (Gr); mendyk; mindyt (Mo); men-dyk (Sy); mendyk (By); mendiggi; mendiggira (Sa); mindaitch (Bk); mindaitch (MB); kojer minditch (Nga); minda mindajung (Ngi); mindaitch (J); mindaitch (K); minditch (Bu); mig-geree (Hm); mondie (Ol); minditj (CK); mentitj (Do); mindich (Da); minditch (Be); miänäq (Vb); mendik (At); menditj (Wt); mindatj (De); mindytch (Ri); mendatj, menditj (Mi)
mereny	food	marrin (Ni); maryn (Ly); maryne (Gr); dadjamaryn (Mo); mar-ryn (Sy); dadjamaryn (By); marine (Ba); maryne (Ar); marring (Gi); maring (Gm); marine (He); murine (SHK); marino (Mr); marine (Sc); marine (Sm); maringe (Ta); marrain (Bt); marrain (Bk); marrin (MB); mērin (Nga); marrain (Ngi); marrain (J); marrain (K); murring (Rw); marighn (Bu); mereny (CK); makan (Do); merinj (Be); mäir̃ny (Vb); marandj, meriny (At); mariny (Wt); marrany (De); murryn (Ri); marany (Mi); maran (Dy)
midjal	light rain, light tears	mitjal (Do); midjal (Wt)
mila	future	me-la (Gr); mila (Mo); mila (By); meela (Ba); mila (Be); mila (Wt)
milkar	fresh, new	mil-gar (Gr); milgar (Mo); mil-gar (Sy); milgar (By)

mir	spear-thrower	meroo (Ar); meero (Bt); meera, meero (Bk); meer, meero, meerr (Bd); miera, meara, mero (Ba); miro (By); meara (Bu); miro (Cy); mirr, mirra, mirru (De); mear (Du); mir (Do); mero (Go) mer-ro, meer-ra, me-ra, mirr, mir-ro (Gr); meero (Hc); mee-ro (Hm); meera (Hs); meero (J); meer, meera (K); me-ara (Ki) meero (Kn); meero (Ly); miro (Mi); meero : Throwing stick (Mr); meero (MB); miro (Mo); mīr (Nga); meeroo, meero (Ngy); meera, meero (Ngi); mi-ro (Sy); miur̃ (Vb)
miran	poise (to prepare a spear before throwing)	miran (Mo); miran (By)
mirnitj	face	mee-nyte (Gr); minyt (Mo); minyt (By); minitcha (Bt); minnaitch (Bk); minitch (MB); meenitch (Nga); minnaitch (J); minnitch (K); mii (Vb)
miyal	eye	menel (Bn); me-al (Ki); meal (Ni); meeal (Ly); mihal, meal (Du); da-mil (Gr); mel (Mo); mel (Sy); mel (By); miel (Sa); meeal (Rh); maya (Ba); male (Ar); maleger (Gi); mail (Go); meail (Gm); meeyal (Hc); mial, mell (He); mial (SHK); meal (Kn); meal (Mr); mail (Sc); meal (Sm); miirl (Ta); meal (Wd); mîel (Wa); mēal (Bt); mēal, meeal (Bk); meal (MB); meeal (Nga); mēl, mel (Ngi); meal (J); meeal, meel (K); miawl, miall, miell (Rw); mairler, mairl (Bu); malbeling (Ol); mel, miyal, miyel (Do); meeowl (Da); meirl (Be); mii(y)äl (Vb); miyal (At); miyal (Wt); myaal, mayel (De); mel (Ri); miyat (Mi)

miyal-bt	blind	miel bet (Sa); mēal burt (Bk); meeal burt (Nga); mēl-burt (Ngi); meal burt (J); mee'al burt (K); miiäl-puutt (Vb); miyal burt (At); miyal boort (Wt); miyal-bart (De); meowlboort (Wi); miyalboort (Mi)
miyaliny	wanting, desiring	mi-er-uk (Gr);
miyalakeniny	giddy	(see miyal, keniny); miiäl-qäinniny (Vb)
miyalyan	cry tears	mal-yang-win (Gr); mealyet (Bt); melyin gwerdin (Bk); milyan (MB); mēlin (Nga); mēlyin (Nga); mēlyin wēling (Nga); mēlyin (Nga); mel-yet (Ngi); mēl-yet, merangin (Ngi); mel-yern (K); mel jan (Do); miiäl-yiin (Vb)
mookiyang	useless, bad	mukiyaŋ (Do); mookiyong (Wt); mujăng (Jm)
mokorong	pig	maggorong (Mo); mâg-go-rong (Sy); makkerong (J); mak'korong (MB); makarang (Mi)
mooly	nose	mo-il (F); tar-mul (Ki); moolya (Ly); mool-ya (Gr); mulya (Mo); mul-ya (Sy); mul-ya (By); modda (Sa); molyah (Rh); molya (Ba); moolya (Ar); mullur (Gi); molya (Go); mowall (Gm); moolya (Hc); moolya (He); molyoomel (SHK); moolya (Kn); moolya (Mr); moolya (Sc); moolia (Sm); mooli (Ta); moolya (Wd); mulla (Wa); moolya (Bt); mulya (Bk); moolya (MB); moil (Nga); mulya (J); mulya (K); mullyi, moilya (Rw); mulyer (Bu); moul-yah (Hm); moil-ya (Ol); moolyarup (Gl); mulj (Do); mualy (Vb); moyley (At); moly, mooly, moolya (Wt); mulya (De); mulya (Ri); moolya (Mi)
moolyabiny	hateful, sulky	mool-ya-bin (Gr); mul-yabin (Mo); mulyabin (Ngi); moolyoobiny (Wt)

moolarda	demons	mulard(a) (De); maaloo (Ga); moo-lar-da, moo-latdá (Gr); mallo (Sa)
moorart	full, satisfied	moo rad-a (Gr); murada (Mo); murada (By); murat (Sa); mgweeree (Bt); moorart (MB); moorart (Ngi); kwejjat murrerdup (J); moorart (K); murrart (Bu); muṛaṭ (Do); muarart (Vb); moorart (Wt); murrart (De)
moorditj	strong, fast	moor-doo-een (Gr); murduin murduin (Mo); bidi-murduin (By); moordaitch (Bt); moordaitch (Bk); moorditch wun (MB); moordeej (Nga); moorda moordeetch (Ngi); moordaitch (J); moordeetch (K); mooditch–yen (Bu); muṭitj (Do); muerdity (Vb); murditj (At); moordidjabiny (Wt); murdatj, murditj (De); moorditj (Mi)
moordiyap	hurry	mur-rigo (Gr); mur-ri-jo (Sy); murrijo (By); murdiup gul (Rh); moordeeup (Nga); murrdipp (Ra); mooditch (Bu); muṭip, yaṛap (Do); mirreeup (Da); muert-e-qäinn-quull (Vb); moordip (Wt)
mooriyak	murder, killing with magic	meerung jingun (Bt); moorik-iny (Mi); mūriăk bōmin, mooreeuk bomin (Nga);
moorn, moorni	dark	mohurn (Ni); mooru (Ly); moheurn (Du); mo-an (Gr); mo-ăn (Mo); mo-ân (Sy); mo-an (By); moan (Sa); moorn (Gm); mooret (Hc); moordang (He); munderlook (Mr); moordong (Wd); mowerna (Bt); moorn (Bk); mooarn (MB); moarn (Ngi); mowin, moorn (J); moowern (K); mooarn (Bu); maranock (Ol); muṇ, muṇit (Do); moonie (Da); maugurn, maurn (Vb); murn (At); moonawooliny (Wt); muwam, murn (De); moorn (Wi)

moort	family	mat-ta (Gr); matta (Mo); mata (Bt); mata (Bk); maat (MB); māt (Nga); mat (Ngi); moorurt (J); moorurt (K); muur̃urt (Vb); mat, mart (At); moort (Wt); murdukumeno (Ri); moort, moordinan (Mi)
naak	beg	ngaggow (By); naga (Bt); naaga burra (Bk); naagin (Ngi)
naap	paint, adorn	nab-bow (Gr); năbbow (Mo); nabow (By); nape (Sa); nabbain (Bt); nabbain (Bk); nabbain (MB); naba, nabbain (Ngi); nabba jerung (J); nabbin (K); naab (Vb)
naar	burn	ngar-ra (Gr); narrow (Mo); nar-row (Sy); narbow (By); narancatagn (Sa); nahr (Gm); nara (Bk); nāra (J); narawen (Nga); kala narree (K); naṛinj (Do); naar (Vb); nariny, naariny (At); naariny (Wt)
nadjal	why	natjil (Do); naitchoo (K); naggio (Sa); natjil (Wt).
nakal	little, gentle	na-gu (Gr); nagăl (Mo); nagal (By); narkle (Ta); nuggal (Wa); naagul (Bt); naagal (Bk); naagul (MB); nag-ul, naagul (Ngi); naggal (J); nāgul (K); naag(a/i)l, naagl (Vb); naarkul (At)
nanap	stop	nïan-nûp (Gr); nannăp (Mo); nan-nâp (Sy); nannap (By); nannup (Go); nan yin (Bk); nanyak (MB); naan nyin (Nga); nyinnain (Ngi); nanna nginna (J); nan yak, nanup (K); nan-nup (Hm); naan(-) (Vb); nganop (Wt); nhanap (De); nan nap (Ri)
natj	what?	nail (Gr); nait (Mo); na-aj? (Bt); naaj (Bk); naatch (MB); naaj (Nga); naaitch (Ngi); naitch, naaj (K); na-, nal, natj (Do); naa (Vb); nadjak (At); naatj, nadja, nayidja (Wt); na it? (Ri); naalj? (Mi)

ngaangk	mother, sun	nanga (Ly); ngan-ga (Gr); nganga (Mo); ngan-ga (Sy); nganaga batta (By); n-anga (nasal n) (Sa); narnk (Rh); nanga (Ba); nangga (Ar); nungon (Gi); knockan (Go); ngangk (Gm); oongar (Hc); nganga (He); ngonk (SHK); ngungan (Kn); nganga (Mr); ngungan (Sc); nongan (Sm); kun (Ta); nanga (Wd); gnanga (Wa); ngaienung (Bt); nganga (Bk); nganga (MB); bol ngan gaiung (Nga); ngangan (Ngi); ngarn-garng (Is); nganga (J); nganga (K); ank, ngank (Rw); ngarngarn (Bu); ng-yun-gen (Hm); ŋaŋk (Do); ngank (Da); nunk, (Hs); ngaangk (Be); ŋaaŋgann (Vb); ngangananap (At); ngaangk, ngangk (Wt); ngangk (De); nangan (Ri); yonga (Dy)
ngaarn	eat	ngan-now (Gr); gwineen (Mo); ngan-now (Sy); ngannow (By); n-anin (nasal n) (Sa); gabba knunging (Ba); gabbee ngannow (Ar); gabba nganning (Cr); kabbee nanning (Go); gab-anong (Hc); gabbi nganin (He); kaip karnee (SHK); nganna (Kn); ngan (Mr); ngarannin (Sc); nanning (Sm); ngungar (Ta); gabby-nanang (Wd); guaning (Wa); geba nganning (Bt); gabba ngannin (Bk); gabba ngannin (MB); ngannin (Nga); gabba ngo ganning (Ngi); gabba ngannin (J); gab nganning (K); ngarnie (Bu); kepa ŋaninj (Do); gnannor (Da); ngarn (Be); ŋaan- (Vb); mariny nganiny (At); keba nganiny (Wt); ngarn (De); nalgoowin (Ri); nganiny (Mi)
ngabang	cover, put on	nappang wanja (Mo); nappang-wanja (By); ngabbungeetch, ngaboungeej (Bk); ngabbung ee (MB); ngaabungin (Nga); nabbang (Ngi); nga'bung'eej (J); ngabbungeej (K)

ngat	repeatedly	ngatti-ngatti (By); ngutta (J); ngut (MB); ngatti (Mo); ngat-ta-ngat-ti (Sy); ŋaitt (Vb)
ngaitj	I	ad-jo (Gr); adjo (Mo); ngad-jo, ngan-ya (Sy); adjo (By); n-agia; n-agna (nasal n) (Sa); nauyia (Go); ngeit (Gm); ngika (Mr); nange (Wd); nganna, ngaija (Bt); ngaija (Bk); ngaija (MB); ngai (Nga); ngaija (Ngi); ngaija (J); ngaija (K); ŋaat (Vb); ngetj (At); ngad jo (Ri); ngadja (Mi); ŋaat (Vb)
ngalak	we two, our	ngalluk (J); ngaluk (K); ngulluk (Be)
ngalang	our	ngillelung (Mo); ngilling (Bt); Ngullagoo (MB); ngailo (Nga); ngarlartung (Bu); ŋaḷaŋ (Do); ngarlang (At); ngalang (Wt)
ngalar	we, all of us (including listener)	ar-lin-gul (Gr); ngala (Mo); ngal-a-ta (Sy); ngalla, ngala (By); gnela (Sa); ngilla (Bt); ngallee (Bk); ngunnaitch (MB); ngail bul (Nga); ngela (Ngi); ngallee (J); ngalla (K); ngarlark (Bu); ŋal- (Do); ŋaaluur (Vb); ngal (At); ngalak (Wt)
ngama	waterhole	ngamar (Mo); gnamar (Mo); amar (By); ngarn-mar gabba (J); ŋamar (Do); ŋamaṛ (Do); ŋaamär̃ (Vb); ŋaambär̃ (Vb); ngama, ngamar (Wt); ngamari (Wt)
nganang	my	nganyany (Wt); ŋaanaŋ (Vb); nganyang (Do); ngannung (Jm); ngarnang (Bs); ngunung (Da); nganung (Ngy); nganung, nganang (Ngi)
ngany	me	ngany (Do); ngaan, ngainya (Jm); ngan-ya, anna (Mo); n·ana (Sa); gnan (Wa); nganna (Bt); nganya (Bk); nganya (MB); ngain, ngan (Nga); nganya (Ngi); nganyee, ngunna (J); nganya (K); ŋaan (Vb); ngaing (At); ngaany (Wt); ngan ya (Ri)

ngarda	down, below	ar-din-ung (Gr); ngardăgăn (Mo); ngar-dâk (Sy); ngardak (By); ngardar (Bk); ngarda nyin (MB); ngarda nyin (Nga); boogoo ngurdee (Ngi); ngardee (J); ngarda ngoondeen (K); ngardal (Bu); ŋaṭa, ŋaṭa njininj (Do); ngardi (Be); ŋaardar̃ (Vb); ngarda (At); ngarda (Wt); ngardi (De)
ngarril	ribs	naral (Ly); nar-ra (Gr); ngarri, ngarrilgul (Mo); ngar-ril (Sy); n-aragl (Sa); nguril (Gm); narile (Sm); ngaralya (Bt); ngarral (Bk); ngarrail (MB); ngaril (Nga); ngarrail (Ngi); ngarrail (J); ngaril (K); ngargil (Bu); ŋaṛilj (Do); ŋaarily (Vb); ngarily, nguritj (At); ngirl (Wt); ngarrily (De)
ngiyan	who?	ngan (Gr); ngan; nganni (Mo); nginni (By); gninei? (Sa); nanning (Bt); ngeem (Bk); ngeen (MB); ngīn (Nga); ngeenung (Ngi); neen, ngeen (J); nyeen (K); ngeand (Bu); ngeean (Da); ŋäininy (Vb); nginy? (At); nginang (Wt); ngando (Ri)
ngoobalyong	bloody	ngoo-bool-yer (Gr); ngubul-ya (Mo); ngubal-ya (By); n-opoton (Sa); gnuppilong (Wa); noobilyong (Bk); ngobilyung (MB); ŋuupiillauŋ (Vb); ngawbelyang (At); ngobooloong (Wt)

ngoondan	brother	ngundu (Mo); ngobern, norran, ngondo (Mo); ngun-du (Sy); ngu-ban (Sy); n-undun (Sa); knooda (Ba); ngooban (Ar); goont (Cr); knunden (Gi); knondan boorong (Go); ngoont (Gm); knundan (Mr); gnundun (Wa); eenyee nganung woordoo (Bt); ngoondain (Bk); ngoondan (MB); ngoondin, ngundăn, ngoondeen (Nga); ngoondan (Ngi); ngoondun, ngoondan (J); ngoondun (K); Bal nganung ngoondun (K); ŋun, ŋunt (Do); ngoon (Da); ngoony, ngoordja (Be); ŋun, ŋunäy, ŋunni, ŋuunt, ŋunniqaar, ŋuundann (Vb); ngoon, ngooni, ngoorn, ngoorden, ngoont (Wt); ngan du (Ri); ngunt, ngundan, ngunda (De); ngoon, ngoonden (Wi)
ngoonyong	sweet, honey flower, nectar	ngon-yung (Gr); ngoonyung (K); ngon-yăng (Mo); ngungang (Sc); ngoonyong (Nga); ngoonyang (Mi); ngunyung (At); ngoonyong (MB); ngoonyoong (Wt)
ngoop	blood	oop, ouop (Du); ngoo-boo (Gr); ngubu baru (Mo); ngu-bo (Sy); ngubow (By); n·opa (Sa); knooba (Ba); ngooboo (Ar); knober (Gi); noope (Go); ngop (Gm); opa (Hc); ngoopoo (He); ngoop (SHK); ngoobur (Kn); ngupa (Mr); nguepa (Sc); nooba (Sm); naba (Wd); gnoap (Wa); ngooba (Bk); ngoba (MB); ngoop (Nga); ngoba (Ngi); ngoba (J); ngoba, naba (K); yup, up (Rw); ngooper (Bu); ŋop, ŋup (Do); ngoop (Da); ŋuup, ŋuap (Vb); ngawp (At); ngop (Wt); ngu:p (De); ngoorp (Wi)
ngoornda-djinang	dream	ngoont jinnongur (Wr); ngoorda jinong (Wl)

ngoornt	lie down	ngwoon-dow (Gr); bidjar ngwundow (Mo); ngwundow (By); nyinnung ngeera (Bt); ngoonda (Bk); ngoonda (MB); ngūndīn (Nga); ngoonda (Ngi); ngoonda (J); ngoondeen (K); ngoondin (Bu); ngoorndaloiny (CK); ŋuṇṭinj, ŋuṇinj (Do); ngoorndiny (Da); ngoorndininy (Be); ŋuardd (Vb); biyu ngurndiny (At); nookert ngoorndiny (Wt); ngurnt (De)
ngoorr	character, manner	ngo-ro (Gr); ngoro (Mo); ngo-ro (Sy); n-uranan-an (Sa); ngurr (At)
ngorlak	teeth	ur-luk (F); or-lock (Ki); orlock (Ni); ollog, orlok (Du); nal-go (Gr); nalgo (Mo); nalgo (Sy); nalgo (By); n-olgo (Sa); norlock (Rh); knollak (Ba); ngalgo (Ar); nolger (Gi); nolga (Go); ngorlok (Gm); nulga (Hc); naulga, ngorlok (He); ngoorlok (SHK); knolga (Kn); ngulla (Mr); ngulga (Sc); nolga (Sm); nalgo (Wd); gnallok (also sometimes gnālok) (Wa); nalgo (Bt); ngolga (Bk); ngorlok (K); ngolga (MB); ngorlok (Nga); ngolga, ngorlok ? (Ngi); ngolga (J); ŋaḷak, ŋoḷak (Do); ngorluk (Da); ŋurluq (Vb); ngawrluk (At); ngorlak (Wt); ngarlku (De); ngorlak (Mi)
ngwidam	serious, dignified	ngwidăm (Mo); ngwidane (By)
ngwirin	beautiful, pretty	ngwir-re, ngwir-ryne (Gr); ngworryn ngworryn (Mo); nyweeree (Bt); ngoorong ngoora (J); ŋuerany, ŋueranyaŋ (Vb)
ni!	hark!	ni (Do); ni (Da); ni (Vb); ni (Wt); ni (Mi)
ninat	worm	nee-nat (Gr); ninat (Mo); tinat (Sa)

nitj, nidja	here, this	ne (Ni); ne (Du); nidja (Mo); nyag-ga (Sy); n'yagga (By); nichia (Sa); neeja (Cy); nyee? inyee? (Bt); neeja (Bk); naajo (K); neeja (MB); neej, neejuk (Nga); nyee (Ngi); neej (J); nghe (Bu); nidjak (CK); ni-, nitja, ninj (Do); nicha (Da); nitch (Be); niäty (Vb); nik? (At); nidja (Wt); nidja (Ri); nidja (Mi)
noitj	dead	noit (Ni); noit (Du); no-dytche (Gr); noyt (Mo); nodytch (By); noytch (Cy); noitch (Gm); nojja (MB); noyja (Ngi); notj (Do); noych (Da); noatch, noitch (Hs); nuiity (Vb); nootj (Wt); nhotj (De); noyitj (Mi)
nookert	sleep	no-go-ro (Gr); nogoro (Mo); nocorcorin (Sa); ngorgut (Nga); noogat (K); nukeṭ ŋuṇṭinj (Do); naugurt (Vb); nuggat (At); nookat (Wt)
noombit	blossom	numbit, numbirt, nyoombeed (Ba); numbit (Sy); ngoombit (Ly); numbit (Do)
noort	stench	noor-doo (Gr); nurdu (Mo); nur-do (Sy); nurda (Ba); noordoo (Ar); nuart (Cr); nurte (Gi); nooda (Go); noorda (Hc); noort (SHK); noordo (Mr); noorda (Sc); noorda (Sm); nyeedoo (Bt); noorda (Bk); goonyee-noorda (J); noorda (MB); noort (Nga); nyooda (Ngi); noord (K); nooda (Bu); noort (Da); nuart (Vb); nurdu (At); noordoo (Wt); nhotj (De)
nop	boy, son	nehp, nehbitur (Ni); no-pine (Gr); nopyn (Mo); nopogn (Sa); noop (Cr); nobarach (Gi); nop (Go); nawp (Gm); nop (SHK); naubejet (Sm); nopine (Wd); nooba (Bt); nobba (Bk); nobba (Ngi); nor-pa (Is); nor-pa (Is); nobba (J); nob (K); nobb (Rw); norba (Bu); nop (Do); nop (Da); nop (Hs); noorbaritch (Be); nuabiny (Vb); nawbing, nopiny (At); nap (Wt); nhoba (De); nop (Wi)

norn	snake	norne (Ni); norn (Du); noorn-noo (Gr); nona (Mo); noner (Gi); noorna-boogura (Bt); noorna (Bk); nôrn (Nga); norna (Ngi); noo-na (Is); norna (J); gnawn (Ra); nuner (Bu); norn (Hm); nornalup (Gl); nuṇ (Do); norm (Hs); noorn (Be); nuarn (Vb); nurn (At); noorn (Wt); nhom (De); norn (Ri); norn (Mi); norra (Dy)
nyidiny	cold	gnitin (Sa); ngitding (Ar); ngiating (Cr); knitine (Gi); neeting (Go); ngiting (Gm); witine (Hc); ngittang (He); nittin (Kn); ngitting (Mr); ngitbine (Sc); netyne (Sm); weating (Wd); ngeerajin (Bt); nyittang (Bk); ngitting-ngitting (J); nyeetin (MB); ngeeting (Nga); ngittang, (Ngi); nyitting (K); ngitignuck (Bu); njitinj (Do); ngertiny (Da); nyiiddiŋy (Vb); niding (At); nyidiny (Wt); ngiding, nyiding (De); nyidiny (Mi)
nyin	sit, be	ngin-now (Gr); nginnow (Mo); ngin-now (Sy); n'yinnow (By); gninaco (Sa); knining (Ba); ngimow (Ar); yinnung (Cr); nying (Gm); urayining (Hc); nginee (He); nginin (SHK); nyning (Sm); ngunting (Ta); narda nyinna (Bt); nyin (Bk); ngarda nyin (MB); ngarda nyin (Nga); ngardee nyinna (Ngi); nan-yinna, nyinnain (J); ngarda nyin (K); nginie (Bu); noonegin (Gl); njin-, njininj (Do); nyinilanginy (Be); nyiän- (Vb); ninitj (At); nyinanginy (Wt); nyin, ngin (De); nyin-iny (Mi)

nyoona, nyoondak	you	nounlok (Du); n'yun-no (Sy); nunda (Sa); nonduck (Gi); noonda (Go); yinuk (Gm); noonda (Hc); ngintuk (SHK); nunda (Mr); noonak (Sm); quinuk (Ta); nunda (Wd); guindok (Wa); noonda (Bt); noonda (MB); nyinok (Nga); noonda (Ngi); yenok (J); noonda (K); noonduck (Bu); nyoondook (CK); njunṭ-, nyunta- (Do); noonuk (Da); noonook (Be); niündaqq (Vb); nyindak, nyunak (At); noonook (Wt); noonda (Mi)
nyoonang	your	n'yu-rang (Sy); n'yurang (By); noonong (Bt); noonong (Bk); noonong (MB); noonong (Ngi); noona (K); noonung (Bu); nyinanga (CK); njunaŋ (Do); niunaŋ (Vb); nyurangak (Ri)
nyoongar	person, human	nyoonger (Ly); yung-ar (Mo); ion-ar (Sa); yung-ar (Cy); nungal (Ba); yoongar (Ar); nunger (Gi); yoongar (Go); noongar (Gm); youngar (Hc); youngar (He); noongar (SHK); youngar (Kn); yungar (Mr); nungar (Sc); youngar (Sm); youngar (Ta); yungar (Wd); yunga (Wa); nyoongara (Bt); yoongar (Bk); yoongar (MB); yūngar (Nga); nyoongar (Ngi); yoongar (J); nyoongar (K); nung-a (Rw); yungar-yogg (Bi); ngungar (Bu); n-yoong-ah (Hm); yonga (Ol); noongar (Da); nunghar (Hs); nuuar̃ (Vb); nungar (At); noongar (Wt); nyoongar (Ri); nyungar (Wi); nyoongar (Mi)
nyorn	alas	njoŋ (Do); nyorn (Da); nyorn (Wt); nyon (Mi)
wa?	hey? right?	wâ (Nga); wa? (Do); waa (Vb)

waab	play	wimberner (Ni); waubbăniranwin, waubbowin, waubbawangowin (Mo); wab-bow (Sy); uaperan (Sa); wabba (Bt); wab wonga (Bk); wabbain (MB); wâba (Nga); wabba (Ngi); wabba (J); wab gowing (K); wabba (Bu); wapinj, waṛpinj (Do); warpuliny (Be); waub (Vb); warbiny (Wt); waba (De)
waabar	player	wauber (Vb)
waal	cry out, call, scream, wail	walrar (Du); ualan (Sa); wēling (Bk); werla (J); wallain (MB); wālin (Nga); wēl-ing (K); wallung (Bu); walinj, welinj, wulinj (Do); wal-waliny (Da); winjaliny (Be); waal (Vb); wal waliny (Wt); wal, wel (De)
waam	stranger	warba (Mo); uame (Sa); warrba (Bt); wam (Bk); womma (MB); waam (Nga); womma (Ngi); wam, wamma (J); wam-al-eeja (K); gaign wommer (Bu); wam (Wt)
waangk	speak, talk, say	wanga (Gr); wăngow (Mo); wan-gow (Sy); barrawangow (By); uanga (Sa); wanga (Bt); wonga (Bk); wanga (MB); wângin (Nga); wanga (Ngi); wongi (TH); wanga (J); wang (K); wonga (Bu); won-gee (Hm); waŋk (Do); waŋkinj (At); wank (Da); waarŋg (Vb); wangadan (Wt); wangk (De); wanging (Wi); waangki-ny (Mi)
waangkar	speaker	(see waangk)
waarlar	carelessly, suddenly	waarlar (Vb); werlany (Da); wal-lar-ra (Gr); wallarra (Mo); wilya-wilyan (Ngi).

walak-walak	separate, spread out	wal-la-kah (Ki); kor-tda, walluck-walluck (Gr); wallăk-ijow, minytwallăkijow, wallăkwallăk, wallu (Mo); wala walagon (Bk); wat-wat (Ngi); wallak wallak (J); walla wallagon (J); warla-warloch, goorda-goorda (J); warlaqq, waurlaqq-waurlaqq (Vb)
walbarn	heal	wal-byne (Gr); walbyn (Mo); walbyn (By); walburning (Bt); gwabbaning (Ngi); walburn (Bk); walburn, walburning (MB); walyak walbarn, walburn (J); walburn (K)
wara	bad, fail	warra (Ly); wurrah (Rh); wurra (Cr); warra (Go); wurra (Gm); wurra (Hc); warra (He); worra (SHK); worthy (Mr); wadang (Ta); werra (Bk); werra-werra (J); werra (Nga); wetgah (TH); warra (K); worra (Rw); warra (Bu); warramut (Le); wara (CK); waṛa (Do); warrah (Da); warra (Be); waara (Vb); ngurr-a-warra (At); warabiny (Wt); warra, werra (De); warralı (Wi); wara (Mi)
warda	renown, fame, news	warda (Mo); waart (Vb); war-da (Gr)
wardakadak	hero, person of renown	wardagadăk (Mo); wardakuttuk (Sc); wardagadup (Sm); wardaguttuk (Bt); warda kadak (Wt)
wardar	watcher, observer	(see warda); warder, waarder (Vb)
wardarn	ocean	gabee-wodin (Ly); odern (Sy); odern (By); uotan (Sa); wadarn (Bt); wattarn (Bk); wattarn (MB); wâdarn (Nga); waddarn (Ngi); wottarn (Is); waddarn (J); waddarn (K); waddarndi (Bi); wattarn (Bu); wuadarn (Vb); wawrdon (At); wadarn (De); wotharn (Na)

wardong	crow, raven	quog-gum, wardung (Gr); wardang (Mo); war-dang (Sy); uara (Sa); wurdang (Ar); wardung (Cr); wardung (Gm); warda (Hc); wordong (He); woodung (Kn); wordong (Mr); wardang (Sm); wartung (Ta); wardang (Wd); wordung (Bt); wordong (Bk); wordong (MB); wawding, wording (Rw); wurdam (Hm); wagoora (TH); waṭaŋ (Do); warrdong (Da); wording, warding (Hs); wardang (Wt); wardang (De); wardang (Mi)
wariny	hanging	uaran (Sa); boornok warrawinja (Bt); warrowin yeera (Bk); warritch (MB); warra weenjan (Ngi); warra (J); yeera warra weenj (K); waṛinj (Do); wariny (At); waarintja (Wt)
warn	do	noonda ninya wunnitch (MB); noonda boogain wunna (J); waṇinj (Do); wooniny (Da); warniny (Wt)
werdam	kill	werdam (Nga); wantaŋinj (Do); wardamit (Bo); werdamin (No); wurt-am-ur (Gr); wandanginy (Wt)
weyak	coward	wai-uk (K); waiak (No); wainger (Bu)
weyarn	afraid, fear, grief	wyen (Mo); wy-en (Sy); uaindalco (Sa); weeyenee (Bt); waiawē (Bk); waience (MB); wēyen (Nga); weyen (Ngi); weyan (J); waien (K); waian (Bu); wi-ah (TH); waayaliny (CK); weyaṇinj (Do); wayarniny (Da); wäiyänn (Vb); kweyiny (Wt); wayarn (De); weyaninj (Wi); wayan-iny (Mi)
widiwidang	shake, shiver	widdee widdung (Bk); weedang (Ngi); widda widdung (MB); witting witting (J); burrong widdee widding (K)

wilki	red ochre, paint	wil-gi (Sy); uilghi (Sa); wilghee (Cy); wilgee (Bt); wilgee (Bk); wilga (MB); wilgee (Ngi); wilgee (J); willgi (Rw); wilgerka (Bu); wilga (Gl); wilgee (Da); wilgie (Hs); wileq (Vb); wilgi (At); wilki (Wt); wilak (De); wilki (Mi)
windjar, windji	where?	in-djalla, wingalla, winjal (Gr); winjalla; winji (Mo); win-ji, win-jal (Sy); ingat (By); uandaa? (Sa); winjal, injal (Bt); winjal (Bk); winjal (MB); māt winjal (Nga); injal, winjee (Ngi); winjal? (J); winjal (K); injal (Bu); wanthella (TH); windjar (CK); wintja? (Do); winjar (Da); wäindyal (Vb); windjak? (At); wingi (Ri); windja? (Mi)
winyan	pitiful, indisposed	wan-yurdu (Mo); winyann (Vb); winyan (Wt); winyan (Mi)
wirawoorliny	whirlwind	wărh-răl (Mo); kooro willin (Nga); warriwillah (Ol); willy (Da); wily-wily (Wt)
wirlo	bush stone curlew	weelya (Bt); weeloo (Nga); weelow (Le); wee-la (Ol); wiluna (Gl); wilj, wilu (Do); weerlo (Da); wheeow (Hs); wiüly (Vb); wilor, willo (At); werloo, wirlo (Wt); wilo (Mi); weelawodda (SW)
wirn	ghost, spirit	wearn (Gi); wē yen nardup dardagup (Bk); weernel (K); weeurn (MB); Wē-yel-um (Ngi); wajjurn, wâjăm (Nga); weya-we (J); wata murnong (J); wiṇ, wen (Do); wernitj (Be); wirnit, win, wern, wirn (Wt); wiyarn, wern, wen (De)

wirndang	weary	windo; wendang (Mo); windo (Sy); windang (Ar); windang (Go); windong (Sc); wendang (Wd); weenta (MB); wede (Nga); weendarng (Bu); win-dong (Hm); wiürddäy (Vb); windang (De); windong (Ri)
wirnitj	evil, haunted	winnaitchung (Bt); winnaitchung (Bk); winnaitch (MB); winnaitch (Ngi); weenitch koola burdeet (J); weeneetch (K); wäiyännity (Vb)
wirt	empty, weak	weṭinj (Do); daggurn wirt (K); wirt (At); werrert (J); wirt, werdiny (Wt)
wongin	alive	wan-gen (Mo); won-gin (Sy); wingainung (Ngi); wongin (Wt); wangin (Wo)
woola!	hooray!	woolah (Da); woola (Wt)
woolkar	guilt	wool-gar (Gr); wulgar (Mo); wulgar (Ri); woolgar (Wt)
woombabaan	vain	wumbubin (Mo); oombain-ooombain, woombain woombain, woombubbin, ngwoombain-ngwoombain (Bk); woomba paan (MB); oomain-oomain (Ngi); woombup, woombubbin (J)
woorrar	a long way	woorie (Ni); oor-rar (Gr); urrar (Mo); u-rar (Sy); woorah (Rh); wooree (Bt); woorar (Bk); woorar (MB); woorerr (Nga); woorarr (Ngi); wooree (J); woorie (Bu); wuṛaṛ (Do); wuarar (Vb); wurri (At); bookootjwoorar (Wt); wurrar (De)
woordak	shade	urac (Sa); woordak, wurdok (Nga); wuurdaq (Vb)

woort	throat	warrat (Bn); wurt (F); wurt (Ki); woort (Ni); waart (Ly); woort (Du); wardo (Mo); war-do (Sy); uoro (Sa); wart (Gm); wardoo (Bt); wardoo (Bk); warda (MB); ward (Nga); warda (Ngi); wardoo (J); warda (K); warder (Bu); wor-da (Ol); woṭ (Do); wort (Da); waurt (Vb); wawrt (At); wort (Wt); wardu (De)
woort-birn	choke	wart been (Nga); wârt bīn (Nga)
worl	sky	waullu (Mo); wau-lu (Sy); ualo; uolo (Sa); woolaran (Cr); woolelan (SHK); warla (Mr); woalu (Wa); warla (MB); dooitch warl (Nga); warla (Ngi); warlok (K); yallonee (Hm); woḷ (Do); waurl (Vb); worl (At); worl (Wt)
wort	away	waterboort (Ly); watto (Mo); wat-to (Sy); uadauigin (Sa); watbilli (Gm); wat-ai-yenna (Ngi); watercarrie (Le); woṭ (Do); wort (Be); wautt (Vb); wawt (At); witj (Wt); wart (De)
wort-bili	that way	(see wort)
wowak	breathe	waug (Mo); waug (Cy); wark (Ta); woogera (Bt); woggarr (Bk); wagarr (MB); wagarr (Ngi); wagarr (J); wager (Bu); waug (Vb)
yaak	stand	yugow (Mo); yurgow (Sy); ira-yugow (By); yook (Bk); yeeruk gool (Nga); yookain (Ngi); yooka (J); yonger, yuckie (Bu); yaakiny (CK); qääyünity yuag (Vb); yaakiny (Wt); yuk (De); yaakiny (Mi)
yaarn	how? how now? what's up?	yanman (Bt); yarn (MB); yaanman (Ngi); yarn? (J); nargn (Bu); nygar (Da); yaan (Vb)
yaawin	moon	yowing (Ta); yaawiny (Vb); yawiny (De)

yakain	turtle	ng-yakyn, yagyn (Mo); ye-kyn (Sy); yakkan (Bk); yaggan (MB); yagain (Nga); yaggan (K); yokine (Gl); yarginy (Da); yaaginy (Vb); yokiny (Wt); yakany (De); yakany (Mi)
yalak	wait (exclamation)	yalaka (Do); yaalaq (Vb)
yeyi	now	yyi (Mo); yyi (Sy); iain (Sa); yeyur (Ba); yiee (Ar); yeahe (Cr); yeaye (Go); yiai (He); yee (SHK); yadgar (Kn); jea (Mr); yeable (Sc); yaiya (Sm); yaga (Wd); yeeya (Bt); yē-yee (Bk); ye-ya (MB); yee (Nga); yē-ya (Ngi); ye-ya (J); ye-ee (K); ajayyer (Bu); yhi (Hs); yiäy (Vb); yi (At); yey (Wt)
yira	up	yeeramanugaween (Ly); e-ra (Gr); ira (Mo); i-ra-bin (Sy); ira (By); ira (Sa); erar (Kn); yaraga yookan (Bt); eerap (Bk); yardok (J); yarragut (MB); yeera burrong nyinnin (Nga); eera-man (Ngi); yeera gool (K); yearanger (Bu); yiragan (Ol); yaṛa, yiṛa, yaṛaŋ (Do); yiär̃a (Vb); yara (At); yira (Wt); yirra (De); yira (Mi)
yok	woman	yock (Ni); iok (Du); yago (Mo); ya-go (Sy); iaco (Sa); yago (Cy); yorka (Ba); yoonga yago (Ar); yoker (Gi); yokka (Go); yawk (Gm); unganya yocka (Hc); yokka (He); york (SHK); jakker (Mr); yoka (Sc); yoka (Sm); yago (Wd); york (Wa); yaago (Bt); yog koojong, biderr yog, birderel yok (Bk); yogga (MB); yog (Nga); yogga (Ngi); york-ka (Is); yogga (J); yog (K); yokk (Ra); yorger (Bu); yo-ker (Hm); jackoh (Ol); yokan (CK); yok (Do); yok (Da); york (Hs); yaugurt (Vb); yawk (At); yok, yoka, (Wt); yaku (De); yoka (Ri); yoka (Mi)

yong	give	yong-a (Mo); ian (Sa); yunge (Cy); yonga (Bt); yunga (Bk); yong (MB); yongin (Nga); yonga (Ngi); yanga, yonga (J); yong (K); yangie, yungie (Bu); yaanginy (CK); yaŋinj (At); yaŋinj (Do); yuaŋ (Vb); ngoongoor (Wt); yungka (De); yoongama (Mi)
yokang	feminine	(see yok)
yokangkar	women	(see yok)
yoodan	tie	yu-tarn (Sy); yuttarlgar, yuttarn, yurjang, yudarn (Mo); yoodurn gwert (Bk); yoordaning (MB); yoodarn (Ngi); burder, yootun (J); yutininj (Do); yüiddern, yur̃ar̃aŋ (Vb); yoodiny, yoodininy, yootininy (Wt); yudarn (De)
yoomp	poison, magic	yump (Nga); yump (Do); yuump (Vb); yoomp (Wt)
yoornt	yellow	yundo (Mo); yoornda, kanjin (J); yoornda (K); yuunt (Vb)
yoowarl	toward	yualăng (Mo); yooalgonga (Bt); yooal-ai-anning (Ngi); yuḷpuḷi (Do); youaal (Hs); yuall (Vb); yualbilli (At); yuwal (De)
yoowarl-bili	this-way	(see yoowarl)
yoowart	not, no, none	yuat (Mo); yu-a-da (Sy); iuat; iuad (Sa); wuadda (Ba); yoo-ad-da (Ar); uadar (Gi); youat (Go); what (Gm); uad (Hc); uadar (He); ooad (SHK); yooard (Kn); whad (Mr); yooat (Sc); ooarda (Sm); wadder (Wd); yoo'oga (Bt); yooaddee (Bk); yooat (MB); yooat (Nga); yooat, yooadda (Ngi); yooat (J); yooat (K); yonader (Bu); yuwat (Do); yuart (Da); uart (Be); yuaat (Vb); yuat (At); yoowart (Wt); yuwad, yuwada (De); yuada (Ri); yoowat (Mi)

yoran	alright, innocent	you-ree (Hm); yuagan (Vb)
yorl	paperbark tree	yorla (Ngi); yorla (De)
yowir	drunk	yowir (Mo); yoweereega (Bt); yowering (Bk); yowering (MB); yowering, yoweraga (Ngi); yowerung (J); yemat yowerung (K)

Notes

1. Introduction

1 Rose, Deborah Bird. *Nourishing Terrains: Australian Aboriginal Views of Landscape and Wilderness*. Canberra: Australian Heritage Commission, 1996.

2 Malthouse Theatre's *The Shadow King* (2013) was an adaptation of Shakespeare's *King Lear* presented in English and a variety of Indigenous languages.

3 *Standing up tall for Noongar*. Office of the Registrar of Indigenous Corporations, Australian Government, n.d., https://www.oric.gov.au/publications/spotlight/standing-tall-noongar.

4 For a map of Aboriginal and Torres Strait Islander languages that reflects the names and locations preferred by Indigenous communities see the Gambay map produced by First Languages Australia (https://gambay.com.au), and the 50 Words map from the Research Unit for Indigenous Language, University of Melbourne, which hosts recordings of 50 words in many of these languages provided by language speakers (https://50words.online).

5 *1267.0 – Australian Standard Classification of Languages*. Australian Bureau of Statistics, 2016, https://www.abs.gov.au/ausstats/abs@.nsf/mf/1267.0.

6 Australian Institute of Aboriginal and Torres Strait Islander Studies et al. *National Indigenous Languages Report*. Canberra: Commonwealth of Australia, 2020.

7 Rademaker, Laura. *Found in Translation: Many Meanings on a North Australian Mission*. Honolulu: University of Hawai'i Press, 2018; Capell, Arthur. Linguistic change in Australia. In *Diprotodon to Detribalization: Studies of Change Among Australian Aborigines*, edited by A.R. Pilling and R.A. Waterman, 240–55. East Lansing: Michigan State University Press, 1970.

8 Marmion, Doug, Kazuko Obata, and Jakelin Troy. *Community, Identity, Wellbeing: The Report of the Second National Indigenous Languages Survey*. Canberra: Australian Institute of Aboriginal and Torres Strait Islander Studies, 2014.

9 Douglas, Wilfred. *The Aboriginal Languages of the South-West of Australia*. Canberra: Australian Institute of Aboriginal Studies, 1968.

10 Colbung, Ken. Not land rights: but land rites. *Australian Aboriginal Studies* 2 (1988): 103–10, p .107.

11 Austlang.*W41: Noongar/Nyoongar*. Australian Institute of Aboriginal and Torres Strait Islander Studies, 2022, https://collection.aiatsis.gov.au/austlang/language/w41.

12 Eberhard, David M., Gary F. Simons, and Charles D. Fennig, eds. *Ethnologue: Languages of the World*. 23rd edn. Dallas: SIL International, 2020.

13 Bracknell, Clint. Conceptualizing Noongar song. *Yearbook for Traditional Music* 49 (2017): 93–113; Haebich, Anna. *Dancing in Shadows: Histories of Nyungar Performance*. Perth: UWA Publishing, 2018.

14 Bracknell, Clint. Old dogs and ice ages in Noongar Country. In *Everywhen: Australia and the Language of Deep History*, edited by Ann McGrath, Laura Rademaker and Jakelin Troy, 75–92. Sydney: UNSW Press, 2023.

15 Reynolds, Henry. *The Other Side of the Frontier: Aboriginal Resistance to the European Invasion of Australia*. Ringwood: Pelican Books, 1982; Haebich, Anna. *Broken Circles*. Fremantle: Fremantle Press, 2000; Forrest, Roni Gray. *Kukenarup – Two Stories: Historical Accounts of a Massacre Site at Cocanarup near Ravensthorpe WA*. Perth: WA Department of Indigenous Affairs, 2004.

16 Mithun, Marianne. The significance of diversity in language endangerment and preservation. In *Endangered Languages: Language Loss and Community Response*, edited by Lenore Grenoble and Lindsay Whaley, 163–91. Cambridge: Cambridge University Press, 1998, p. 189.

17 McDonald, Jo. Serpents Glen (Karnatukul): new histories for deep time attachment to Country in Australia's Western Desert. *Bulletin of the History of Archaeology* 30, no. 1 (2020).

18 Turner, Margaret Kemarre. *Iwenhe Tyerrtye: What It Means to Be an Aboriginal Person*. Alice Springs: IAD Press, 2010, p.196.

19 L. Bennett, personal communication, March 2022.

20 Tuck, Eve, and K. Wayne Yang. Unbecoming claims: pedagogies of refusal in qualitative research. *Qualitative Enquiry* 20, no. 6 (2014): 811–18, p. 812.

21 Arthur, Jay. The eighth day of creation. *Journal of Australian Studies* 23, no. 61 (1999): 65–74, p .73.

22 Arthur, The eighth day of creation, p. 73.

23 Arthur, The eighth day of creation, p. 73.

24 Allen, Aaron S. Diverse ecomusicologies: making a difference with the environmental liberal arts. In *Performing Environmentalisms:*

Expressive Culture and Environmental Change, edited by John Holmes McDowell, Katherine Borland, Rebecca Dirksen and Sue Tuohy, 89–116. Champaign: University of Illinois Press, 2021.

25 Worster, Donald. *The Wealth of Nature: Environmental History and the Ecological Imagination*. New York: Oxford University Press, 1993; Orr, David W. *Earth in Mind: On Education, Environment, and the Human Prospect*. Washington, DC: Island Press, 1994; Allen, Aaron S. Prospects and problems for ecomusicology in confronting a crisis of culture. *Journal of the American Musicological Society* 64, no. 2 (2011): 414–19.

26 Randall, Martin. *Shakespeare and Ecology*. London: Oxford University Press, 2015.

27 Van Toorn, Penelope. *Writing Never Arrives Naked: Early Aboriginal Cultures of Writing in Australia*. Canberra: Aboriginal Studies Press, 2006.

28 Moghari, Shaghayegh. Racism, ethnic discrimination, and otherness in Shakespeare's Othello and the Merchant of Venice. *International Journal of English and Comparative Literary Studies* 2, no. 4 (2021): 25–41.

29 As stated in 1953 and cited in Rademaker, *Found in Translation*.

30 Knowles, Ric. Festivalizing down under: unsettling the contact zone. *Theatre Journal* 72, no. 4 (2020): 487–500, p.494-5.

31 *Pawâkan Macbeth: A Cree takeover by Reneltta Arluk*. Akpik Theatre, 2019, http://akpiktheatre.com/pawakan-macbeth.

32 Dionne, Craig, and Parmita Kapadia, eds. *Native Shakespeares: Indigenous Appropriations on a Global Stage*. Burlington, VT: Ashgate, 2008.

33 *Our story*. Bell Shakespeare, n.d., www.bellshakespeare.com.au/our-story.

34 Bracknell, Clint. The emotional business of Noongar song. *Journal of Australian Studies* 44, no. 2 (2020): 140–53.

35 Hobson, John, Kevin Lowe, Susan Poetsch, and Michael Walsh, eds. *Re-awakening Languages: Theory and Practice in the Revitalisation of Australia's Indigenous Languages*. Camperdown: Sydney University Press, 2018.

36 Bell, Jeanie. Language attitudes and language revival/survival. *Journal of Multilingual and Multicultural Development* 34, no. 4 (2013): 399–410, p. 408.

37 Bracknell, Clint, and Rachel Nordlinger. Language and knowledge. In *Australian Perspectives on Indigenous Knowledge*, edited by Marcia Langton and Michael-Shawn Fletcher. Melbourne: Melbourne University Press, forthcoming.

38 Turpin, Myfany, Calista Yeoh, and Clint Bracknell. Wanji-wanji: the past and future of an Aboriginal travelling song. *Musicology Australia* 42, no. 2 (2020): 123–47.

39 The inclusion of Hecate and many of the supernatural elements of the play are often attributed to Shakespeare's junior contemporary and collaborator Thomas Middleton. See Daileader, Celia R. Weird brothers: what Thomas Middleton's The Witch can tell us about race, sex, and gender in Macbeth. In *Weyward Macbeth: Intersections of Race and Performance*, edited by Scott Newstok and Ayanna Thompson, 11–20. New York: Palgrave Macmillan, 2010.

2. Waabarangkar! A Noongar Ensemble

1 Morrison, Kyle J. Flow state in Noongar performance. Masters thesis, Edith Cowan University, 2023.

2 Morrison, Flow state".

3 Ryan, Trevor. Keniny Kaadadijiny: restoring and developing dance for Noongar boodjar. Masters thesis, Edith Cowan University, 2022.

4 May, Stephen. Indigenous immersion education: international developments. *Journal of Immersion and Content-Based Language Education* 1, no. 1 (2013): 34–69.

5 Farmer [Bracknell], Kylie. Sonnets in Noongar – the task. *Runway Journal* 31 (2016). http://runway.org.au/sonnets-in-noongar-the-task.

6 Studham, Susan Fenty. Supporting brave spaces for theatre-makers post-#metoo: a Chicago-based study on rehearsing and performing intimacy in theatre. In *Performing #MeToo: How Not to Look Away*, edited by Judith Rudakoff, 68–85. Bristol: Intellect, 2021.

7 Arao, Brian, and Kristi Clemens. From safe spaces to brave spaces: a new way to frame dialogue around diversity and social justice. In *The Art of Effective Facilitation: Reflections from Social Justice Educators*, edited by Lisa M. Landreman, 135–50. Sterling, VA: Stylus Publishing, 2013.

8 Studham, Supporting brave spaces, p. 73.

9 Tan, Marcus Cheng Chye. *Acoustic Interculturalism: Listening to Performance*. London: Palgrave Macmillan, 2012; Connor, Steven. *Beyond Words: Sobs, Hums, Stutters and Other Vocalizations*. London: Reaktion Books, 2014; Ginther, Amy Mihyang. Dysconscious racism in mainstream British voice pedagogy and its potential effects on students from pluralistic backgrounds in UK drama conservatoires. *Voice and Speech Review* 9, no. 1 (2015): 41–60.

10 Oram, Daron. Decentering listening: toward an anti-discriminatory approach to accent and dialect training for the actor. *Voice and Speech Review* 15, no. 1 (2021): 6–26, p. 17.

11 Bell, Jeanie. Language attitudes and language revival/survival.

12 Techmeier, Mary. Music in the teaching of French. *The Modern Language Journal* 53, no. 2 (1969): 96; Fonseca Mora, Carmen. Foreign language acquisition and melody singing. *ELT Journal* 54, no. 2 (2000): 146–52.
13 Ellis, Peter Berresford, and Seumas Mac a' Ghobhainn. *The Problem of Language Revival*. Inverness: Club Leabhar, 1971, p. 144.
14 Bracknell, Kylie. Noongar words and philosophy are the true hero in our Macbeth adaptation Hecate. *The Guardian*, 14 February 2020. https://www.theguardian.com/commentisfree/2020/feb/14/noongar-words-and-philosophy-are-the-true-hero-in-our-macbeth-adaptation-hecate.
15 Vivienne Binyarn Hansen, via Facebook, 17 February 2020.
16 Crawley, S. Open letters demand university does more to tackle racism. *Varsity*, 26 June 2020. https://www.varsity.co.uk/news/19541.
17 Brenzinger, Matthias, et al.. *Language vitality and endangerment*. International Expert Meeting on UNESCO Programme Safeguarding of Endangered Languages, Paris, 2003.
18 Haebich, Anna. *Dancing in Shadows: Histories of Nyungar Performance*.

3. On Noongar Language in Hecate

1 Bracknell, Clint, Amy Budrikis, and Roma Yibiyung Winmar. Maya-kwobabiny: re-embedding language at Kepa Kurl, Western Australia. *Language Documentation & Conservation* 16 (2022): 319–40.
2 Haebich, *Dancing in Shadows*.
3 *W41: Noongar/Nyoongar*. AIATSIS.
4 Kickett-Tucker, Cheryl S. Moorn (black)? Djardak (white)? How come i don't fit in Mum? Exploring the racial identity of Australian Aboriginal children and youth. *Health Sociology Review* 18, no. 1 (2009): 119–36.
5 Thieberger, Nicholas. *Linguistic Report on the Single Noongar Native Title Claim*. Beckenham: South West Aboriginal Land and Sea Council, 2004, p. 7.
6 Bunbury Noongar Aboriginal Progress Association. *Nyungar Nyinalanginy Wangkininy: Nyungar Language Conference*. Bunbury: Bunbury Noongar Aboriginal Progress Association, 1990.
7 Whitehurst, Rose. *Noongar Dictionary*. East Perth: Noongar Language and Cultural Centre, 1992.
8 Gina Williams, personal communication, 19 October 2018.
9 McCarron, Robyn. Noongar language and literature. *SPAN: Journal of the South Pacific Association for the Commonwealth Literature and Language Studies* 36 (1992); Whitehurst, *Noongar Dictionary*.
10 Wooltorton, Sandra, and Glenys Collard. *Noongar Our Way*. Bunbury: Noongar Language and Culture Centre, 1992, p .ix.

11 Winmar, Ralph. *Walwalinj: The Hill that Cries*. Manning, WA: Dorothy Winmar, 1996; Bennell, Tom, and Glenys Collard. *Kura*. Bunbury, WA: Kurangkurl Consultancy, 1993.

12 Della Rae Morrison, personal communication, 19 October 2018; Breen, Marcus, ed. *Our Place, Our Music*. Canberra: Aboriginal Studies Press, 1989; Haebich, Anna. *For Their Own Good: Aborigines and Government in the South West of Western Australia 1900 to 1940*. Nedlands: UWA Press, 1989.

13 Bourke, Keane. Indigenous languages being Taught to 10,000 West Australian school kids. *ABC News*, 4 July 2022. www.abc.net.au/news/2022-07-04/wa-students-learn-indigenous-languages-at-record-rate/101194088.

14 *Shakespeare's words*. Shakespeare Birthplace Trust, n.d., www.shakespeare.org.uk/explore-shakespeare/shakespedia/shakespeares-words/; *Shakespeare text statistics*. Open Source Shakespeare, n.d., www.opensourceshakespeare.org/statistics/.

15 Thieberger, Nicholas, Rachel Nordlinger, and Jill Vaughan. *50 words in Australian Indigenous languages*. University of Melbourne, 9 November 2020. https://pursuit.unimelb.edu.au/articles/50-words-in-australian-indigenous-languages.

16 Thieberger, *Linguistic Report*.

17 Brewer, Charlotte. Shakespeare, word-coining, and the OED. *Shakespeare Survey* 65 (2013): 345–57; Hope, Jonathan. Who invented 'gloomy'? Lies people want to believe about Shakespeare. *Memoria Di Shakespeare: A Journal of Shakespearean Studies* 3 (2017). 21–45, p. 45.

18 Hope. Who invented 'gloomy'?

19 Brown, Robert. Papers and correspondence of Robert Brown [microform], M1193, M2494-2496. Canberra: AIATSIS Audiovisual Archive, 1800–1855; Symmons, Charles. Grammatical introduction to the study of the Aboriginal language of Western Australia. *Western Australian Almanack*. Perth, 1842.

20 Thieberger, Nicholas. *Digital Daisy Bates*. 2017. http://bates.org.au.

21 Laves, Gerhardt. Papers of Gerhardt Laves Ms/2189, Items 2.18-2.27. Canberra: AIATSIS Archive, 1929–1932.

22 Henderson, John, Hannah McGlade, Kim Scott, and Denise Smith-Ali. A protocol for Laves' 1931 Noongar field notes. Perth: University of Western Australia and AIATSIS, 2006; Henderson, John. Capturing chaos: rendering handwritten language documents. *Language Documentation & Conservation* 2, no. 2 (2008): 212–43; Henderson, John. Language documentation and community interests. In *Keeping Languages Alive: Documentation, Pedagogy, and Revitalization*, edited by Mari C. Jones and Sarah Ogilvie, 56–68. Cambridge: Cambridge University Press, 2013.

23 Hale, Ken. *Balardung and Mirning language elicitation. OGRADY-HALE_01 (014053-014055)*. Canberra: AIATSIS Archive, 1960.

24 Douglas, Wilfred. *Language elicitation, narratives and songs from south-west Western Australia. Douglas_W01 (A001322-A001324).* Canberra: AIATSIS Audiovisual Archive, 1964–1967; von Brandestein, Carl Georg. *Songs, messages, texts and language elicitation from south-eastern Western Australia. Von-Brandenstein_C04 (A002150-A002159), Take 35 (002158b 002159a) and Tape 37 (002159a).* Canberra: AIATSIS Audiovisual Archive, 1967–1970.

25 Douglas, *The Aboriginal Languages*, 1968; Douglas, Wilfred. *Illustrated Dictionary of the South-West Aboriginal Language*. Claremont, WA: Edith Cowan University, 1996.

26 von Brandenstein, Carl Georg. Nyungar anew. Canberra: Department of Linguistics, Research School of Pacific Studies, Australian National University, 1988.

27 Thieberger. *Linguistic Report*.

28 Broadbent, Sylvia M. Rumsen I: methods of reconstitution. *International Journal of American Linguistics* 23, no. 4 (1957): 275–80.

29 Thieberger, *Linguistic Report*.

30 Douglas, *The Aboriginal Languages*.

6. A Noongar Grammar and Glossary

1 Efi, Tui Atua Tupua Tamasese Taisi. Clutter in Indigenous knowledge, research and history: a Samoan perspective. *Social Policy Journal of New Zealand* 25 (2005): 61–69, p. 66; Morgan, Mindy J. *The Bearer of This Letter: Language Ideologies, Literacy Practices, and the Fort Belknap Indian Community*. Lincoln: University of Nebraska Press, 2009.

2 Douglas, *The Aboriginal Languages*; von Brandenstein. Nyungar anew; Dench, Alan. Comparative reconstitution. In *Historical Linguistics 1995: Selected Papers from the 12th International Conference on Historical Linguistics, Manchester, August 1995, Vol. 1 General Issues and Non-Germanic Languages*, edited by John C. Smith and D. Bentley, 57–73. Amsterdam and Philadelphia: John Benjamins Publishing Company.

3 Bates, Daisy. A few notes on some south-western Australian dialects. *The Journal of the Royal Anthropological Institute of Great Britain and Ireland* 44 (1914) 65–82, p. 66.

4 Douglas, *The Aboriginal Languages*, p. 40.

5 von Brandenstein, Nyungar anew. p. 4.

6 von Brandenstein, Nyungar anew, p. 2.

7 Douglas, *The Aboriginal Languages*, p. 47.

8 von Brandenstein, Nyungar anew, p. 62.

9 see '-er', von Brandenstein, Nyungar anew, p. 3.

10 von Brandenstein, Nyungar anew, p. 23; Douglas, *The Aboriginal Languages*, p. 65.
11 von Brandenstein, Nyungar anew, pp. 64, 65.
12 von Brandenstein, Nyungar anew, p. 62; Douglas, *The Aboriginal Languages*, p. 95.
13 von Brandenstein, Nyungar anew, p. 2.
14 Douglas, *The Aboriginal Languages*, p. 72.
15 see 'met', Douglas, *The Aboriginal Languages*, p. 64.
16 Douglas, *The Aboriginal Languages*, p .40.
17 von Brandenstein, Nyungar anew, p. 1.

Bibliography

1267.0 – Australian Standard Classification of Languages. Australian Bureau of Statistics (ABS), 2016, https://www.abs.gov.au/ausstats/abs@.nsf/mf/1267.0.

50 Words project. Research Unit for Indigenous Language, University of Melbourne, n.d., https://50words.online,

Allen, Aaron S. Prospects and problems for ecomusicology in confronting a crisis of culture. *Journal of the American Musicological Society* 64, no. 2 (2011): 414–19.

Allen, Aaron S. Diverse ecomusicologies: making a difference with the environmental liberal arts. In *Performing Environmentalisms: Expressive Culture and Environmental Change*, edited by John Holmes McDowell, Katherine Borland, Rebecca Dirksen and Sue Tuohy, 89–116. Champaign: University of Illinois Press, 2021.

Arao, Brian, and Kristi Clemens. From safe spaces to brave spaces: a new way to frame dialogue around diversity and social justice. In *The Art of Effective Facilitation: Reflections from Social Justice Educators*, edited by Lisa M. Landreman, 135–50. Sterling, VA: Stylus Publishing, 2013.

Arthur, Jay. The eighth day of creation. *Journal of Australian Studies* 23, no. 61 (1999): 65–74.

Austlang. *W41: Noongar/Nyoongar*. Australian Institute of Aboriginal and Torres Strait Islander Studies, 2022, https://collection.aiatsis.gov.au/austlang/language/w41.

Australian Institute of Aboriginal and Torres Strait Islander Studies, Australian National University and Department of Infrastructure, Transport, Regional Development and Communications. *National Indigenous Languages Report*. Canberra: Commonwealth of Australia, 2020.

Bates, Daisy. A few notes on some south-western Australian dialects. *The Journal of the Royal Anthropological Institute of Great Britain and Ireland* 44 (1914) 65–82.

Bell, Jeanie. Language attitudes and language revival/survival. *Journal of Multilingual and Multicultural Development* 34, no. 4 (2013): 399–410.

Bennell, Tom, and Glenys Collard. *Kura*. Bunbury, WA: Kurangkurl Consultancy, 1993.

Bourke, Keane. Indigenous languages being Taught to 10,000 West Australian school kids. *ABC News*, 4 July 2022. www.abc.net.au/news/2022-07-04/wa-students-learn-indigenous-languages-at-record-rate/101194088.

Bracknell, Clint. Conceptualizing Noongar song. *Yearbook for Traditional Music* 49 (2017): 93–113

Bracknell, Clint. The emotional business of Noongar song. *Journal of Australian Studies* 44, no. 2 (2020): 140–53.

Bracknell, Clint. Old dogs and ice ages in Noongar Country. In *Everywhen: Australia and the Language of Deep History*, edited by Ann McGrath, Laura Rademaker and Jakelin Troy, 75–92. Sydney: UNSW Press, 2023.

Bracknell, Clint, and Rachel Nordlinger. Language and knowledge. In *Australian Perspectives on Indigenous Knowledge*, edited by Marcia Langton and Michael-Shawn Fletcher. Melbourne: Melbourne University Press, forthcoming.

Bracknell, Clint, Amy Budrikis, and Roma Yibiyung Winmar. Maya-kwobabiny: re-embedding language at Kepa Kurl, Western Australia. *Language Documentation & Conservation* 16 (2022): 319–40.

Bracknell, Kylie. Noongar words and philosophy are the true hero in our Macbeth adaptation Hecate. *The Guardian*, 14 February 2020. https://www.theguardian.com/commentisfree/2020/feb/14/noongar-words-and-philosophy-are-the-true-hero-in-our-macbeth-adaptation-hecate.

Breen, Marcus, ed. *Our Place, Our Music*. Canberra: Aboriginal Studies Press, 1989.

Brenzinger, Matthias, Akira Yamamoto, Noriko Aikawa, Dmitri Koundiouba, Anahit Minasyan, Arienne Dwyer, Colette Grinevald, Michael Krauss, Osahito Miyaoka, Osamu Sakiyama, Rieks Smeets, and Ofelia Zepeda. *Language vitality and endangerment*. International Expert Meeting on UNESCO Programme Safeguarding of Endangered Languages, Paris, 2003. https://ich.unesco.org/doc/src/00120-EN.pdf

Brewer, Charlotte. Shakespeare, word-coining, and the OED. *Shakespeare Survey* 65 (2013): 345–57.

Broadbent, Sylvia M. Rumsen I: methods of reconstitution. *International Journal of American Linguistics* 23, no. 4 (1957): 275–80.

Brown, Robert. Papers and correspondence of Robert Brown [microform], M1193, M2494-2496. Canberra: AIATSIS Audiovisual Archive, 1800–1855.

Bunbury Noongar Aboriginal Progress Association. *Nyungar Nyinalanginy Wangkininy: Nyungar Language Conference*. Bunbury: Bunbury Noongar Aboriginal Progress Association, 1990.

Capell, Arthur. Linguistic change in Australia. In *Diprotodon to Detribalization: Studies of Change Among Australian Aborigines*, edited by A.R. Pilling and R.A. Waterman, 240–55. East Lansing: Michigan State University Press, 1970.

Colbung, Ken. Not land rights: but land rites. *Australian Aboriginal Studies* 2 (1988): 103–10.

Connor, Steven. *Beyond Words: Sobs, Hums, Stutters and Other Vocalizations*. London: Reaktion Books, 2014.

Crawley, S. Open letters demand university does more to tackle racism. *Varsity*, 26 June 2020. https://www.varsity.co.uk/news/19541.

Curr, Edward M. *The Australian Race: Its Origin, Languages, Customs, Place of Landing in Australia, and the Routes by which it Spread itself over that Continent*. Vol.1. Melbourne: Government Printer, 1886–1887.

Daileader, Celia R. Weird brothers: what Thomas Middleton's The Witch can tell us about race, sex, and gender in Macbeth. In *Weyward Macbeth: Intersections of Race and Performance*, edited by Scott Newstok and Ayanna Thompson, 11–20. New York: Palgrave Macmillan, 2010.

Dench, Alan. Comparative reconstitution. In *Historical Linguistics 1995: Selected Papers from the 12th International Conference on Historical Linguistics, Manchester, August 1995, Vol. 1 General Issues and Non-Germanic Languages*, edited by John C. Smith and D. Bentley, 57–73. Amsterdam and Philadelphia: John Benjamins Publishing Company.

Dionne, Craig, and Parmita Kapadia, eds. *Native Shakespeares: Indigenous Appropriations on a Global Stage*. Burlington, VT: Ashgate, 2008

Douglas, Wilfred. *Language elicitation, narratives and songs from south-west Western Australia. Douglas_W01 (A001322-A001324)*. Canberra: AIATSIS Audiovisual Archive, 1964–1967.

Douglas, Wilfred. *The Aboriginal Languages of the South-West of Australia*. Canberra: Australian Institute of Aboriginal Studies, 1968.

Douglas, Wilf. *W.H. Atkins Memorial: Nyungar-English, English-Nyungar Dictionary with Equivalents in Standard Orthography*. Kalgoorlie, WA: W.H. Douglas, 1991.

Douglas, Wilfred. *Illustrated Dictionary of the South-West Aboriginal Language*. Claremont, WA: Edith Cowan University, 1996.

Eberhard, David M., Gary F. Simons, and Charles D. Fennig, eds. *Ethnologue: Languages of the World*. 23rd edn. Dallas: SIL International, 2020.

Efi, Tui Atua Tupua Tamasese Taisi. Clutter in Indigenous knowledge, research and history: a Samoan perspective. *Social Policy Journal of New Zealand* 25 (2005): 61–69.

Ellis, Peter Berresford, and Seumas Mac a' Ghobhainn. *The Problem of Language Revival*. Inverness: Club Leabhar, 1971.

Farmer [Bracknell], Kylie. Sonnets in Noongar – the task. *Runway Journal* 31 (2016). http://runway.org.au/sonnets-in-noongar-the-task.

Fonseca Mora, Carmen. Foreign language acquisition and melody singing. *ELT Journal* 54, no. 2 (2000): 146–52.

Forrest, Roni Gray. *Kukenarup – Two Stories: Historical Accounts of a Massacre Site at Cocanarup near Ravensthorpe WA*. Perth: WA Department of Indigenous Affairs, 2004.

Gambay – First languages map. First Languages Australia, n.d., https://gambay.com.au/.

Ginther, Amy Mihyang. Dysconscious racism in mainstream British voice pedagogy and its potential effects on students from pluralistic backgrounds in UK drama conservatoires. *Voice and Speech Review* 9, no. 1 (2015): 41–60.

Haebich, Anna. *For Their Own Good: Aborigines and Government in the South West of Western Australia 1900 to 1940*. Nedlands: UWA Press, 1989.

Haebich, Anna. *Broken Circles*. Fremantle: Fremantle Press, 2000.

Haebich, Anna. *Dancing in Shadows: Histories of Nyungar Performance*. Perth: UWA Publishing, 2018

Hale, Ken. *Balardung and Mirning language elicitation. OGRADY-HALE_01 (014053-014055)*. Canberra: AIATSIS Archive, 1960.

Henderson, John. Capturing chaos: rendering handwritten language documents. *Language Documentation & Conservation* 2, no. 2 (2008): 212–43.

Henderson, John. Language documentation and community interests. In *Keeping Languages Alive: Documentation, Pedagogy, and Revitalization*, edited by Mari C. Jones and Sarah Ogilvie, 56–68. Cambridge: Cambridge University Press, 2013.

Henderson, John, Hannah McGlade, Kim Scott, and Denise Smith-Ali. A protocol for Laves' 1931 Noongar field notes. Perth: University of Western Australia and AIATSIS, 2006.

Hobson, John, Kevin Lowe, Susan Poetsch, and Michael Walsh, eds. *Re-awakening Languages: Theory and Practice in the Revitalisation of Australia's Indigenous Languages*. Camperdown: Sydney University Press, 2018.

Hope, Jonathan. Who invented 'gloomy'? Lies people want to believe about Shakespeare. *Memoria Di Shakespeare: A Journal of Shakespearean Studies* 3 (2017): 21–45.

Kickett-Tucker, Cheryl S. Moorn (black)? Djardak (white)? How come i don't fit in Mum? Exploring the racial identity of Australian Aboriginal children and youth. *Health Sociology Review* 18, no. 1 (2009): 119–36.

Knowles, Ric. Festivalizing down under: unsettling the contact zone. *Theatre Journal* 72, no. 4 (2020): 487–500.

Laves, Gerhardt. Papers of Gerhardt Laves Ms/2189, Items 2.18-2.27. Canberra: AIATSIS Archive, 1929–1932.

McCarron, Robyn. Noongar language and literature. *SPAN: Journal of the South Pacific Association for the Commonwealth Literature and Language Studies* 36 (1992).

McDonald, Jo. Serpents Glen (Karnatukul): new histories for deep time attachment to Country in Australia's Western Desert. *Bulletin of the History of Archaeology* 30, no. 1 (2020).

Marmion, Doug, Kazuko Obata, and Jakelin Troy. *Community, Identity, Wellbeing: The Report of the Second National Indigenous Languages Survey*. Canberra: Australian Institute of Aboriginal and Torres Strait Islander Studies, 2014.

Morgan, Mindy J. *The Bearer of This Letter: Language Ideologies, Literacy Practices, and the Fort Belknap Indian Community*. Lincoln: University of Nebraska Press, 2009.

Morrison, Kyle J. Flow state in Noongar performance. Masters thesis, Edith Cowan University, 2023.

Our story. Bell Shakespeare, n.d., www.bellshakespeare.com.au/our-story.

Randall, Martin. *Shakespeare and Ecology*. London: Oxford University Press, 2015.

May, Stephen. Indigenous immersion education: international developments. *Journal of Immersion and Content-Based Language Education* 1, no. 1 (2013): 34–69.

Mithun, Marianne. The significance of diversity in language endangerment and preservation. In *Endangered Languages: Language Loss and Community Response*, edited by Lenore Grenoble and Lindsay Whaley, 163–91. Cambridge: Cambridge University Press, 1998.

Moghari, Shaghayegh. Racism, ethnic discrimination, and otherness in Shakespeare's Othello and the Merchant of Venice. *International Journal of English and Comparative Literary Studies* 2, no. 4 (2021): 25–41.

Oram, Daron. Decentering listening: toward an anti-discriminatory approach to accent and dialect training for the actor. *Voice and Speech Review* 15, no. 1 (2021): 6–26.

Orr, David W. *Earth in Mind: On Education, Environment, and the Human Prospect*. Washington, DC: Island Press, 1994.

Pawâkan Macbeth: A Cree takeover by Reneltta Arluk. Akpik Theatre, 2019, http://akpiktheatre.com/pawakan-macbeth.

Rademaker, Laura. *Found in Translation: Many Meanings on a North Australian Mission*. Honolulu: University of Hawai'i Press, 2018.

Reynolds, Henry. *The Other Side of the Frontier: Aboriginal Resistance to the European Invasion of Australia*. Ringwood: Pelican Books, 1982.

Rose, Deborah Bird. *Nourishing Terrains: Australian Aboriginal Views of Landscape and Wilderness*. Canbera: Australian Heritage Commission, 1996.

Ryan, Trevor. Keniny Kaadadijiny: restoring and developing dance for Noongar boodjar. Masters thesis, Edith Cowan University, 2022.

Shakespeare text statistics. Open Source Shakespeare, n.d., www.opensourceshakespeare.org/statistics/.

Shakespeare's words. Shakespeare Birthplace Trust, n.d., www.shakespeare.org.uk/explore-shakespeare/shakespedia/shakespeares-words/.

Standing up tall for Noongar. Office of the Registrar of Indigenous Corporations, Australian Government, n.d., https://www.oric.gov.au/publications/spotlight/standing-tall-noongar.

Studham, Susan Fenty. Supporting brave spaces for theatre-makers post-#metoo: a Chicago-based study on rehearsing and performing intimacy in theatre. In *Performing #MeToo: How Not to Look Away*, edited by Judith Rudakoff, 68–85. Bristol: Intellect, 2021.

Symmons, Charles. Grammatical introduction to the study of the Aboriginal language of Western Australia. *Western Australian Almanack*. Perth, 1842.

Tan, Marcus Cheng Chye. *Acoustic Interculturalism: Listening to Performance*. London: Palgrave Macmillan, 2012.

Techmeier, Mary. Music in the teaching of French. *The Modern Language Journal* 53, no. 2 (1969): 96.

Thieberger, Nicholas. *Digital Daisy Bates*. 2017. http://bates.org.au.

Thieberger, Nicholas. *Linguistic Report on the Single Noongar Native Title Claim*. Beckenham: South West Aboriginal Land and Sea Council, 2004.

Thieberger, Nicholas, Rachel Nordlinger, and Jill Vaughan. *50 words in Australian Indigenous languages*. University of Melbourne, 9 November 2020. https://pursuit.unimelb.edu.au/articles/50-words-in-australian-indigenous-languages.

Tuck, Eve, and K. Wayne Yang. Unbecoming claims: pedagogies of refusal in qualitative research. *Qualitative Enquiry* 20, no. 6 (2014): 811–18.

Turner, Margaret Kemarre. *Iwenhe Tyerrtye: What It Means to Be an Aboriginal Person*. Alice Springs: IAD Press, 2010.

Turpin, Myfany, Calista Yeoh, and Clint Bracknell. Wanji-wanji: the past and future of an Aboriginal travelling song. *Musicology Australia* 42, no. 2 (2020): 123–47.

Van Toorn, Penelope. *Writing Never Arrives Naked: Early Aboriginal Cultures of Writing in Australia*. Canberra: Aboriginal Studies Press, 2006.

von Brandestein, Carl Georg. *Songs, messages, texts and language elicitation from south-eastern Western Australia. Von-Brandenstein_C04 (A002150-A002159), Take 35 (002158b 002159a) and Tape 37 (002159a)*. Canberra: AIATSIS Audiovisual Archive, 1967–1970.

von Brandenstein, Carl Georg. Nyungar anew: phonology, text samples and etymological and historical 1500-word vocabulary of an artificially re-created Aboriginal language in the South-West of Australia. Pacific Linguistics, C-99. Canberra: Department of Linguistics, Research School of Pacific Studies, Australian National University, 1988.

Walker, Kath. 'Recording the cries of the people': an interview with Oodgeroo (Kath Walker). *Kunapipi* 10, no. 1 (1988): 17–30.

Whitehurst, Rose. *Noongar Dictionary*. East Perth: Noongar Language and Cultural Centre, 1992.

Winmar, Ralph. *Walwalinj: The Hill that Cries*. Manning, WA: Dorothy Winmar, 1996.

Wooltorton, Sandra, and Glenys Collard. *Noongar Our Way*. Bunbury: Noongar Language and Culture Centre, 1992.

Worster, Donald. *The Wealth of Nature: Environmental History and the Ecological Imagination*. New York: Oxford University Press, 1993.

Acknowledgements

This book is dedicated to our Noongar ancestors who shared, sang, and sustained our beautiful language.

Shakespeare in the Noongar World is the manifestation of many individuals and organisations. We offer sincere thanks to:

Kyle J. Morrison, who conceived the idea of presenting Shakespeare in Noongar.

Kurongkurl Katitjin at Edith Cowan University, which supported Dr Roma Yibiyung Winmar, Dr Amy Burdrikis and the authors to facilitate research and community language gatherings contributing to the creation of *Hecate*.

Members of the Noongar community who participated in the language and ensemble development workshops for *Hecate*, especially senior language speakers Dr Roma Yibiyung Winmar, Judy Bone, Jill Collard, Vivienne Hansen, Mort Hansen, Dr Richard Walley OAM, Professor Len Collard, Barry McGuire, Mitchella Hutchins and Vivian Brockman-Webb.

Yirra Yaakin Theatre Company and former chairperson Clem Rodney (RIP), who championed this project since its inception. Associate presenter Bell Shakespeare, especially artistic director Peter Evans and associate director James Evans. Perth Festival and dramaturg of *Hecate* Kate Mulvany.

About Upswell

Upswell Publishing was established in 2021 by Terri-ann White as a not-for-profit press. A perceived gap in the market for distinctive literary works in fiction, poetry and narrative non-fiction was the motivation. In her years as a bookseller, writer and then publisher, Terri-ann has maintained a watch on literary books and the way they insinuate themselves into a cultural space and are then located within our literary and cultural inheritance. She is interested in making books to last: books with the potential to still be noticed, and noted, after decades and thus be ripe to influence new literary histories.

About this typeface

Book designer Becky Chilcott chose Foundry Origin not only as a strong, carefully considered, and dependable typeface, but also to honour her late friend and mentor, type designer Freda Sack, who oversaw the project. Designed by Freda's long-standing colleague, Stuart de Rozario, much like Upswell Publishing, Foundry Origin was created out of the desire to say something new.